BUREAU FOR PARANORMAL RESEARCH AND DEFENSE

THE SOUL OF VENICE
& OTHER STORIES

Created by MIKE MIGNOLA

JOHANN KRAUS

A medium whose physical form was destroyed while his ectoplasmic projection was out-of-body. That essence now resides in a containment suit. A psychic empath, Johann can create temporary forms for the dead to speak to the living.

LIZ SHERMAN

A fire-starter since the age of 11, when she accidentally burned her entire family to death. She has been a ward of the B.P.R.D. since then, learning to control her pyrokinetic abilities and cope with the trauma those abilities have wrought.

ABE SAPIEN

An amphibious man discovered in a long-forgotten subbasement beneath a Washington, D.C. hospital sealed inside a primitive stasis chamber. All indications suggest a previous life, dating back to the Civil War—an unfolding mystery for Abe.

ROGER

A homunculus made from human blood and herbs. Discovered in Romania, Roger was first brought to life by Liz's pyrokinetic touch. Whether or not he is actually alive may be up for debate, but his child-like love of that life is not.

DR. KATE CORRIGAN

A former professor at New York University, an authority on folklore and occult history. Dr. Corrigan has been a B.P.R.D. consultant for over 10 years, now serving as special liaison to the enhanced-talents task force.

MIKE MIGNOLA'S

B.P.R.D.™

THE SOUL OF VENICE
& OTHER STORIES

Featuring

MIKE MIGNOLA, MILES GUNTHER

MICHAEL AVON OEMING, BRIAN AUGUSTYN

GUY DAVIS, GEOFF JOHNS

SCOTT KOLINS, JOE HARRIS

ADAM POLLINA, & CAMERON STEWART

Editor
SCOTT ALLIE

Assistant Editor
MATT DRYER

Collection Designer
RICHARD E. JONES

Publisher
MIKE RICHARDSON

DARK HORSE BOOKS™

Tom Weddle ♦ *vice president of finance*

Randy Stradley ♦ *vice president of publishing*

Chris Warner ♦ *senior books editor*

Anita Nelson ♦ *vice president of sales & marketing*

Michael Martens ♦ *vice president of business development*

David Scroggy ♦ *vice president of product development*

Lia Ribacchi ♦ *art director*

Dale LaFountain ♦ *vice president of information technology*

Darlene Vogel ♦ *director of purchasing*

Ken Lizzi ♦ *general counsel*

Published by Dark Horse Books
A division of Dark Horse Comics, Inc.
10956 SE Main Street
Milwaukie, OR 97222

First edition August 2004
ISBN: 1-59307-132-9

1 3 5 7 9 10 8 6 4 2

Printed in China

This book collects the B.P.R.D. oneshots *The Soul of Venice*, *Dark Waters*, *Night Train*,
and *There's Something Under My Bed*, published by Dark Horse Comics.

THE SOUL OF VENICE

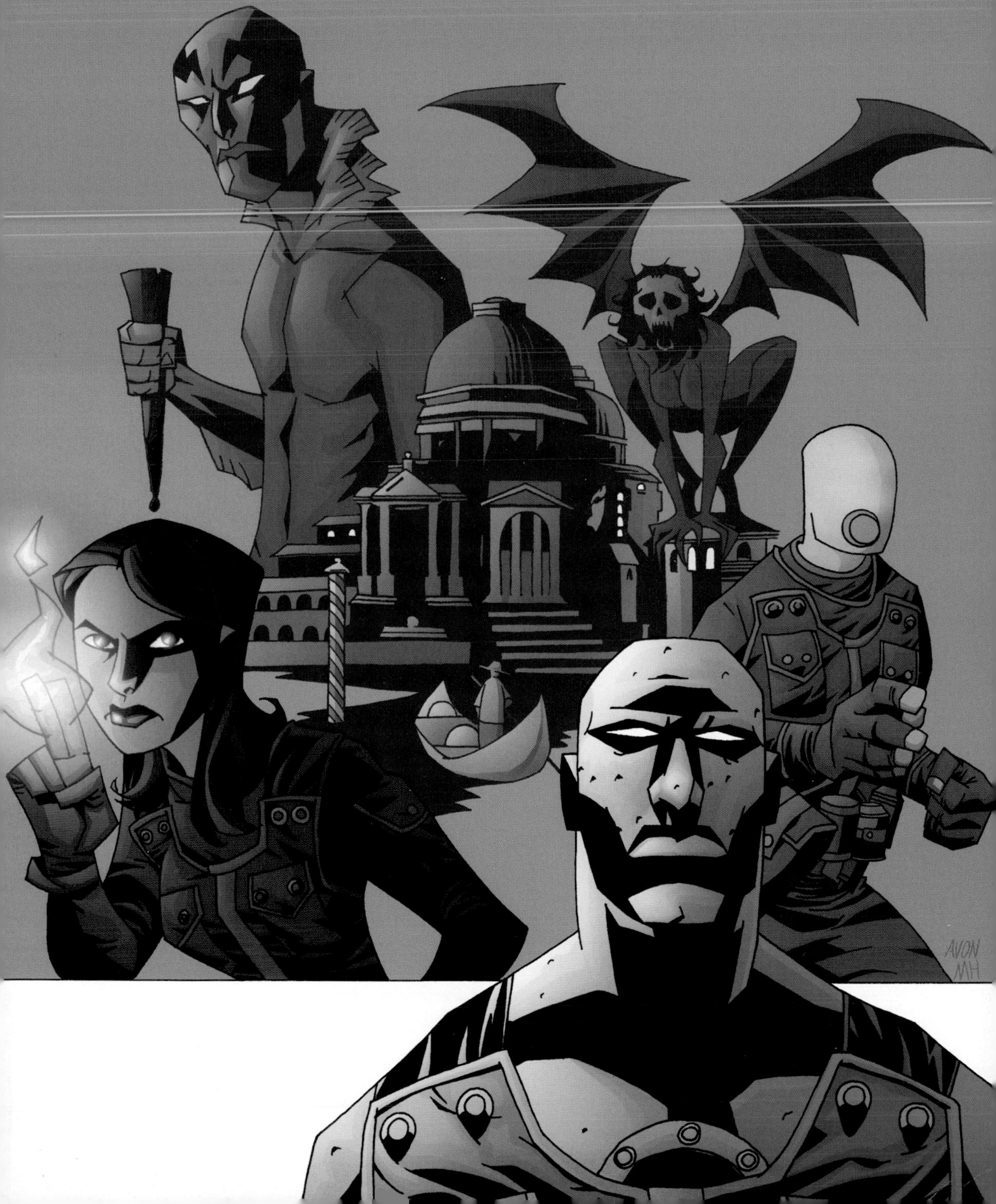
AVON
MH

THE SOUL OF VENICE

Story by
MILES GUNTHER & MICHAEL AVON OEMING
with MIKE MIGNOLA

Art by
MICHAEL AVON OEMING

Colors by
DAVE STEWART

Letters by
KEN BRUZENAK

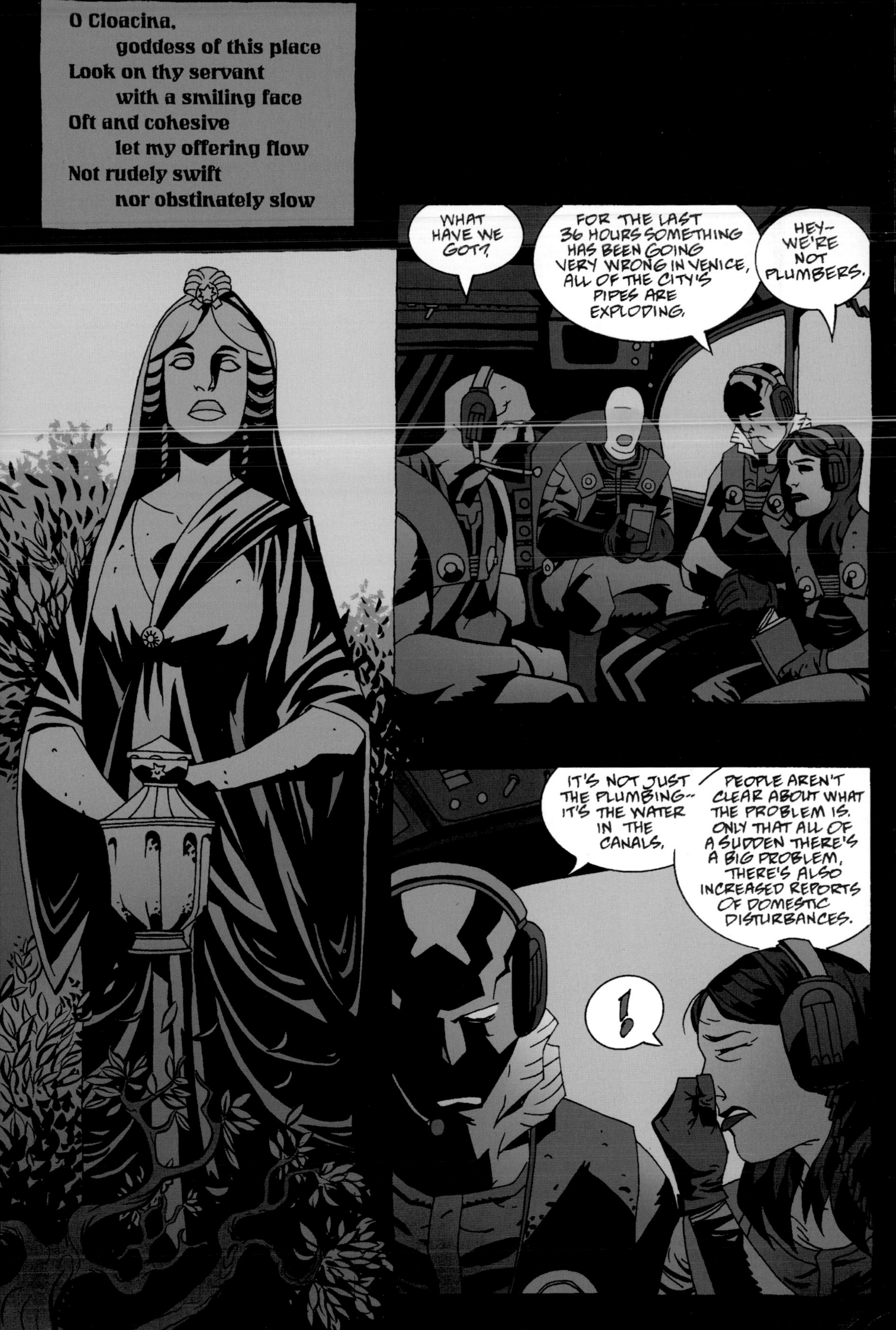

O Cloacina,
goddess of this place
Look on thy servant
with a smiling face
Oft and cohesive
let my offering flow
Not rudely swift
nor obstinately slow
WHAT HAVE WE GOT?
FOR THE LAST 36 HOURS SOMETHING HAS BEEN GOING VERY WRONG IN VENICE. ALL OF THE CITY'S PIPES ARE EXPLODING.
HEY-- WE'RE NOT PLUMBERS.
IT'S NOT JUST THE PLUMBING-- IT'S THE WATER IN THE CANALS.
PEOPLE AREN'T CLEAR ABOUT WHAT THE PROBLEM IS. ONLY THAT ALL OF A SUDDEN THERE'S A BIG PROBLEM. THERE'S ALSO INCREASED REPORTS OF DOMESTIC DISTURBANCES.
!

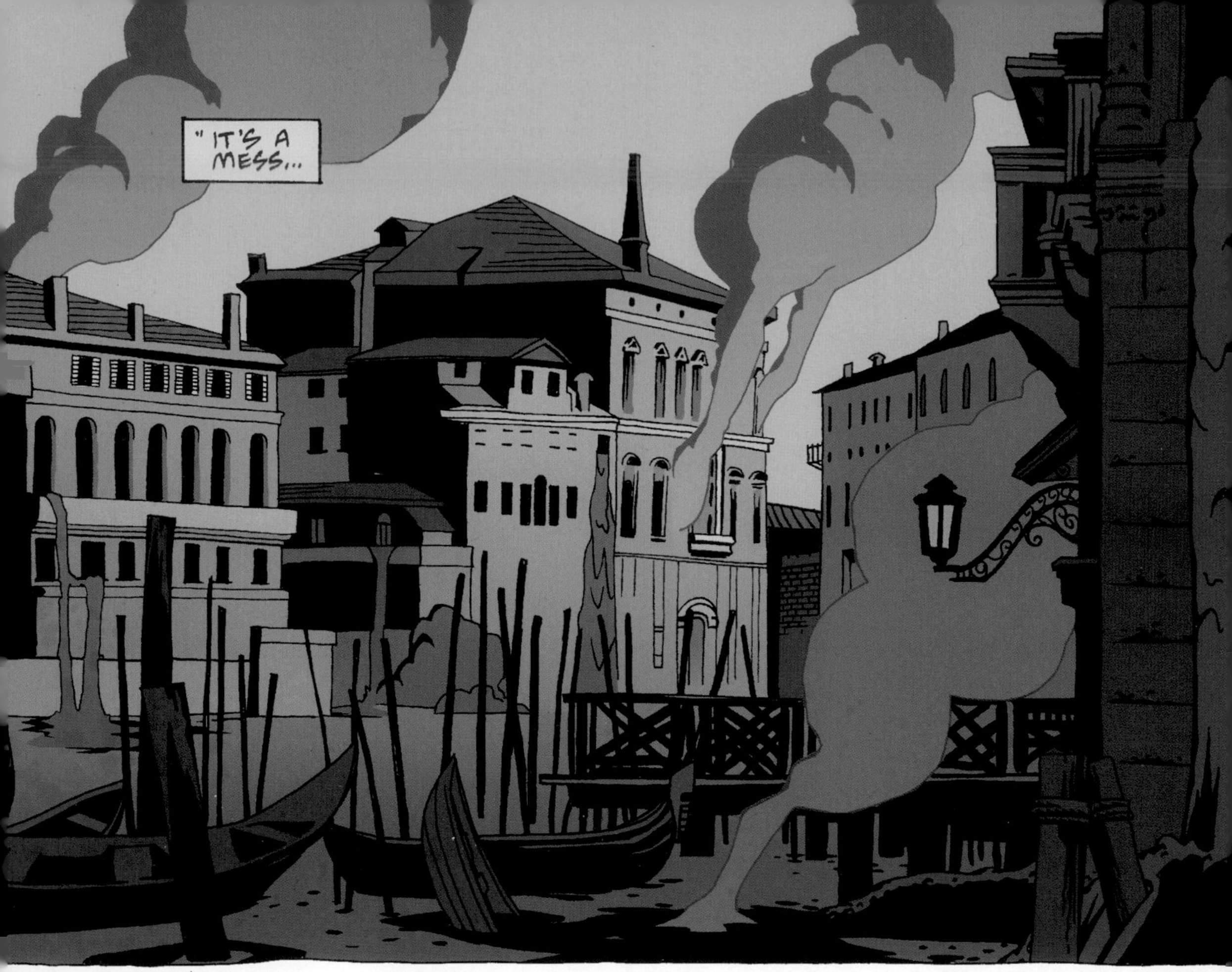
"IT'S A MESS...

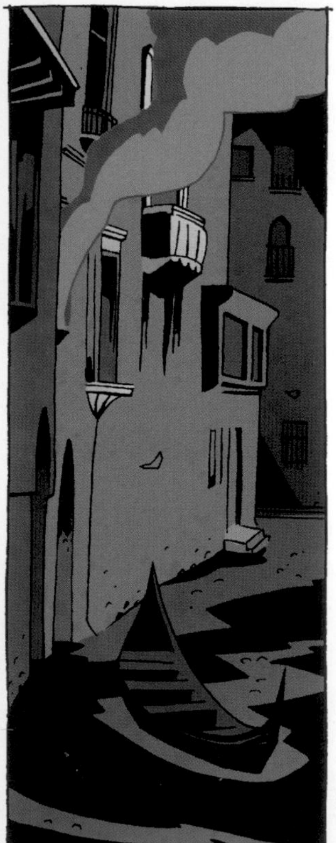

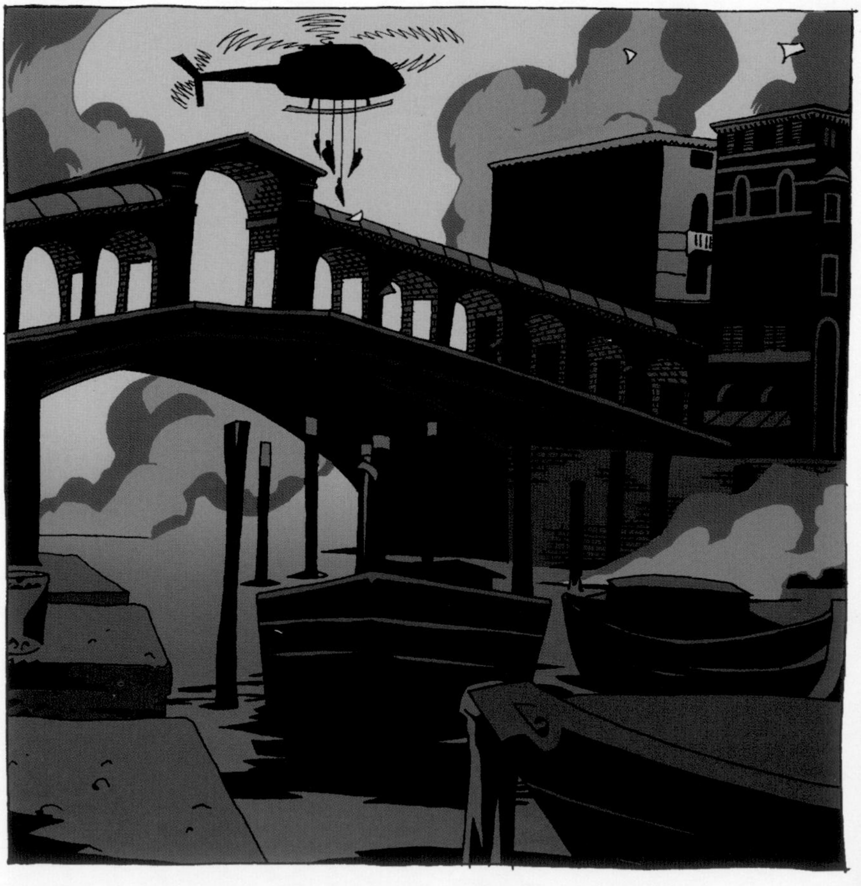

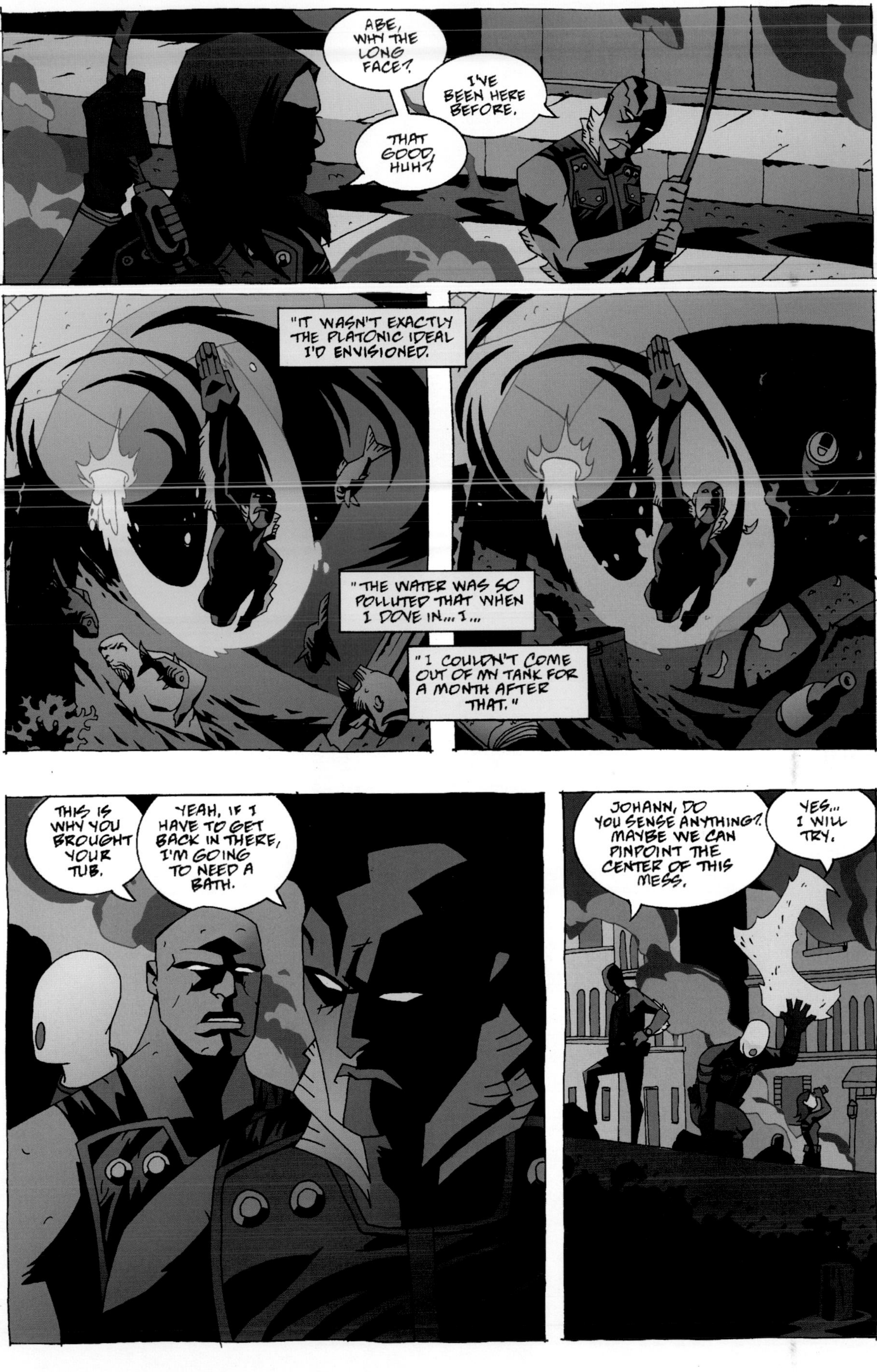
ABE, WHY THE LONG FACE?
I'VE BEEN HERE BEFORE.
THAT GOOD, HUH?
"IT WASN'T EXACTLY THE PLATONIC IDEAL I'D ENVISIONED.
"THE WATER WAS SO POLLUTED THAT WHEN I DOVE IN... I...
"I COULDN'T COME OUT OF MY TANK FOR A MONTH AFTER THAT."
THIS IS WHY YOU BROUGHT YOUR TUB.
YEAH, IF I HAVE TO GET BACK IN THERE, I'M GOING TO NEED A BATH.
JOHANN, DO YOU SENSE ANYTHING? MAYBE WE CAN PINPOINT THE CENTER OF THIS MESS.
YES... I WILL TRY.

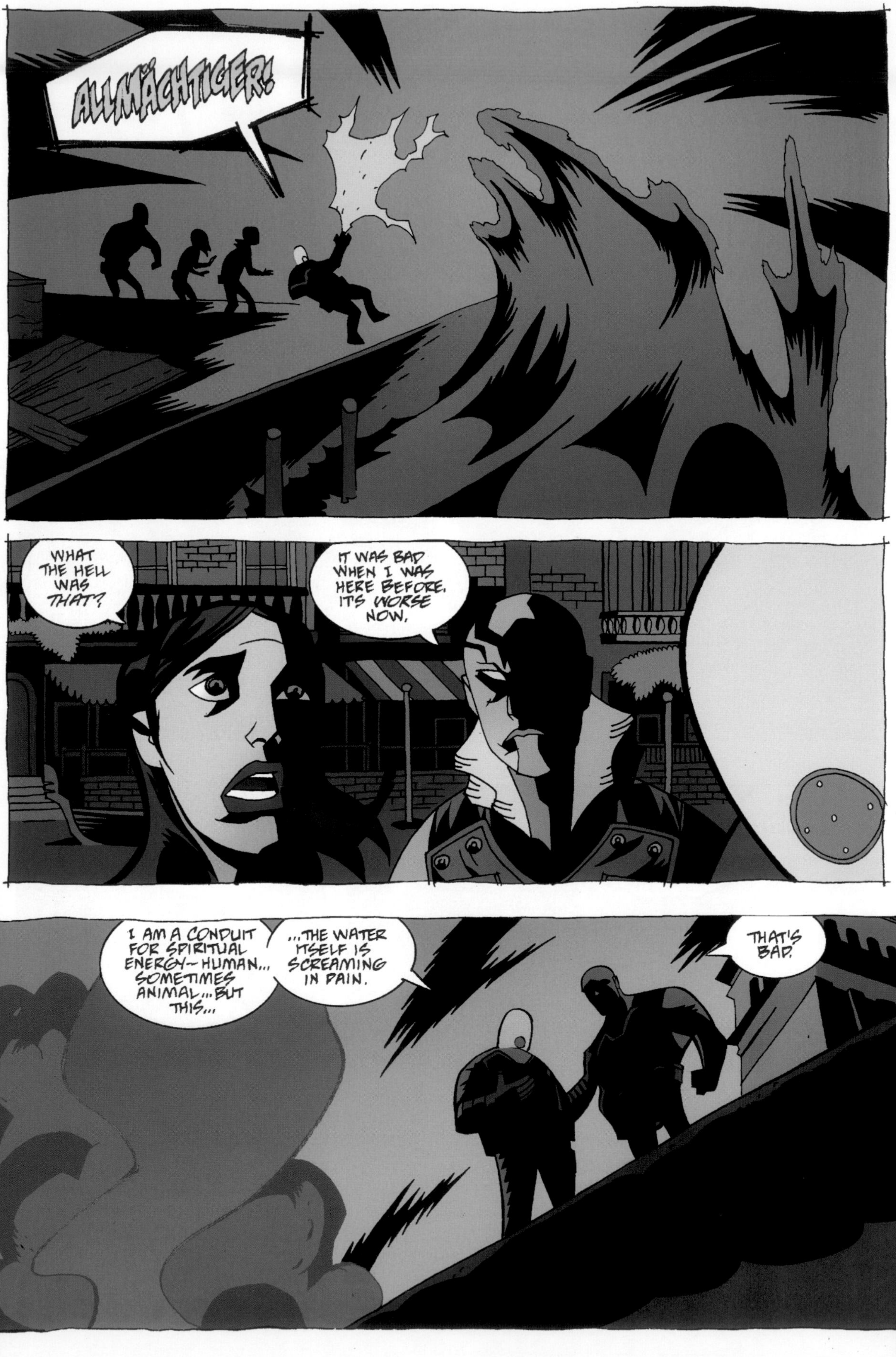
ALLMÄCHTIGER!
WHAT THE HELL WAS THAT?
IT WAS BAD WHEN I WAS HERE BEFORE. IT'S WORSE NOW.
I AM A CONDUIT FOR SPIRITUAL ENERGY-- HUMAN... SOMETIMES ANIMAL... BUT THIS...
...THE WATER ITSELF IS SCREAMING IN PAIN.
THAT'S BAD.

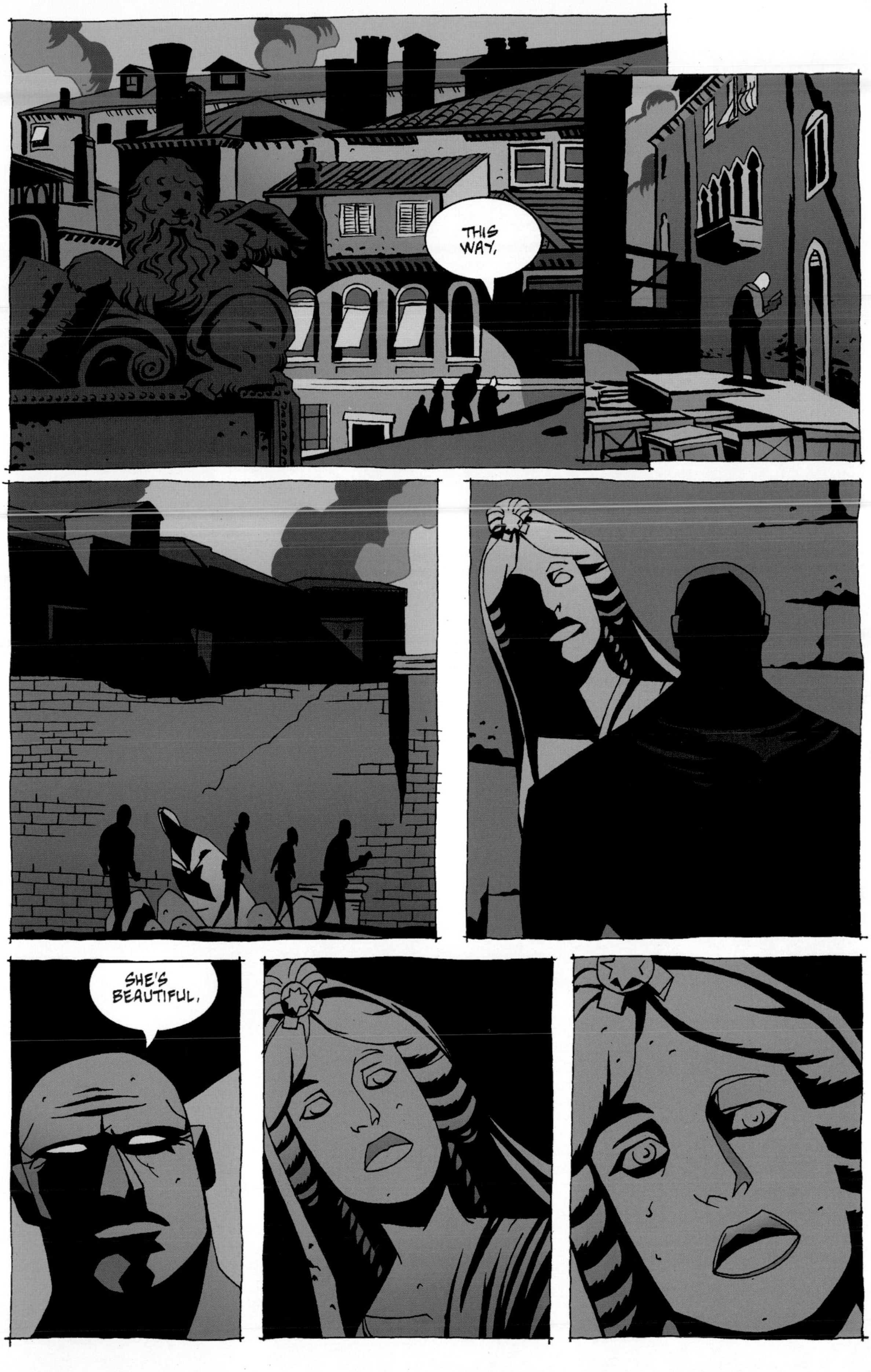
THIS WAY.
SHE'S BEAUTIFUL.

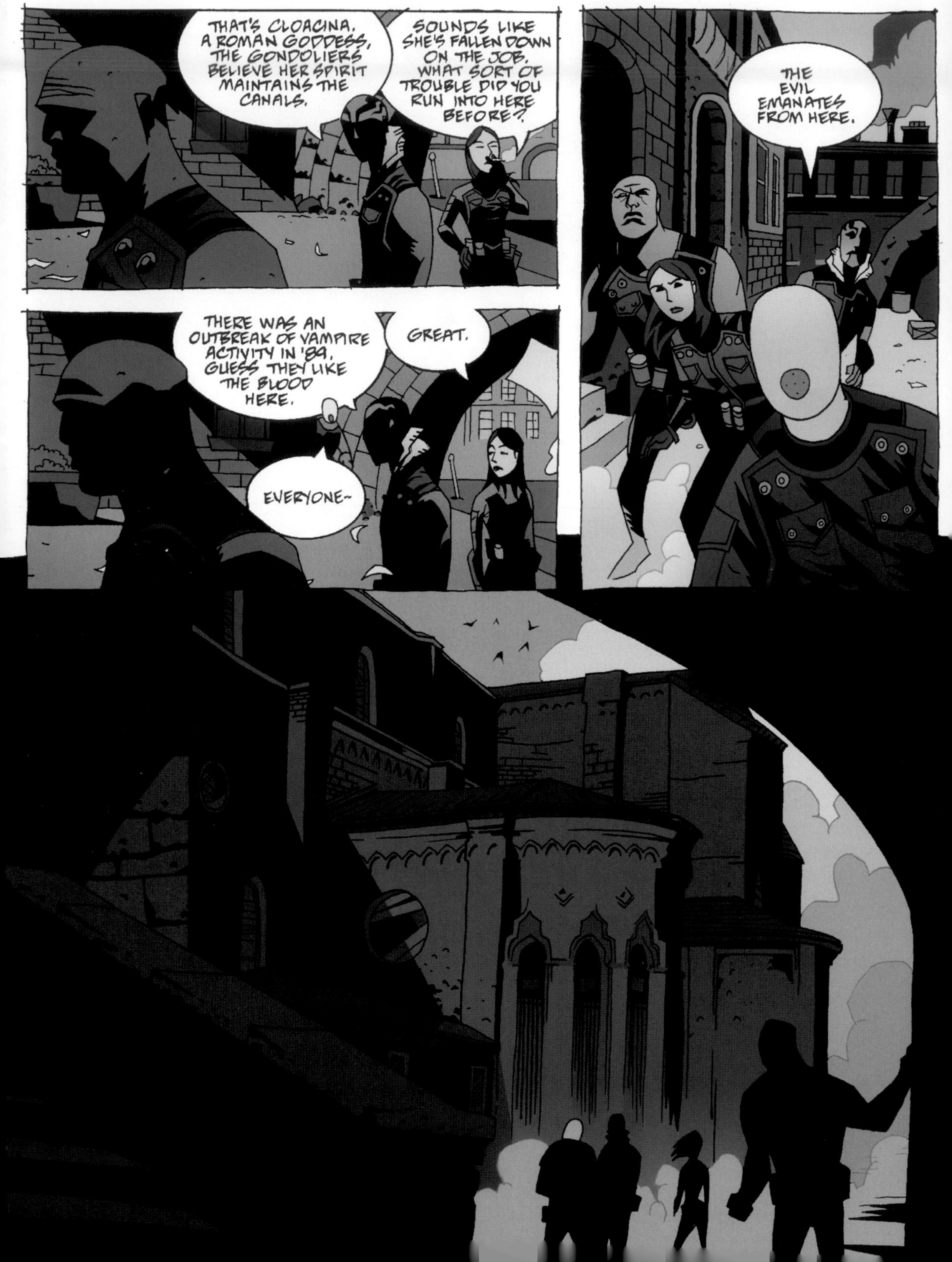
THAT'S CLOACINA, A ROMAN GODDESS. THE GONDOLIERS BELIEVE HER SPIRIT MAINTAINS THE CANALS.
SOUNDS LIKE SHE'S FALLEN DOWN ON THE JOB. WHAT SORT OF TROUBLE DID YOU RUN INTO HERE BEFORE?
THERE WAS AN OUTBREAK OF VAMPIRE ACTIVITY IN '89. GUESS THEY LIKE THE BLOOD HERE.
GREAT.
EVERYONE--
THE EVIL EMANATES FROM HERE.

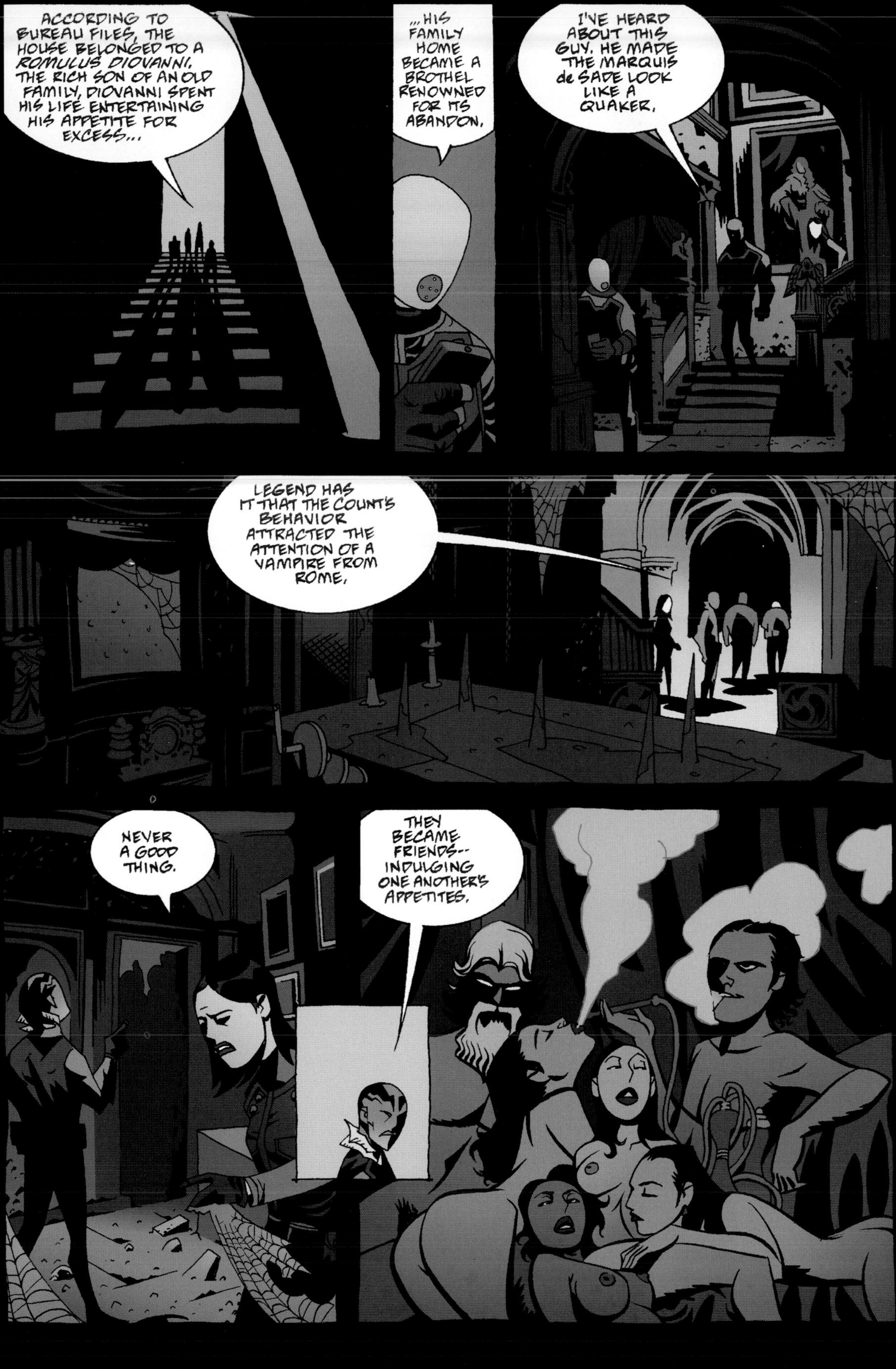
ACCORDING TO BUREAU FILES, THE HOUSE BELONGED TO A *ROMULUS DIOVANNI*. THE RICH SON OF AN OLD FAMILY, DIOVANNI SPENT HIS LIFE ENTERTAINING HIS APPETITE FOR EXCESS...
...HIS FAMILY HOME BECAME A BROTHEL RENOWNED FOR ITS ABANDON.
I'VE HEARD ABOUT THIS GUY. HE MADE THE MARQUIS de SADE LOOK LIKE A QUAKER.
LEGEND HAS IT THAT THE COUNT'S BEHAVIOR ATTRACTED THE ATTENTION OF A VAMPIRE FROM ROME.
NEVER A GOOD THING.
THEY BECAME FRIENDS-- INDULGING ONE ANOTHER'S APPETITES.

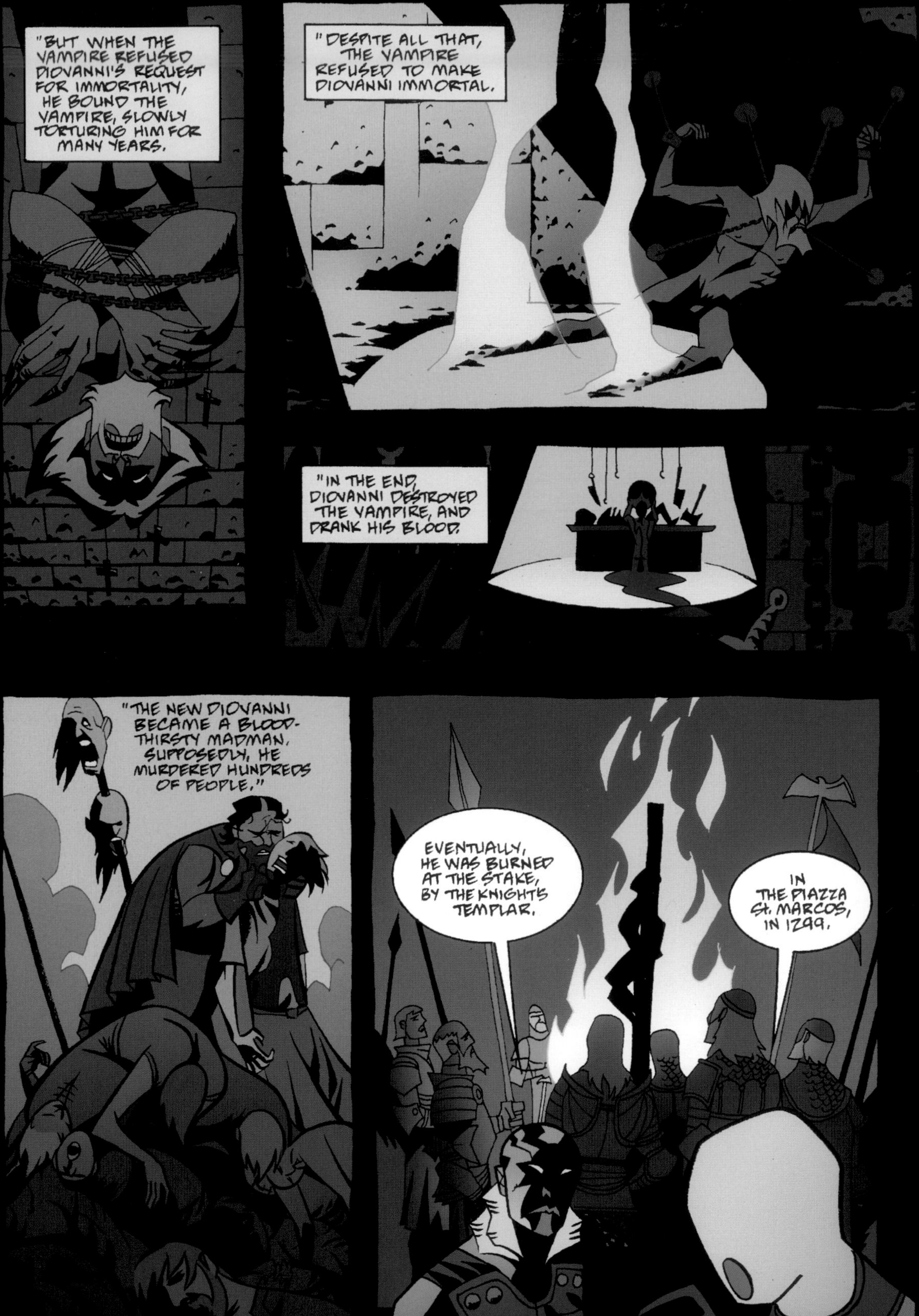

"BUT WHEN THE VAMPIRE REFUSED DIOVANNI'S REQUEST FOR IMMORTALITY, HE BOUND THE VAMPIRE, SLOWLY TORTURING HIM FOR MANY YEARS.
"DESPITE ALL THAT, THE VAMPIRE REFUSED TO MAKE DIOVANNI IMMORTAL.
"IN THE END, DIOVANNI DESTROYED THE VAMPIRE, AND DRANK HIS BLOOD.
"THE NEW DIOVANNI BECAME A BLOOD-THIRSTY MADMAN. SUPPOSEDLY, HE MURDERED HUNDREDS OF PEOPLE."
EVENTUALLY, HE WAS BURNED AT THE STAKE, BY THE KNIGHT'S TEMPLAR.
IN THE PIAZZA St. MARCOS, IN 1299.

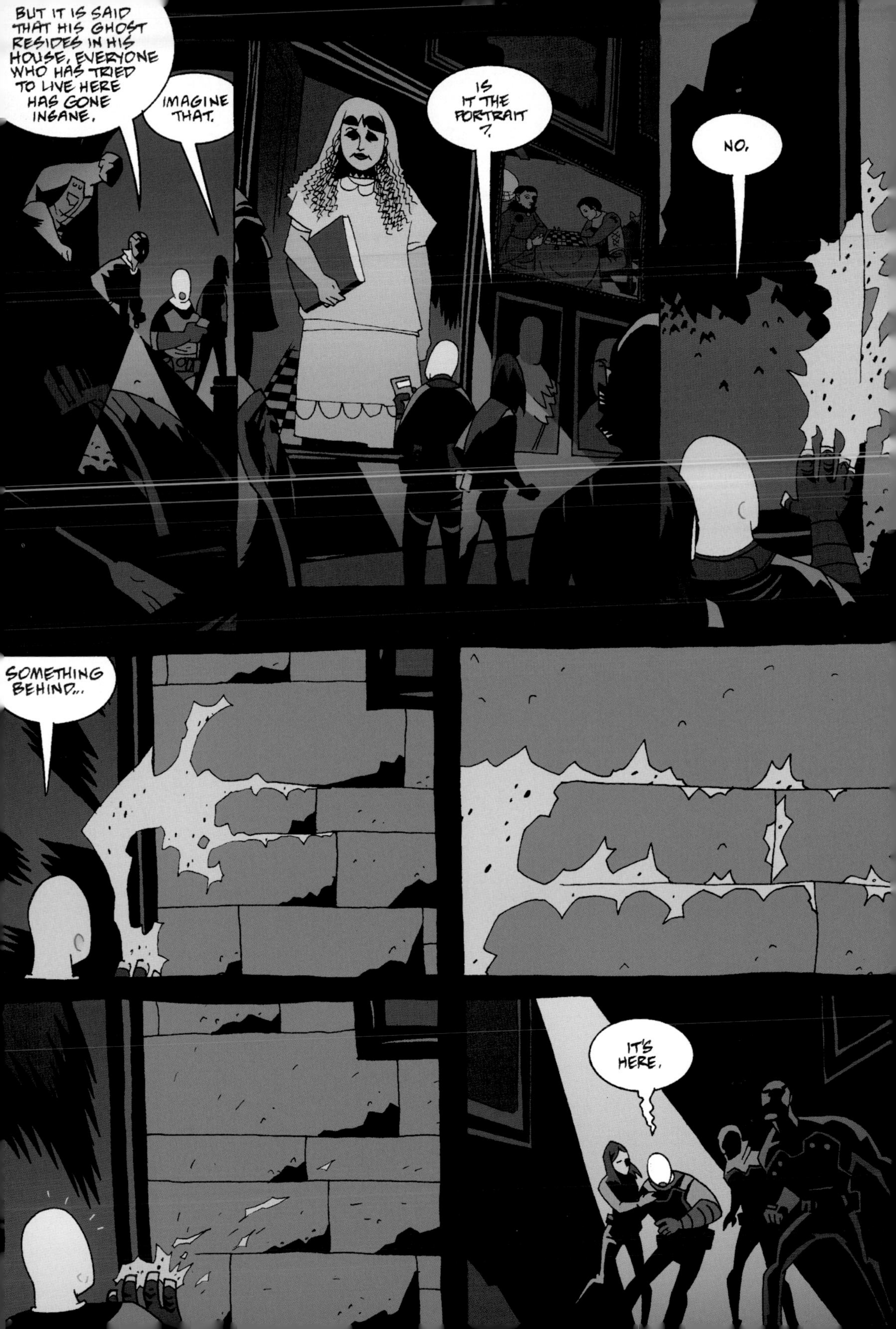
BUT IT IS SAID THAT HIS GHOST RESIDES IN HIS HOUSE. EVERYONE WHO HAS TRIED TO LIVE HERE HAS GONE INSANE.
IMAGINE THAT.
IS IT THE PORTRAIT ?
NO.
SOMETHING BEHIND...
IT'S HERE.

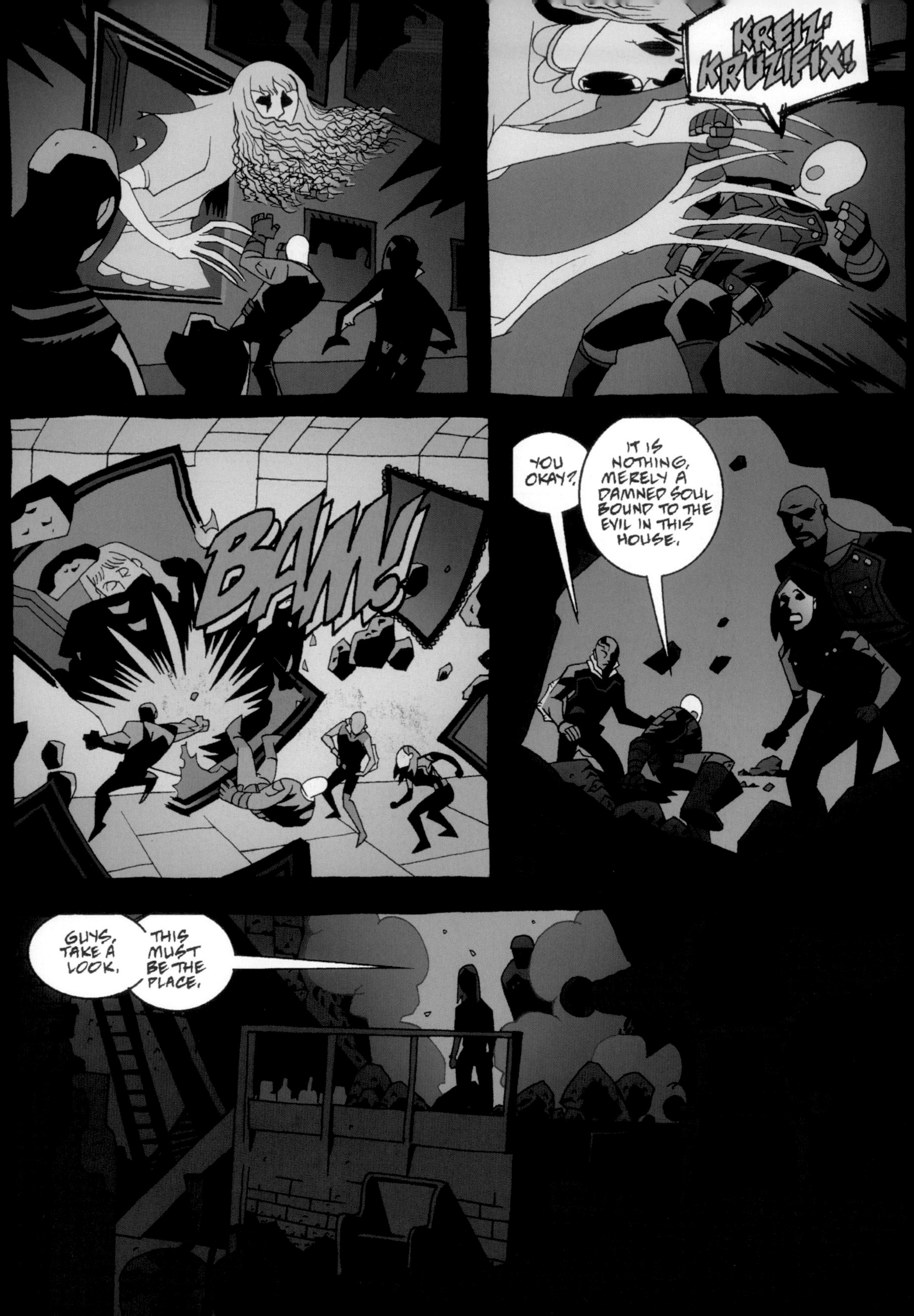
KREIZ-KRUZIFIX!
BAM!
YOU OKAY?
IT IS NOTHING, MERELY A DAMNED SOUL BOUND TO THE EVIL IN THIS HOUSE.
GUYS, TAKE A LOOK.
THIS MUST BE THE PLACE.

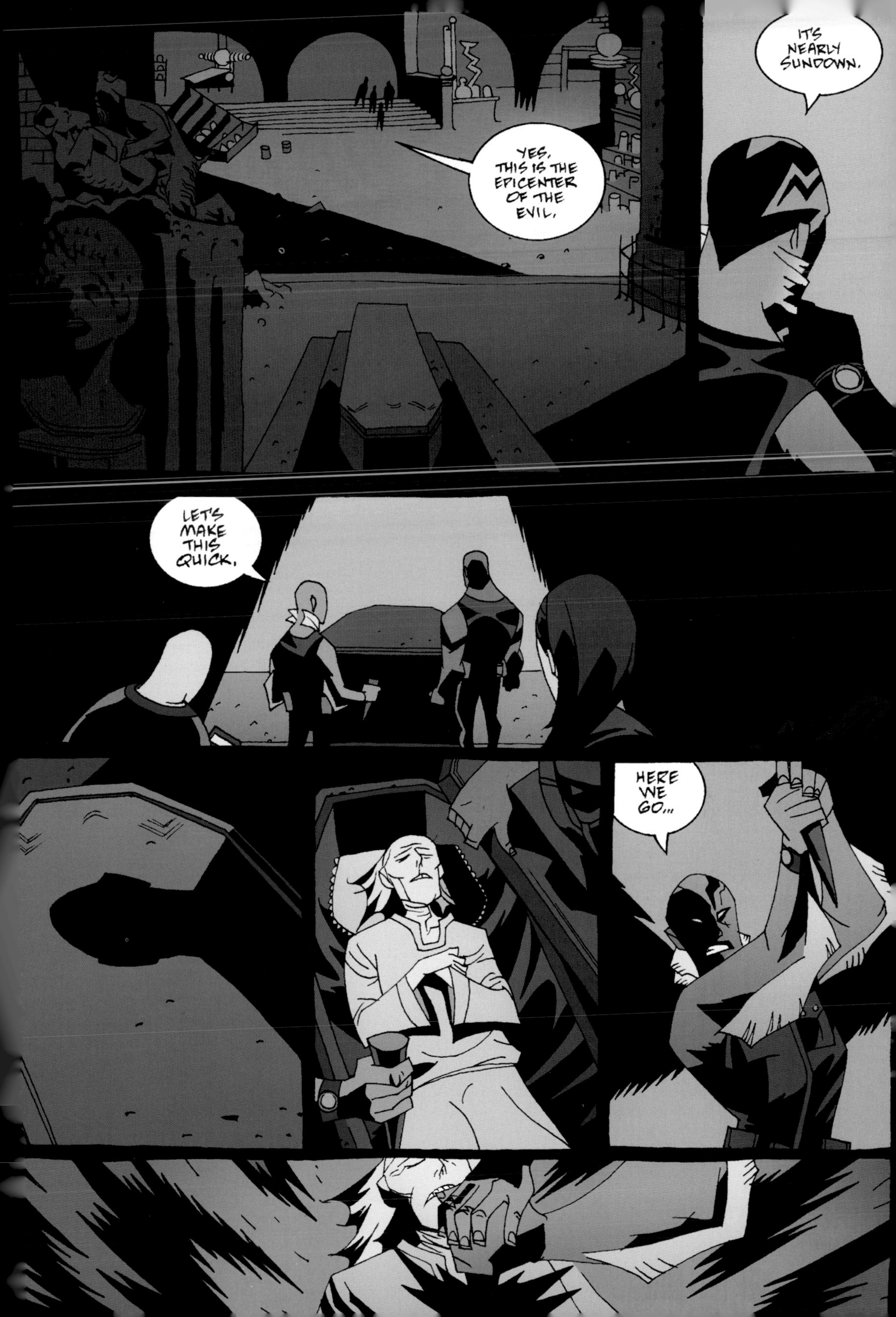
IT'S NEARLY SUNDOWN.
YES, THIS IS THE EPICENTER OF THE EVIL.
LET'S MAKE THIS QUICK.
HERE WE GO...

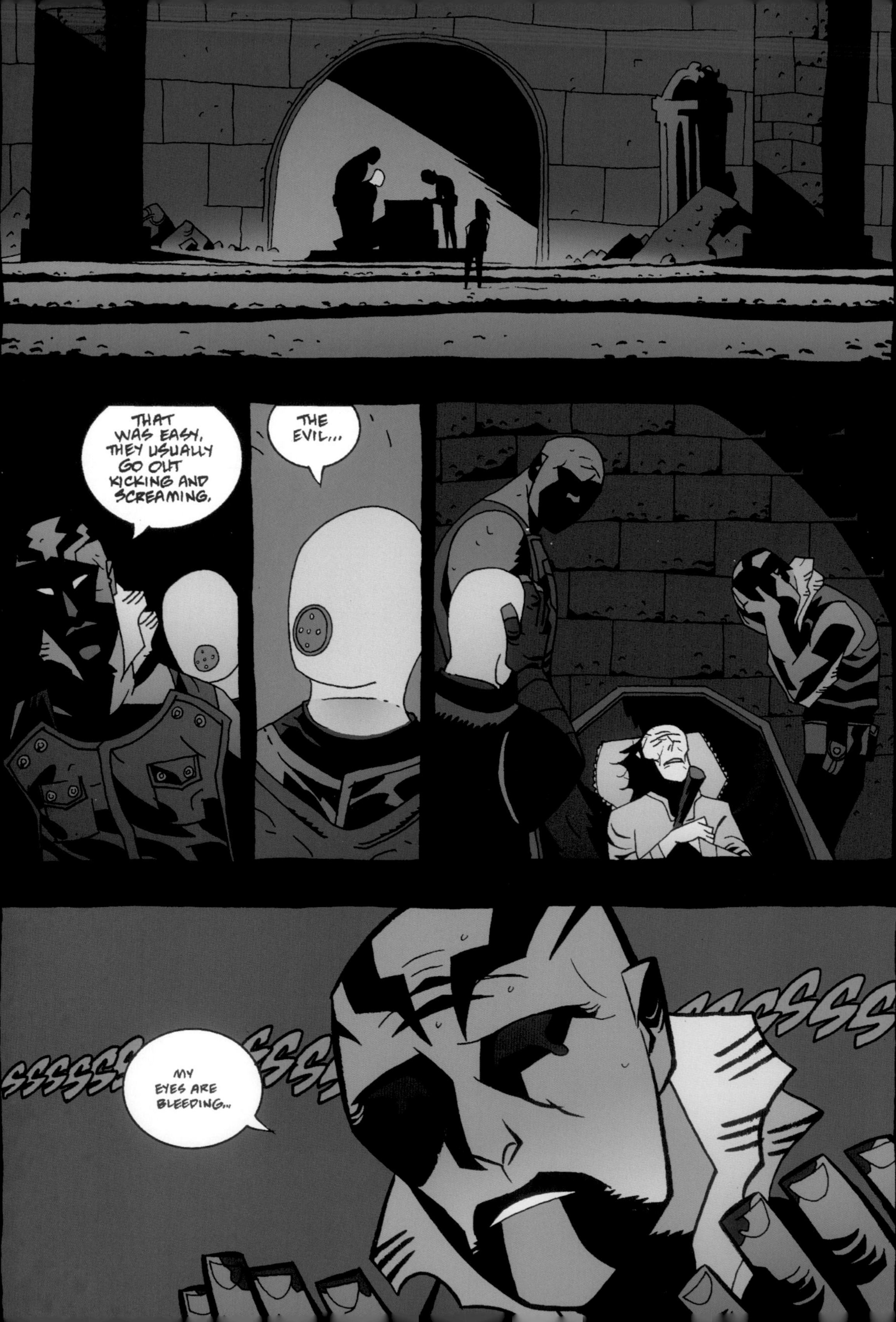
THAT WAS EASY. THEY USUALLY GO OUT KICKING AND SCREAMING.
THE EVIL...
SSSSSS SSSS SSSSS
MY EYES ARE BLEEDING...

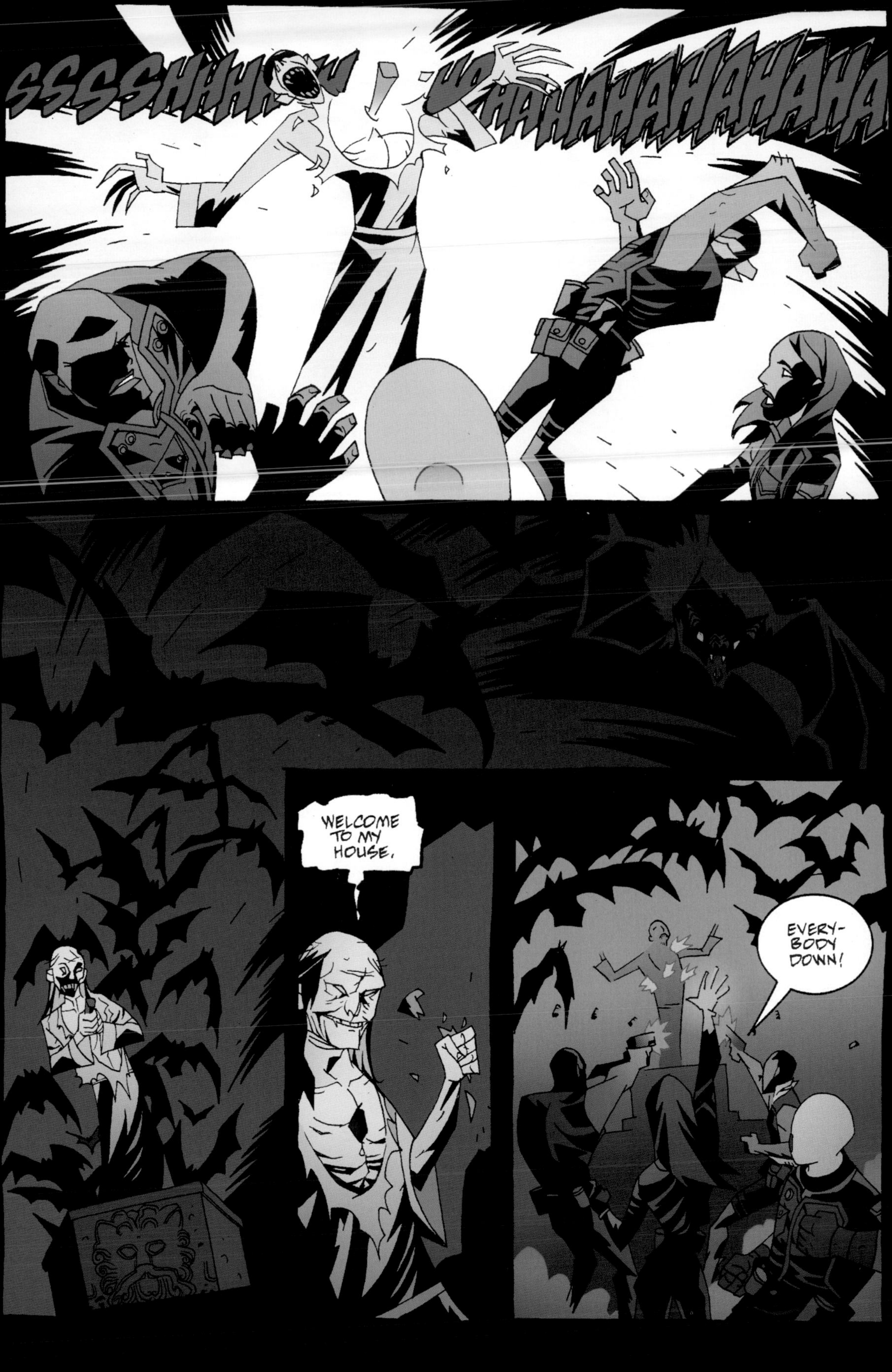
SSSSHHHHOW
WAHAHAHAHAHAHAHA
WELCOME TO MY HOUSE.
EVERY-BODY DOWN!

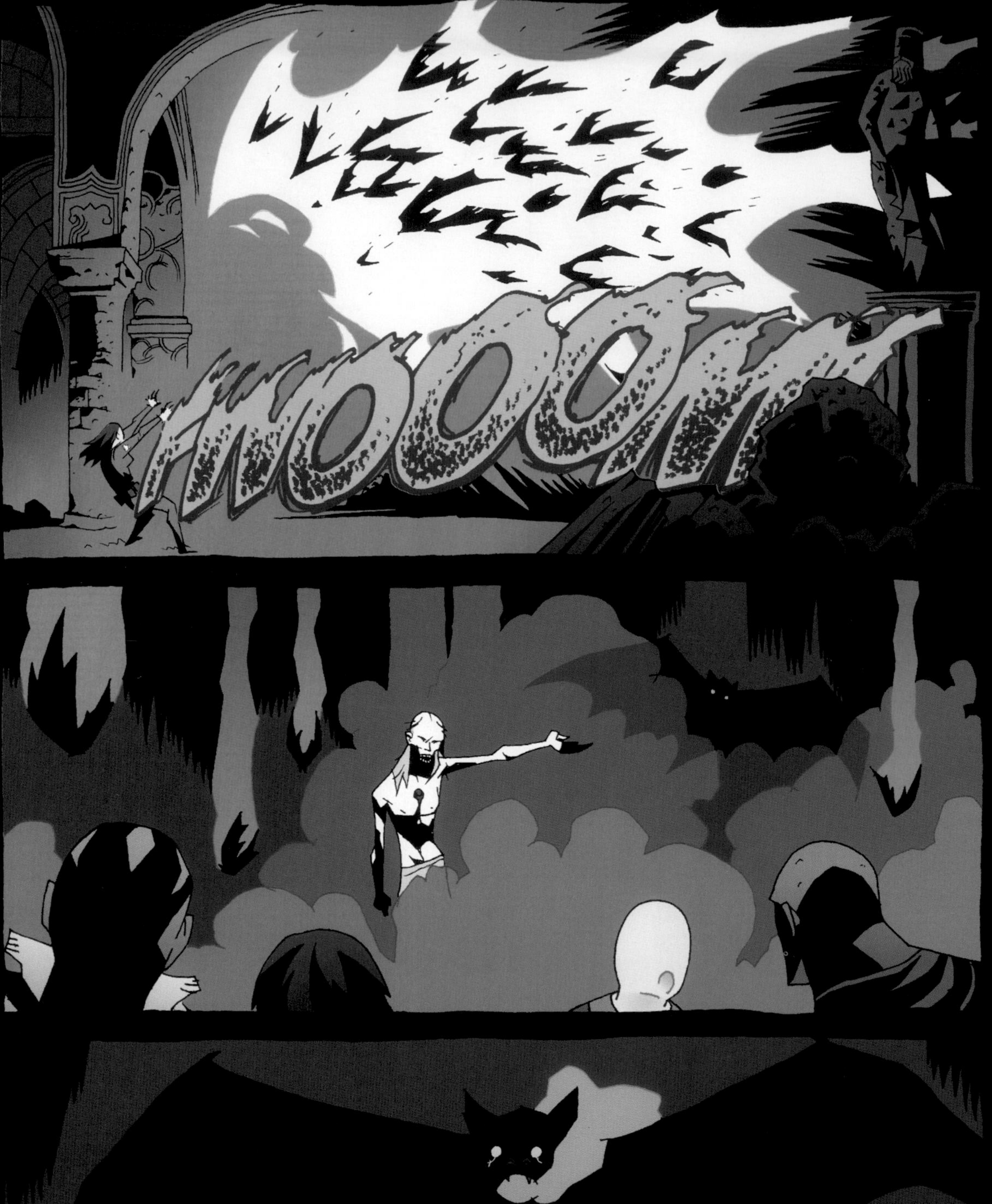
FWOOOM

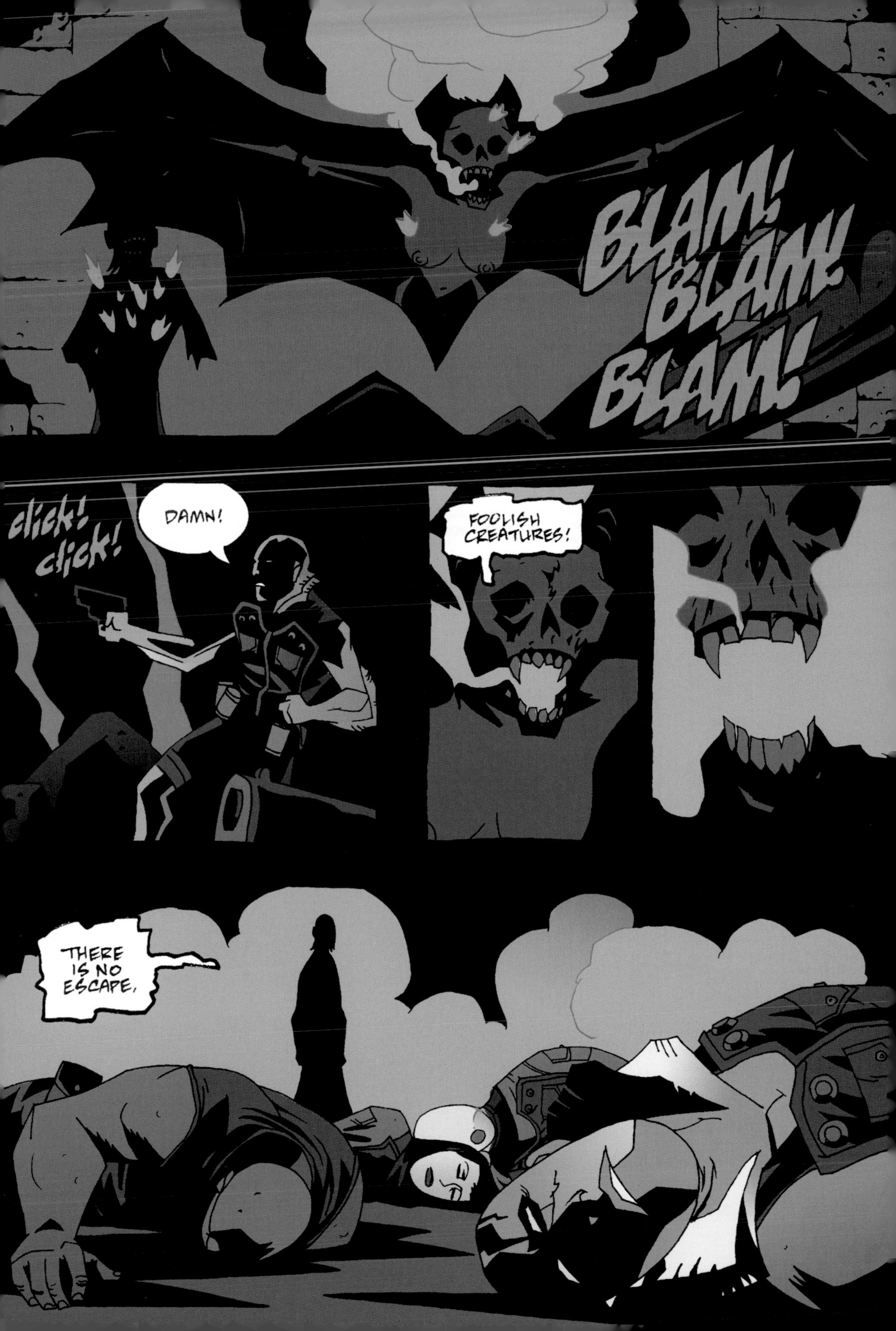
BLAM! BLAM! BLAM!
click! click!
DAMN!
FOOLISH CREATURES!
THERE IS NO ESCAPE,

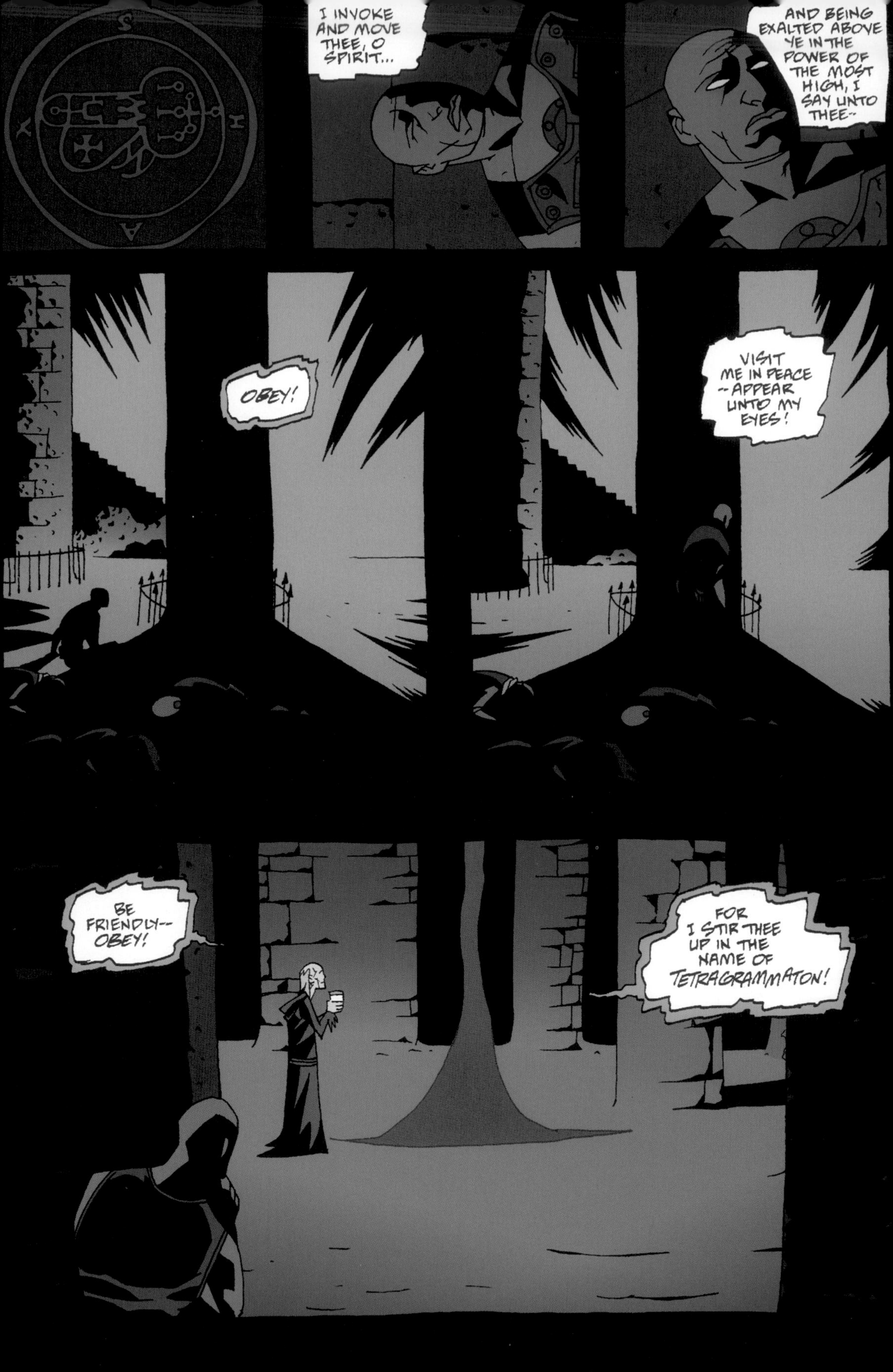
I INVOKE AND MOVE THEE, O SPIRIT...
AND BEING EXALTED ABOVE YE IN THE POWER OF THE MOST HIGH, I SAY UNTO THEE--
OBEY!
VISIT ME IN PEACE --APPEAR UNTO MY EYES!
BE FRIENDLY-- OBEY!
FOR I STIR THEE UP IN THE NAME OF TETRAGRAMMATON!

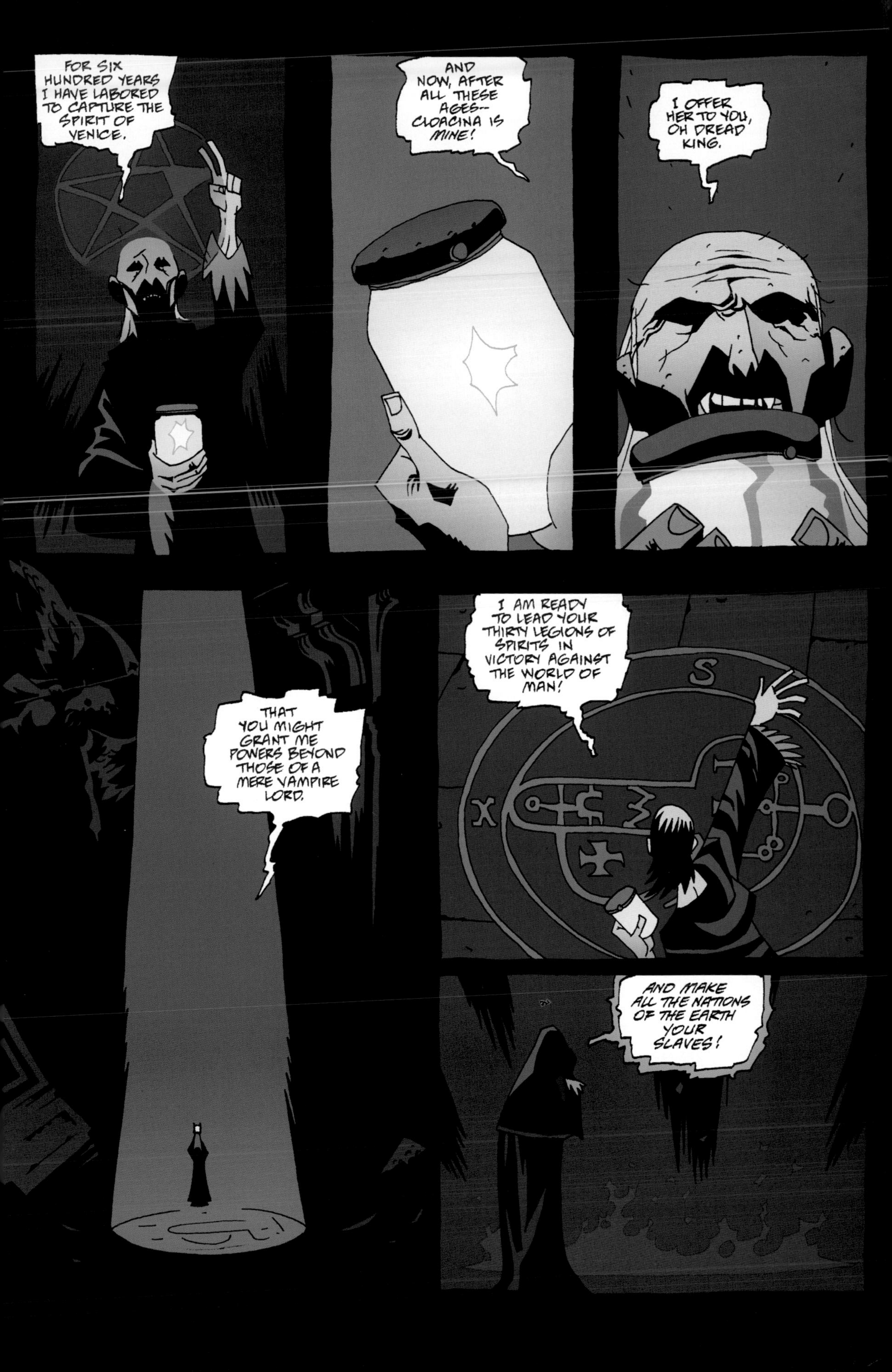
FOR SIX HUNDRED YEARS I HAVE LABORED TO CAPTURE THE SPIRIT OF VENICE.
AND NOW, AFTER ALL THESE AGES-- CLOACINA IS MINE!
I OFFER HER TO YOU, OH DREAD KING.
THAT YOU MIGHT GRANT ME POWERS BEYOND THOSE OF A MERE VAMPIRE LORD.
I AM READY TO LEAD YOUR THIRTY LEGIONS OF SPIRITS IN VICTORY AGAINST THE WORLD OF MAN!
AND MAKE ALL THE NATIONS OF THE EARTH YOUR SLAVES!

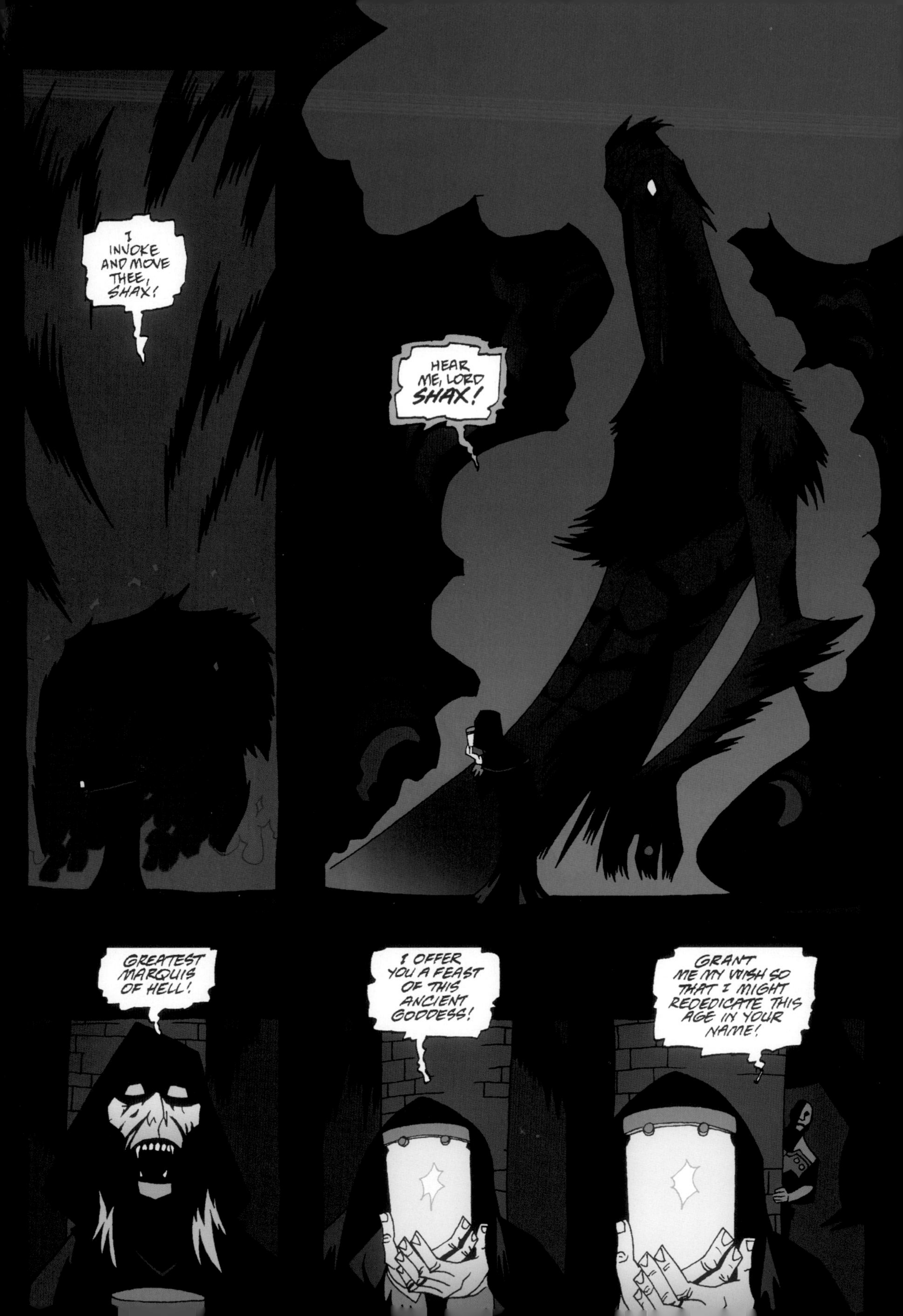
I INVOKE AND MOVE THEE, SHAX!
HEAR ME, LORD SHAX!
GREATEST MARQUIS OF HELL!
I OFFER YOU A FEAST OF THIS ANCIENT GODDESS!
GRANT ME MY WISH SO THAT I MIGHT REDEDICATE THIS AGE IN YOUR NAME!

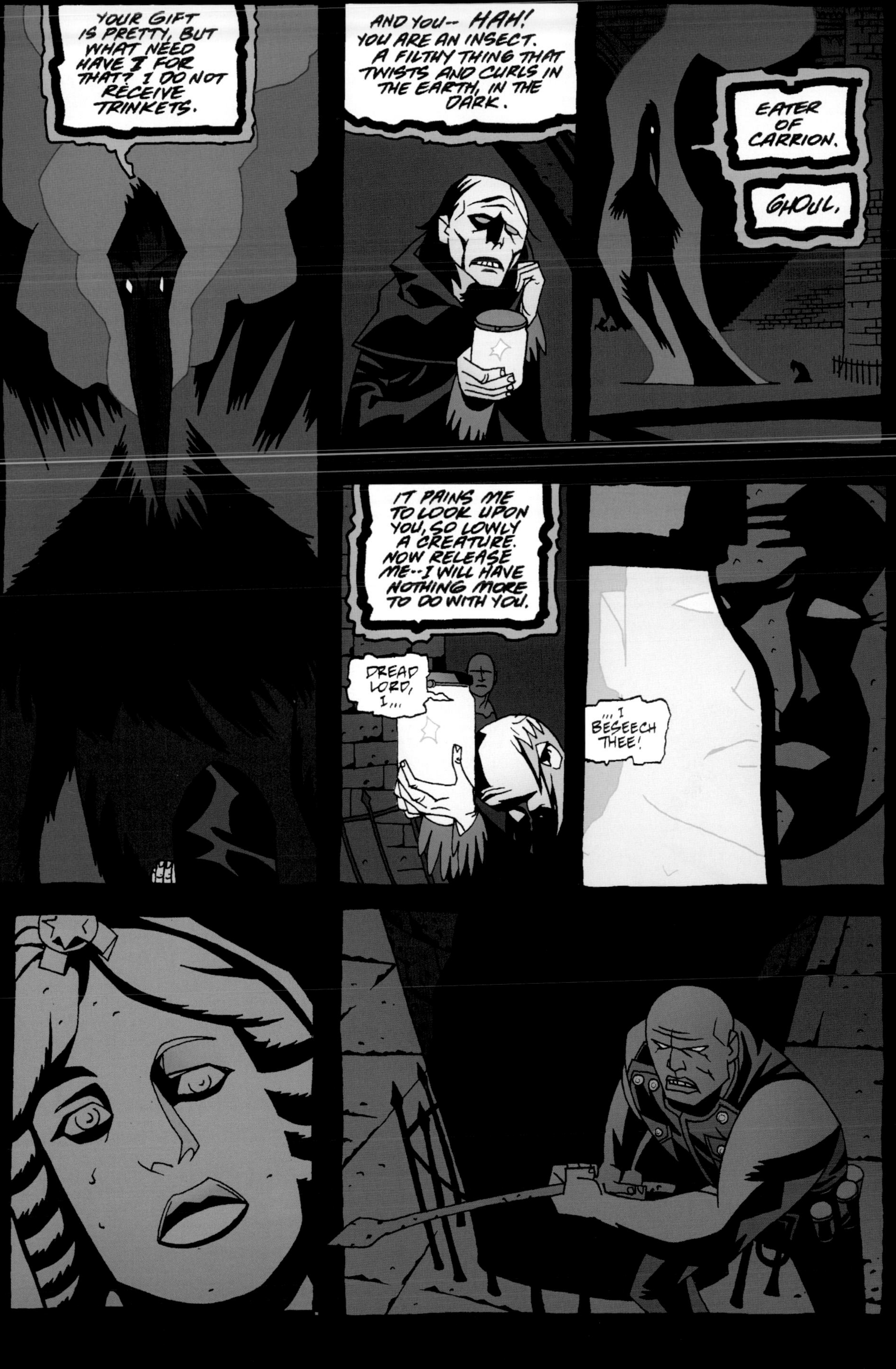
YOUR GIFT IS PRETTY, BUT WHAT NEED HAVE I FOR THAT? I DO NOT RECEIVE TRINKETS.
AND YOU-- HAH! YOU ARE AN INSECT. A FILTHY THING THAT TWISTS AND CURLS IN THE EARTH, IN THE DARK.
EATER OF CARRION.
GHOUL.
IT PAINS ME TO LOOK UPON YOU, SO LOWLY A CREATURE. NOW RELEASE ME--I WILL HAVE NOTHING MORE TO DO WITH YOU.
DREAD LORD, I...
... I BESEECH THEE!

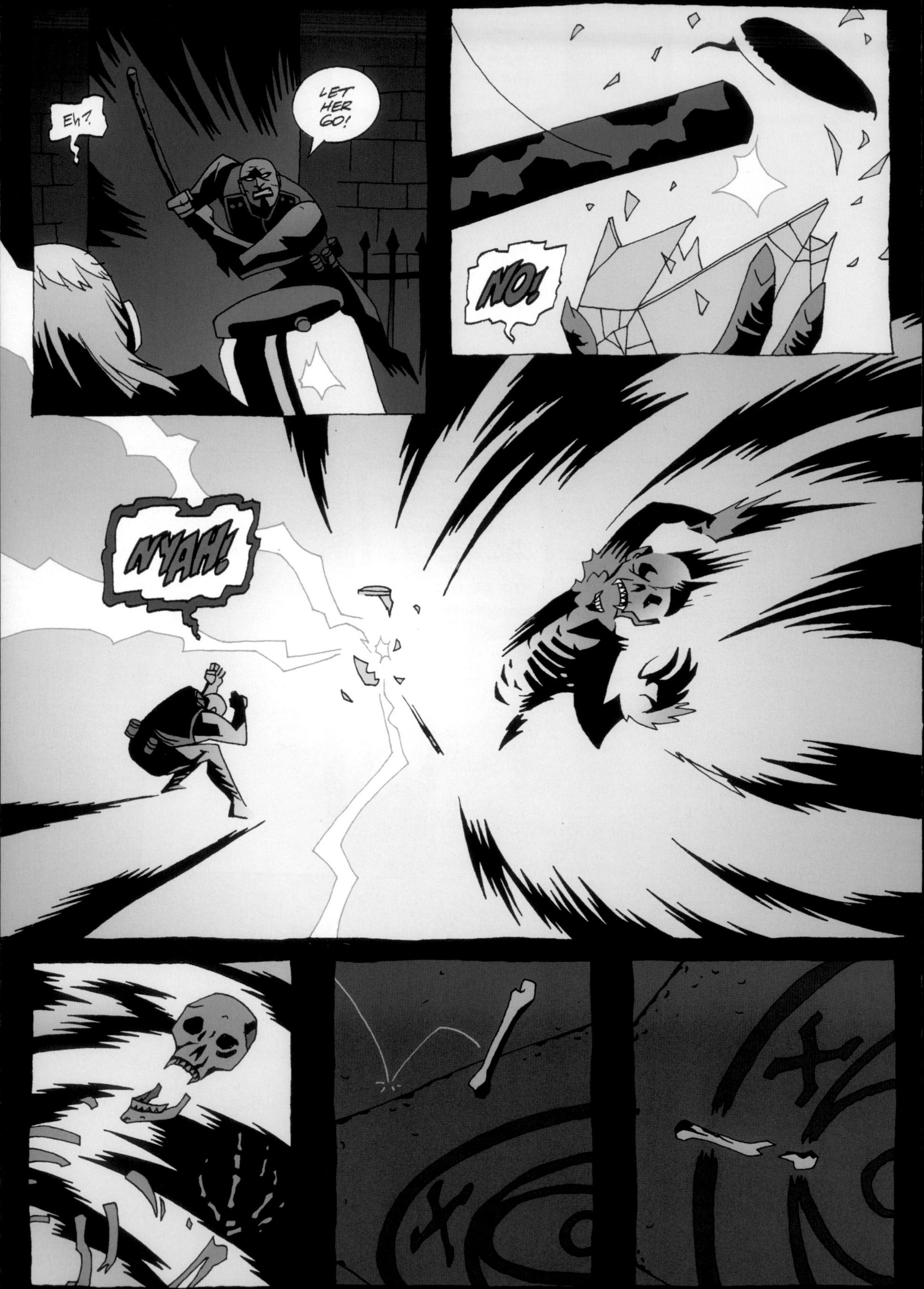

Eh?
LET HER GO!
NO!
N'YAH!

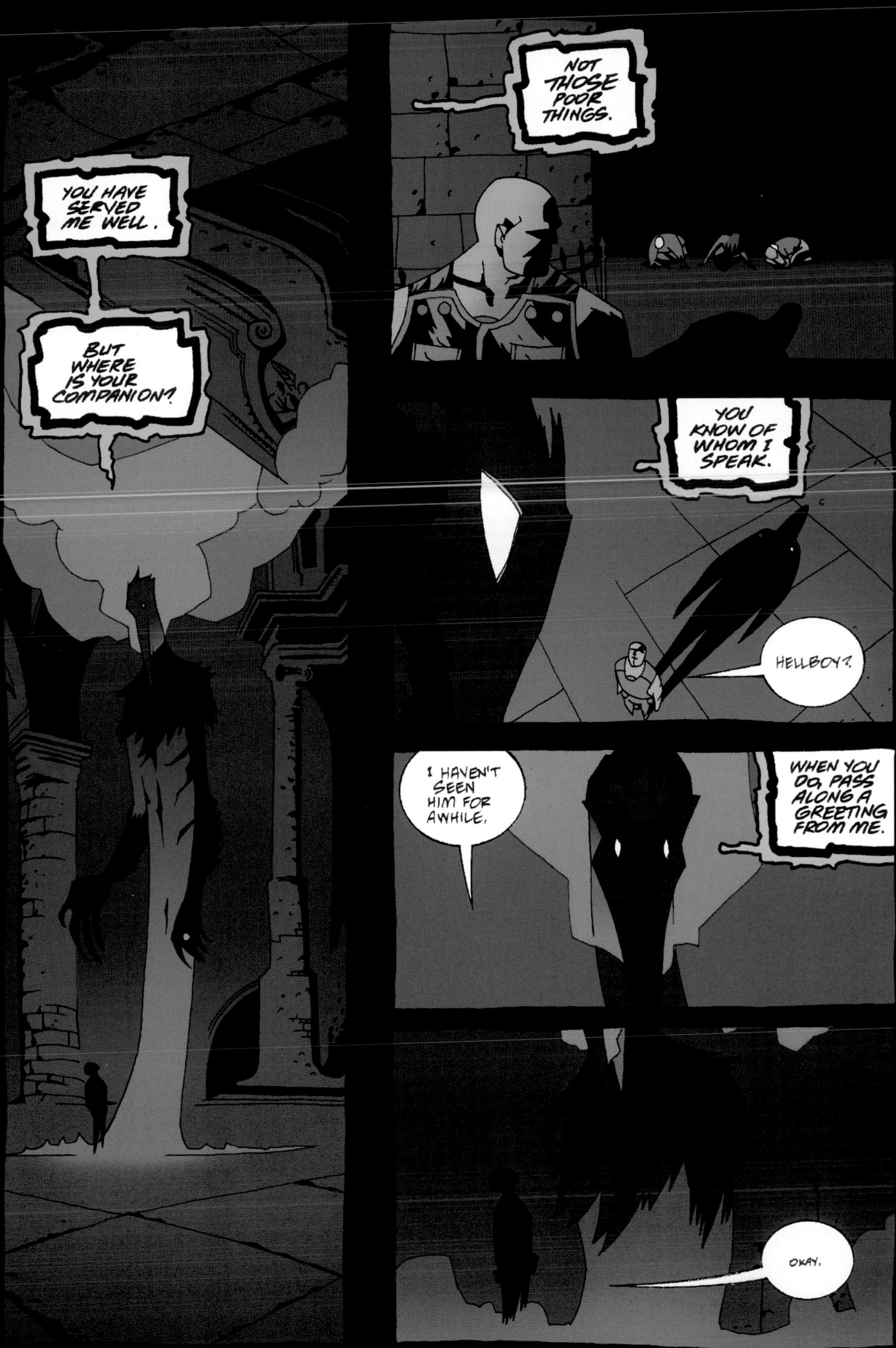
YOU HAVE SERVED ME WELL.
BUT WHERE IS YOUR COMPANION?
NOT THOSE POOR THINGS.
YOU KNOW OF WHOM I SPEAK.
HELLBOY?
I HAVEN'T SEEN HIM FOR AWHILE.
WHEN YOU DO, PASS ALONG A GREETING FROM ME.
OKAY.

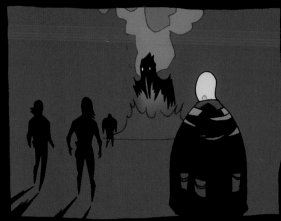

WHO'S THAT?

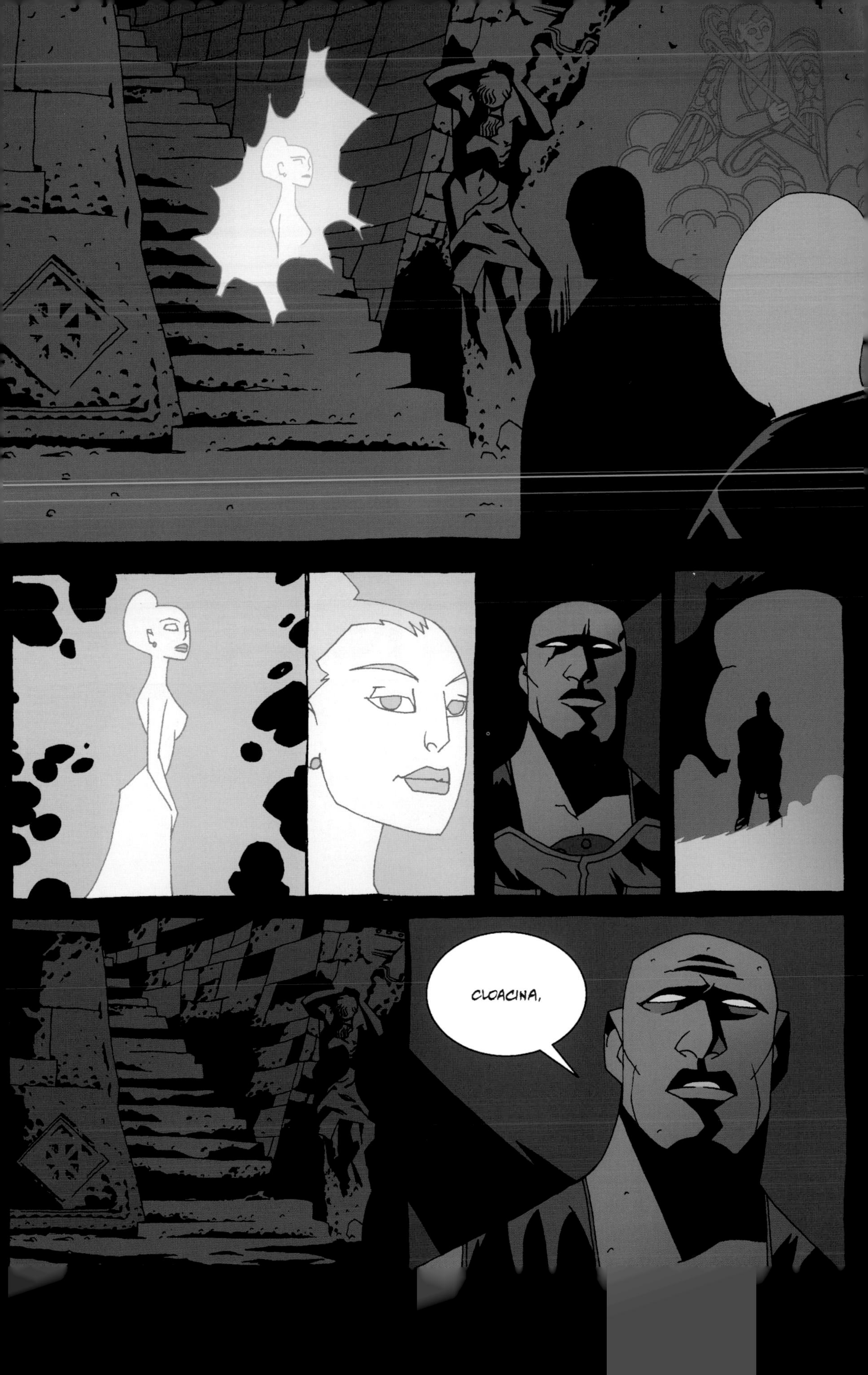
CLOACINA,

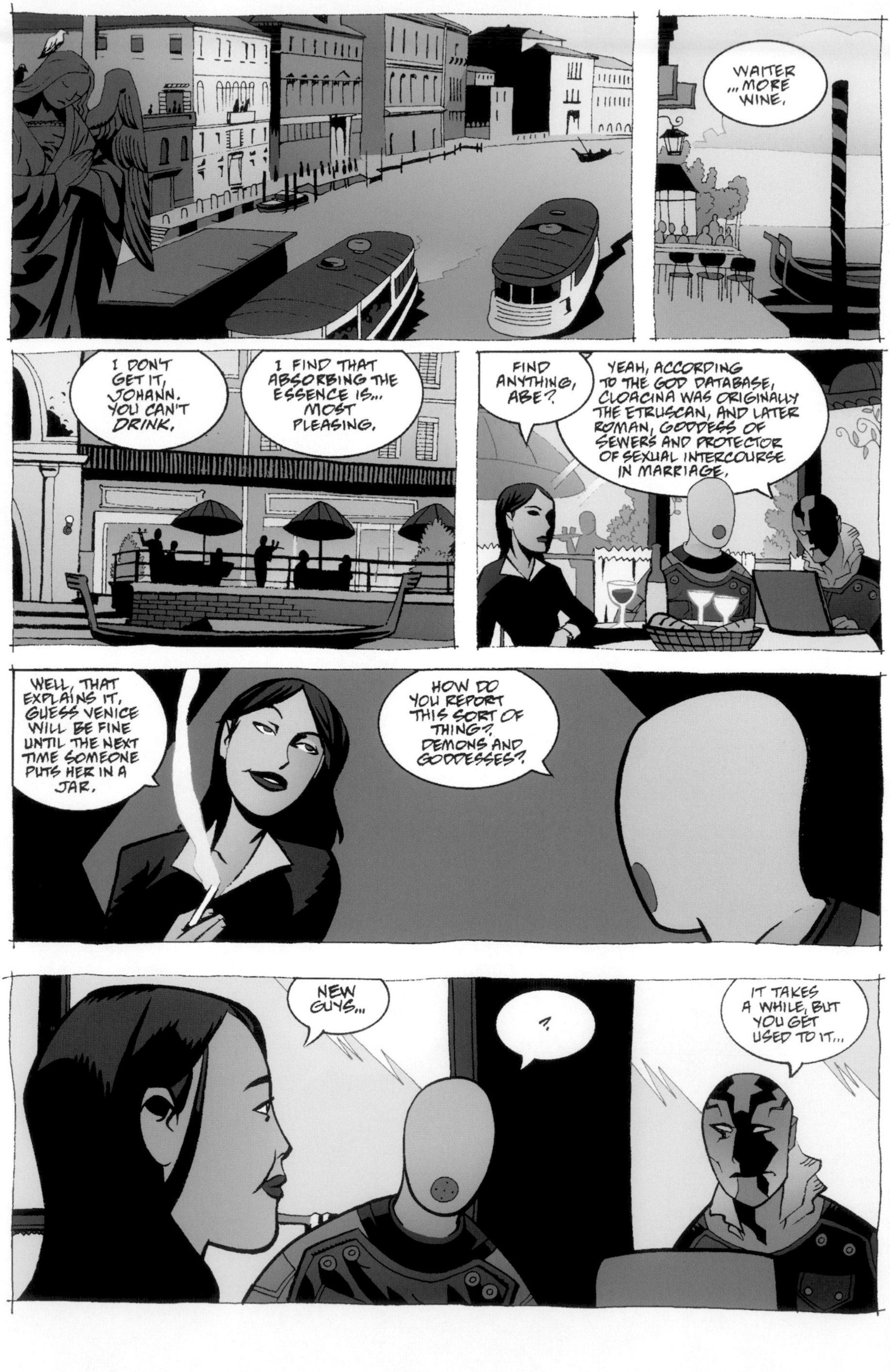
WAITER ...MORE WINE.
I DON'T GET IT, JOHANN. YOU CAN'T DRINK.
I FIND THAT ABSORBING THE ESSENCE IS... MOST PLEASING.
FIND ANYTHING, ABE?
YEAH, ACCORDING TO THE GOD DATABASE, CLOACINA WAS ORIGINALLY THE ETRUSCAN, AND LATER ROMAN, GODDESS OF SEWERS AND PROTECTOR OF SEXUAL INTERCOURSE IN MARRIAGE.
WELL, THAT EXPLAINS IT. GUESS VENICE WILL BE FINE UNTIL THE NEXT TIME SOMEONE PUTS HER IN A JAR.
HOW DO YOU REPORT THIS SORT OF THING? DEMONS AND GODDESSES?
NEW GUYS...
?
IT TAKES A WHILE, BUT YOU GET USED TO IT...

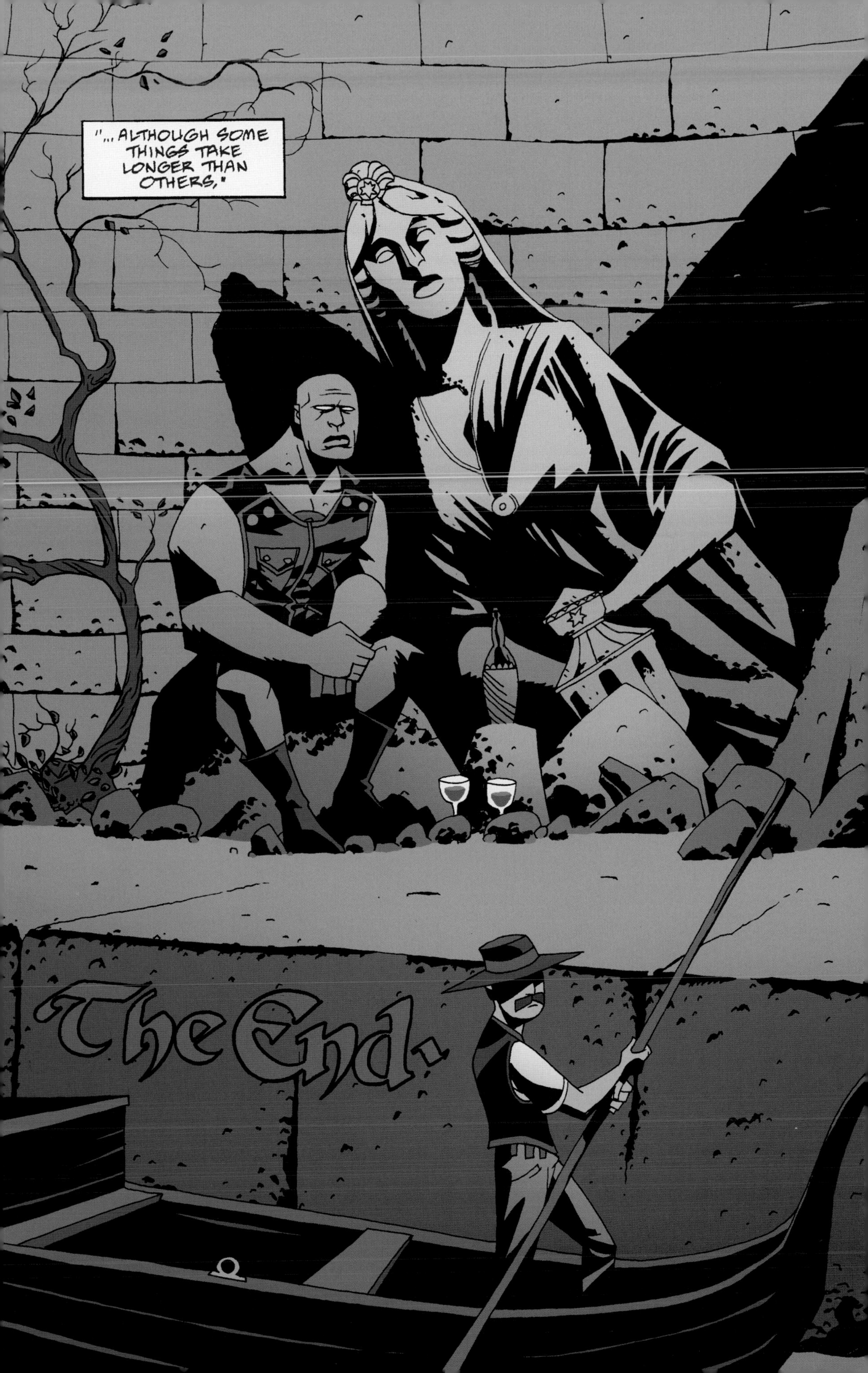
"...ALTHOUGH SOME THINGS TAKE LONGER THAN OTHERS."
The End.

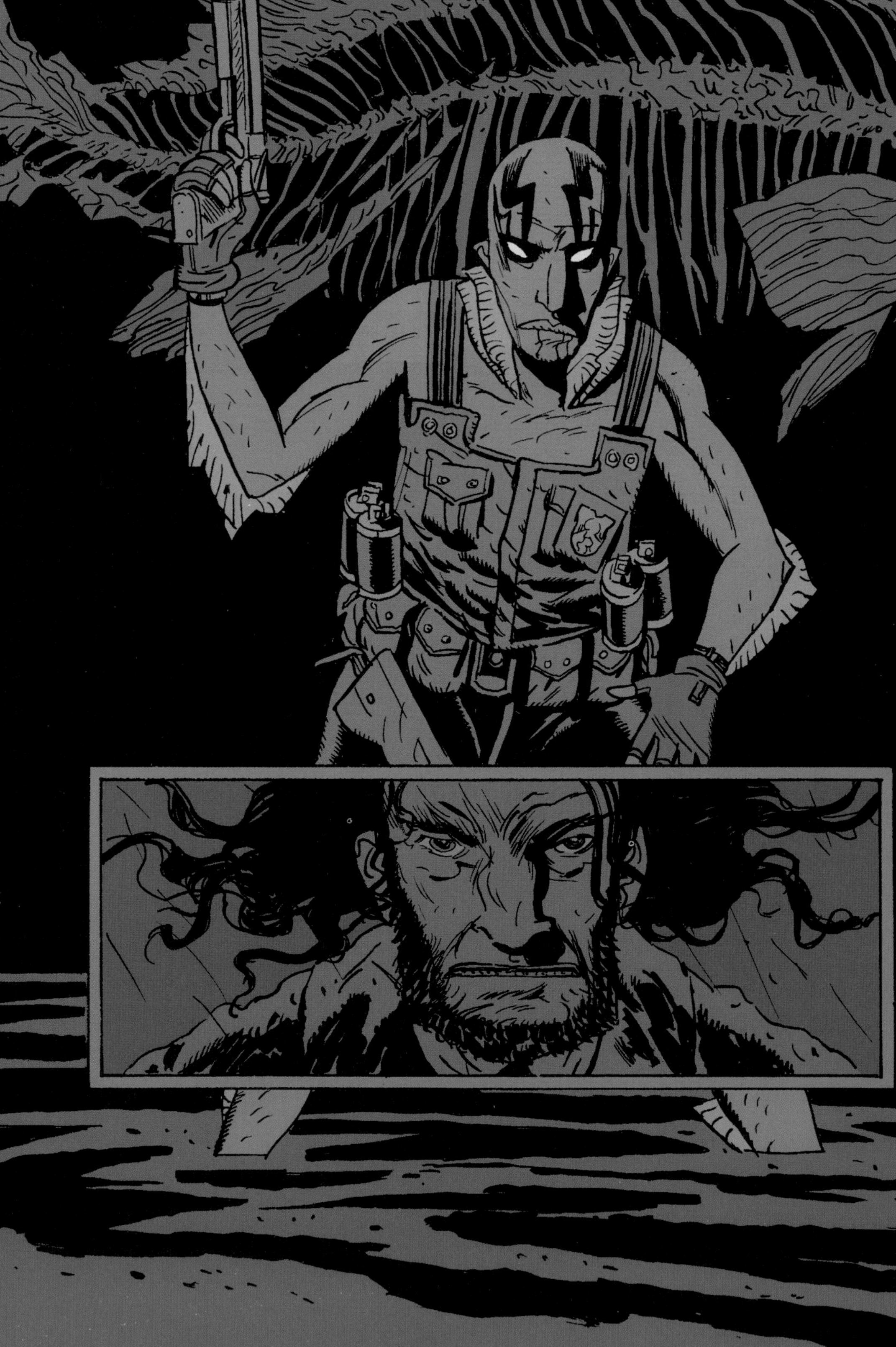

DARK WATERS

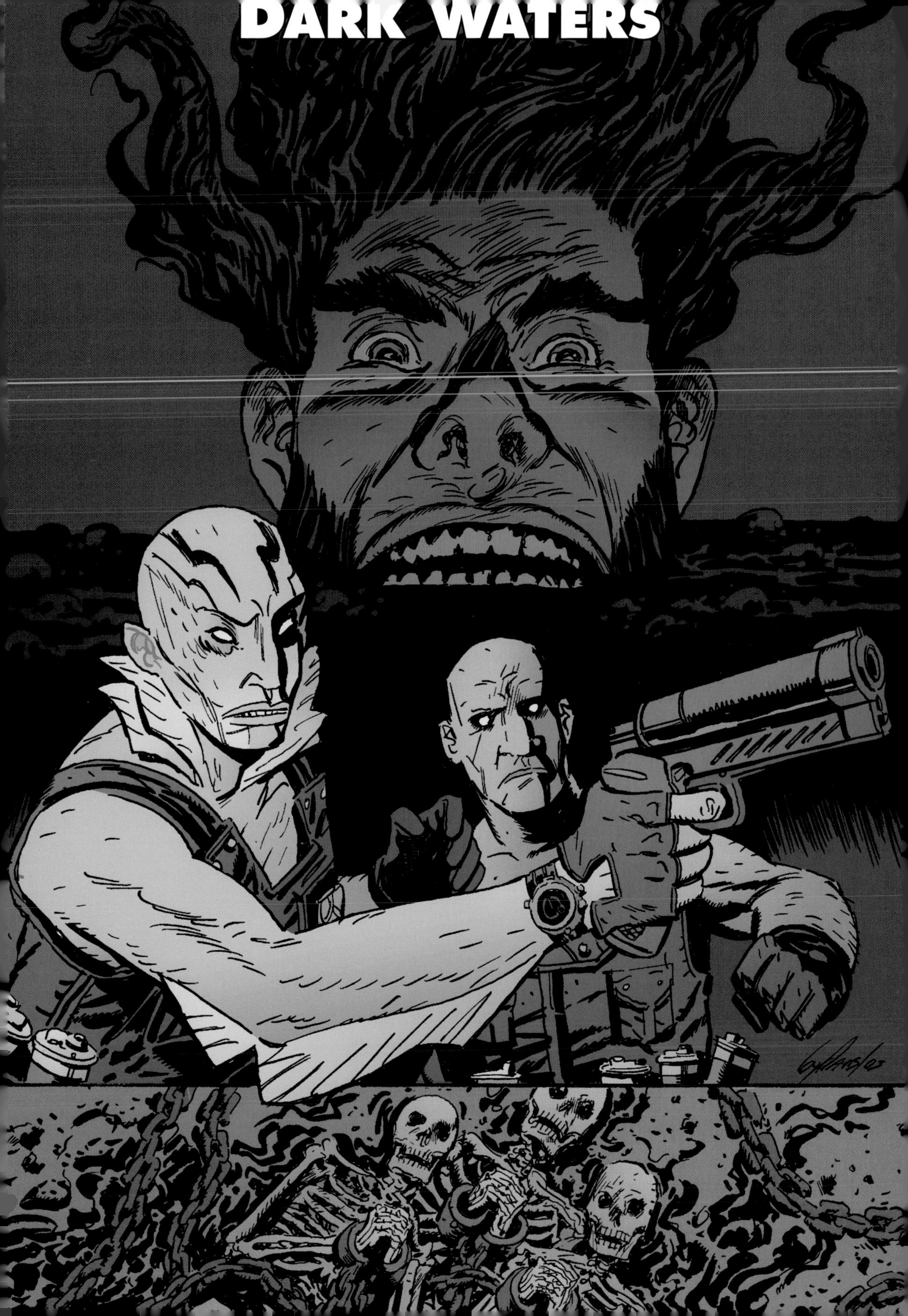

Story by
BRIAN AUGUSTYN

Art by
GUY DAVIS

Colors by
DAVE STEWART

Letters by
MICHELLE MADSEN

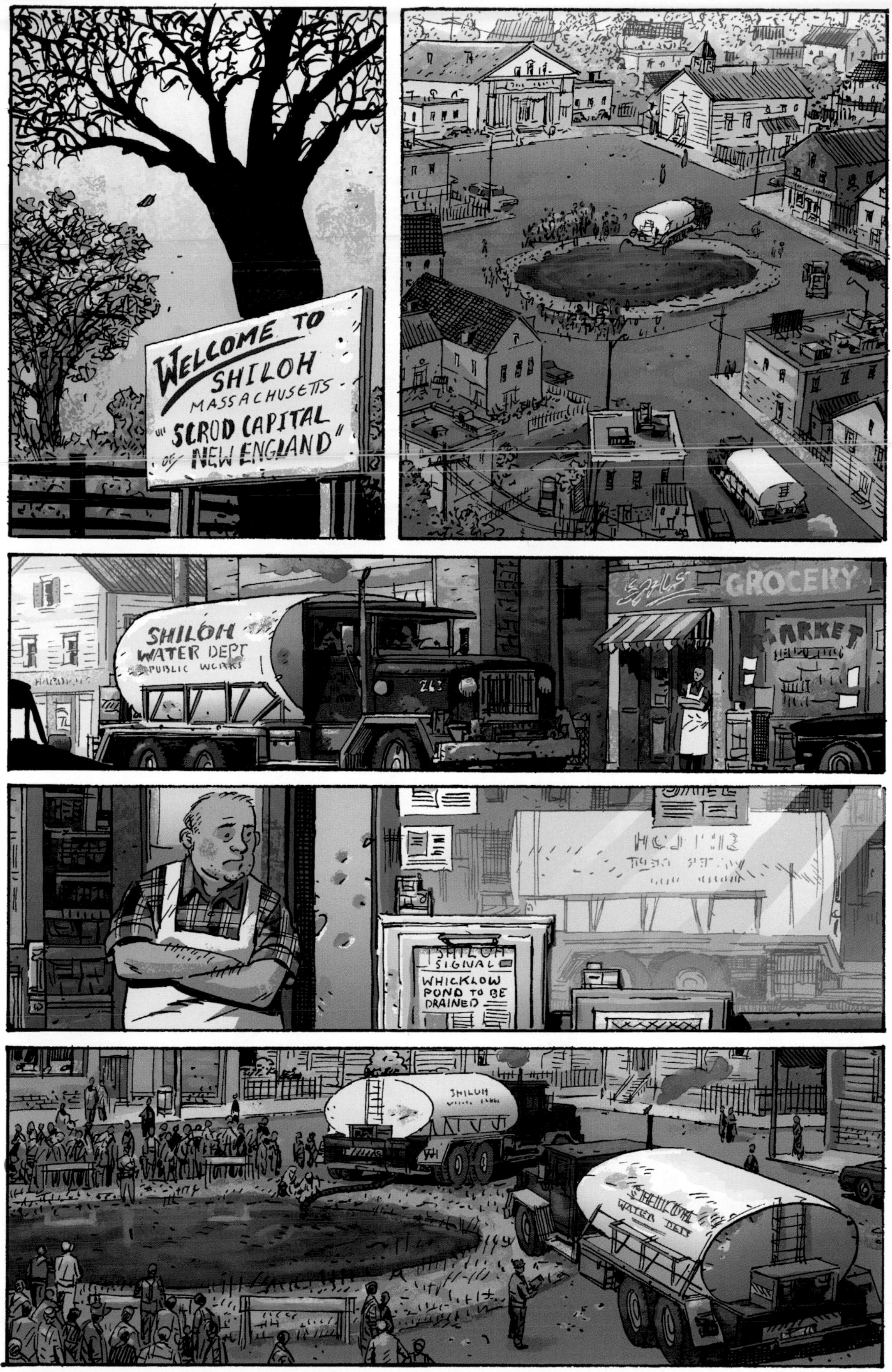
WELCOME TO
SHILOH
MASSACHUSETTS
"SCROD CAPITAL OF NEW ENGLAND"
SHILOH WATER DEPT
PUBLIC WORKS
263
GROCERY
MARKET
SHILOH SIGNAL
WHICKLOW POND TO BE DRAINED
SHILOH
WATER DEPT

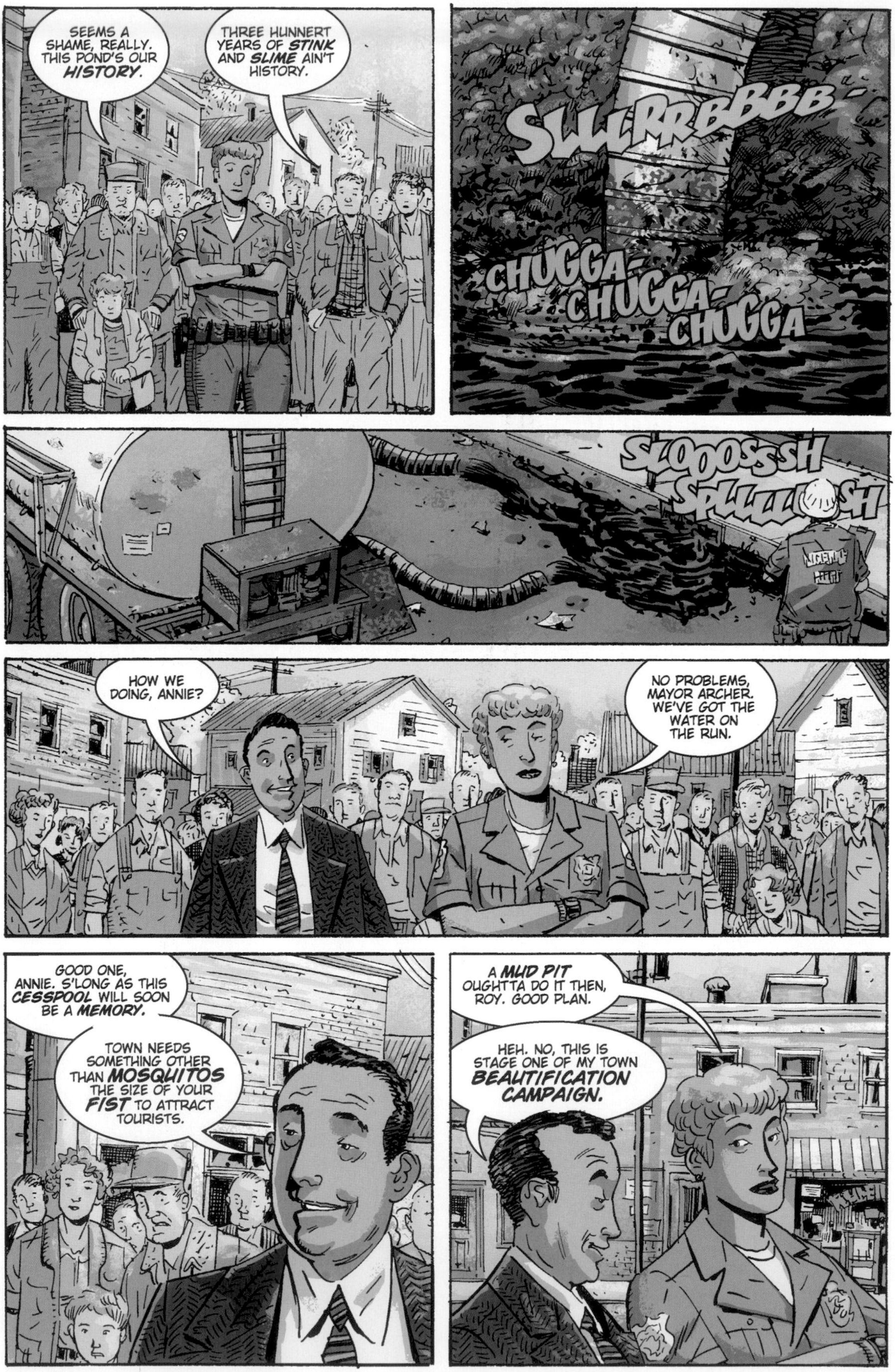
SEEMS A SHAME, REALLY. THIS POND'S OUR HISTORY.
THREE HUNNERT YEARS OF STINK AND SLIME AIN'T HISTORY.
SLLLRRBBBB-
CHUGGA-CHUGGA-CHUGGA
SLOOOSSSH
SPLLLLOSH
HOW WE DOING, ANNIE?
NO PROBLEMS, MAYOR ARCHER. WE'VE GOT THE WATER ON THE RUN.
GOOD ONE, ANNIE. S'LONG AS THIS CESSPOOL WILL SOON BE A MEMORY.
TOWN NEEDS SOMETHING OTHER THAN MOSQUITOS THE SIZE OF YOUR FIST TO ATTRACT TOURISTS.
A MUD PIT OUGHTTA DO IT THEN, ROY. GOOD PLAN.
HEH. NO, THIS IS STAGE ONE OF MY TOWN BEAUTIFICATION CAMPAIGN.

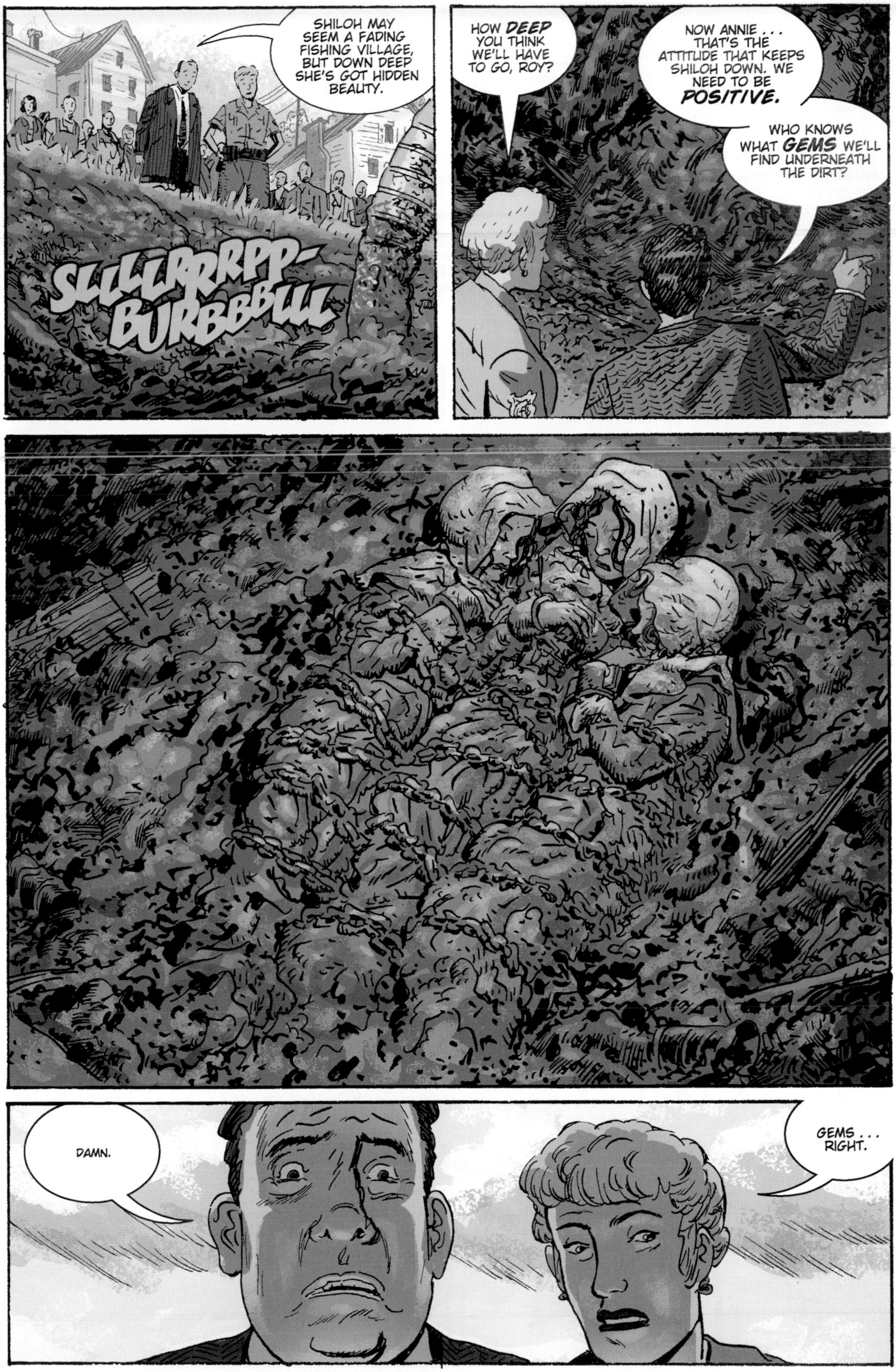
SHILOH MAY SEEM A FADING FISHING VILLAGE, BUT DOWN DEEP SHE'S GOT HIDDEN BEAUTY.
SLLLLRRRRPP-BURBBBLLL
HOW DEEP YOU THINK WE'LL HAVE TO GO, ROY?
NOW ANNIE . . . THAT'S THE ATTITUDE THAT KEEPS SHILOH DOWN. WE NEED TO BE POSITIVE.
WHO KNOWS WHAT GEMS WE'LL FIND UNDERNEATH THE DIRT?
DAMN.
GEMS . . . RIGHT.

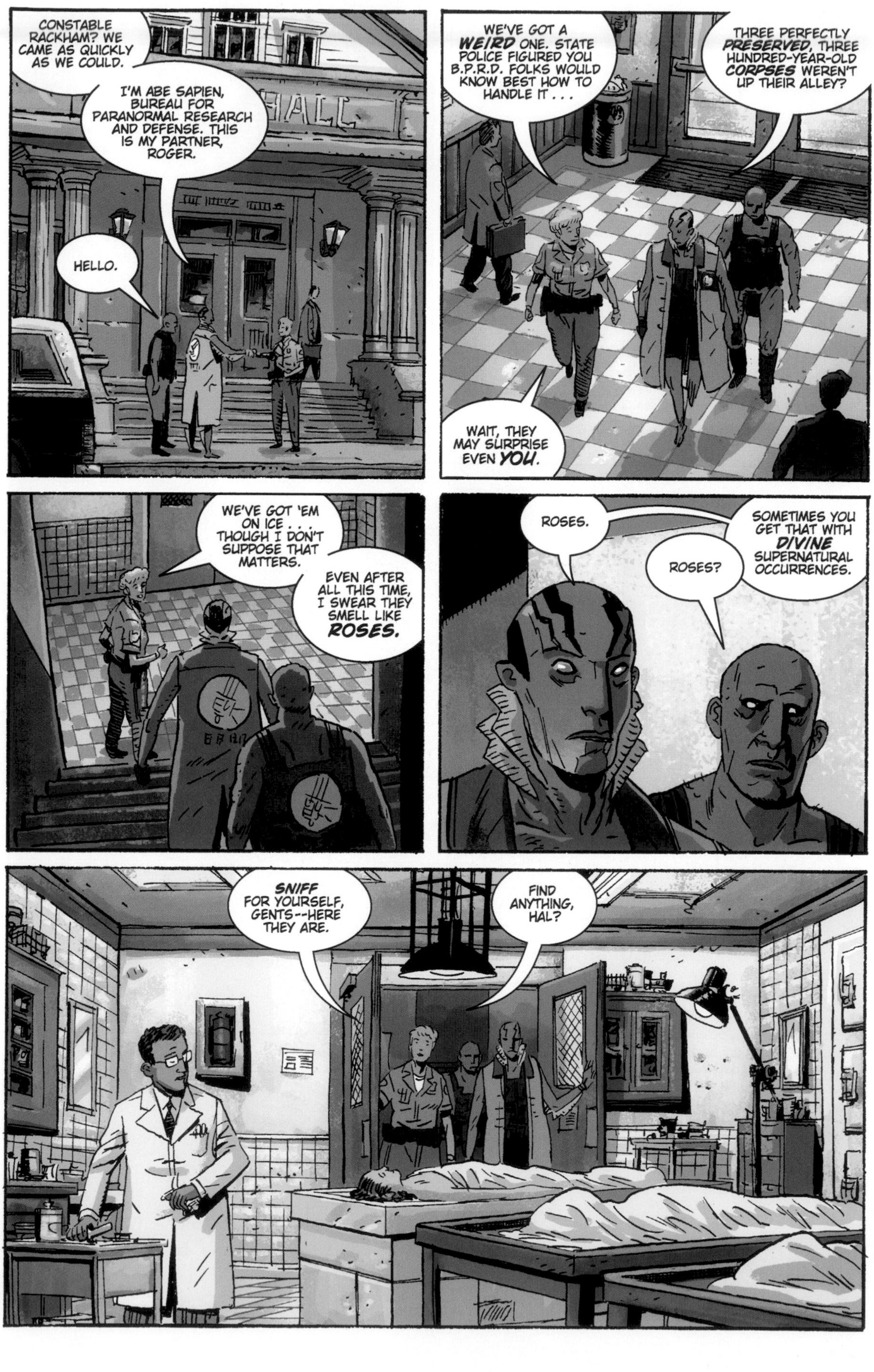
CONSTABLE RACKHAM? WE CAME AS QUICKLY AS WE COULD.
I'M ABE SAPIEN, BUREAU FOR PARANORMAL RESEARCH AND DEFENSE. THIS IS MY PARTNER, ROGER.
HELLO.
WE'VE GOT A WEIRD ONE. STATE POLICE FIGURED YOU B.P.R.D. FOLKS WOULD KNOW BEST HOW TO HANDLE IT . . .
THREE PERFECTLY PRESERVED, THREE HUNDRED-YEAR-OLD CORPSES WEREN'T UP THEIR ALLEY?
WAIT, THEY MAY SURPRISE EVEN YOU.
WE'VE GOT 'EM ON ICE . . . THOUGH I DON'T SUPPOSE THAT MATTERS.
EVEN AFTER ALL THIS TIME, I SWEAR THEY SMELL LIKE ROSES.
ROSES.
ROSES?
SOMETIMES YOU GET THAT WITH DIVINE SUPERNATURAL OCCURRENCES.
SNIFF FOR YOURSELF, GENTS--HERE THEY ARE.
FIND ANYTHING, HAL?

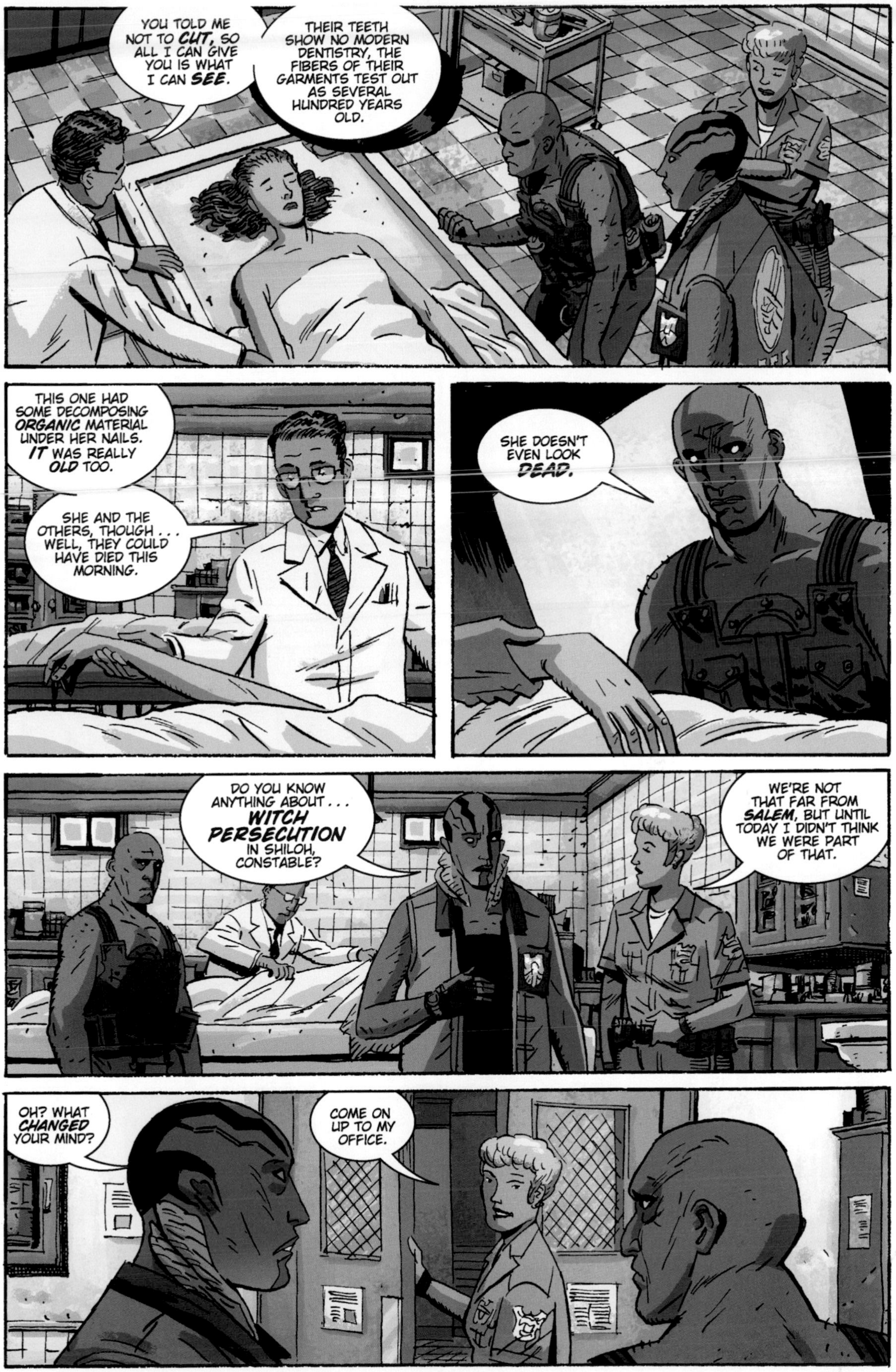
YOU TOLD ME NOT TO CUT, SO ALL I CAN GIVE YOU IS WHAT I CAN SEE.
THEIR TEETH SHOW NO MODERN DENTISTRY, THE FIBERS OF THEIR GARMENTS TEST OUT AS SEVERAL HUNDRED YEARS OLD.
THIS ONE HAD SOME DECOMPOSING ORGANIC MATERIAL UNDER HER NAILS. IT WAS REALLY OLD TOO.
SHE AND THE OTHERS, THOUGH . . . WELL, THEY COULD HAVE DIED THIS MORNING.
SHE DOESN'T EVEN LOOK DEAD.
DO YOU KNOW ANYTHING ABOUT . . . WITCH PERSECUTION IN SHILOH, CONSTABLE?
WE'RE NOT THAT FAR FROM SALEM, BUT UNTIL TODAY I DIDN'T THINK WE WERE PART OF THAT.
OH? WHAT CHANGED YOUR MIND?
COME ON UP TO MY OFFICE.

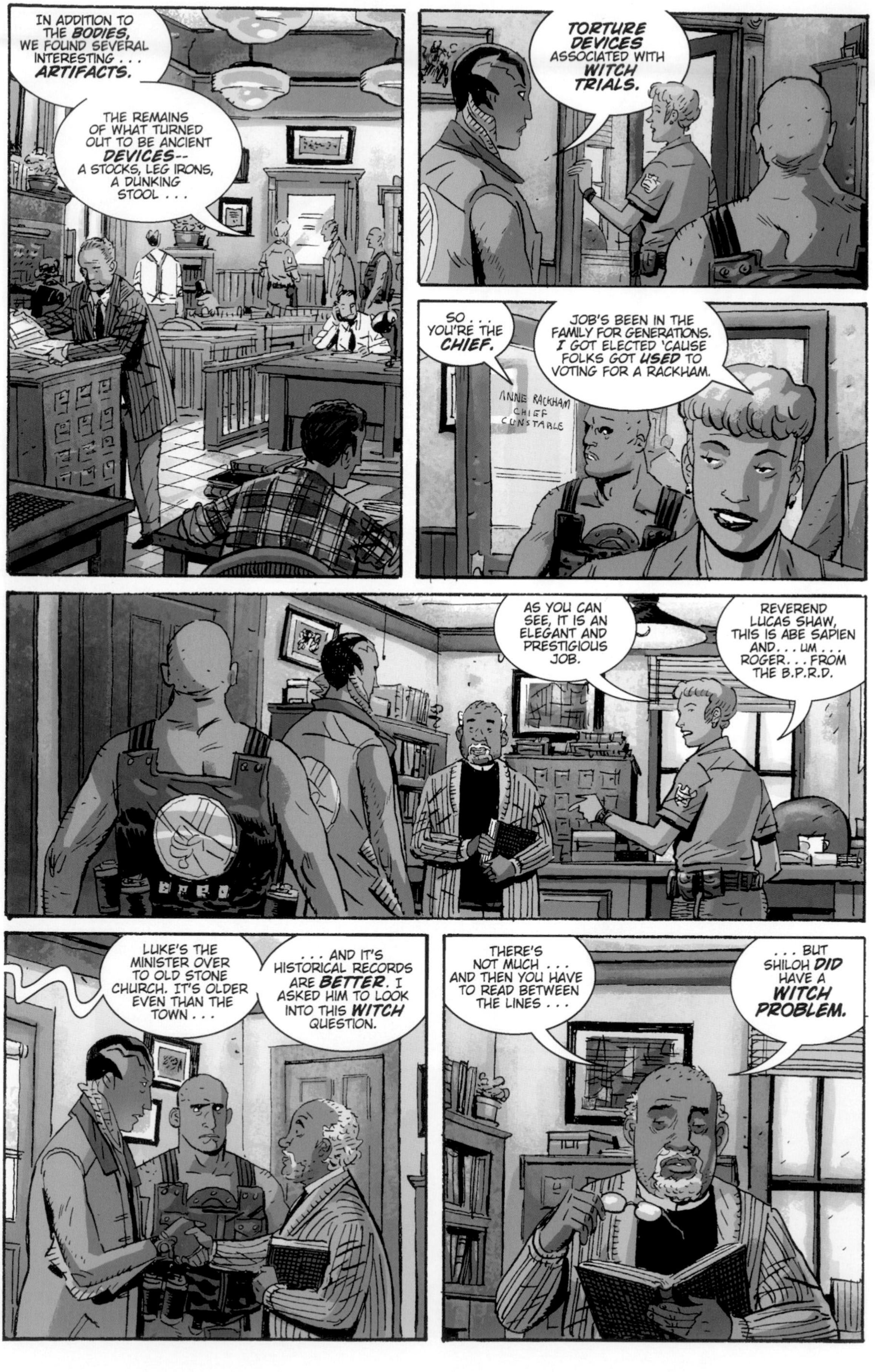
IN ADDITION TO THE BODIES, WE FOUND SEVERAL INTERESTING . . . ARTIFACTS.
THE REMAINS OF WHAT TURNED OUT TO BE ANCIENT DEVICES-- A STOCKS, LEG IRONS, A DUNKING STOOL . . .
TORTURE DEVICES ASSOCIATED WITH WITCH TRIALS.
SO . . . YOU'RE THE CHIEF.
JOB'S BEEN IN THE FAMILY FOR GENERATIONS. I GOT ELECTED 'CAUSE FOLKS GOT USED TO VOTING FOR A RACKHAM.
ANNE RACKHAM CHIEF CONSTABLE
AS YOU CAN SEE, IT IS AN ELEGANT AND PRESTIGIOUS JOB.
REVEREND LUCAS SHAW, THIS IS ABE SAPIEN AND . . . UM . . . ROGER . . . FROM THE B.P.R.D.
LUKE'S THE MINISTER OVER TO OLD STONE CHURCH. IT'S OLDER EVEN THAN THE TOWN . . .
. . . AND IT'S HISTORICAL RECORDS ARE BETTER. I ASKED HIM TO LOOK INTO THIS WITCH QUESTION.
THERE'S NOT MUCH . . . AND THEN YOU HAVE TO READ BETWEEN THE LINES . . .
. . . BUT SHILOH DID HAVE A WITCH PROBLEM.

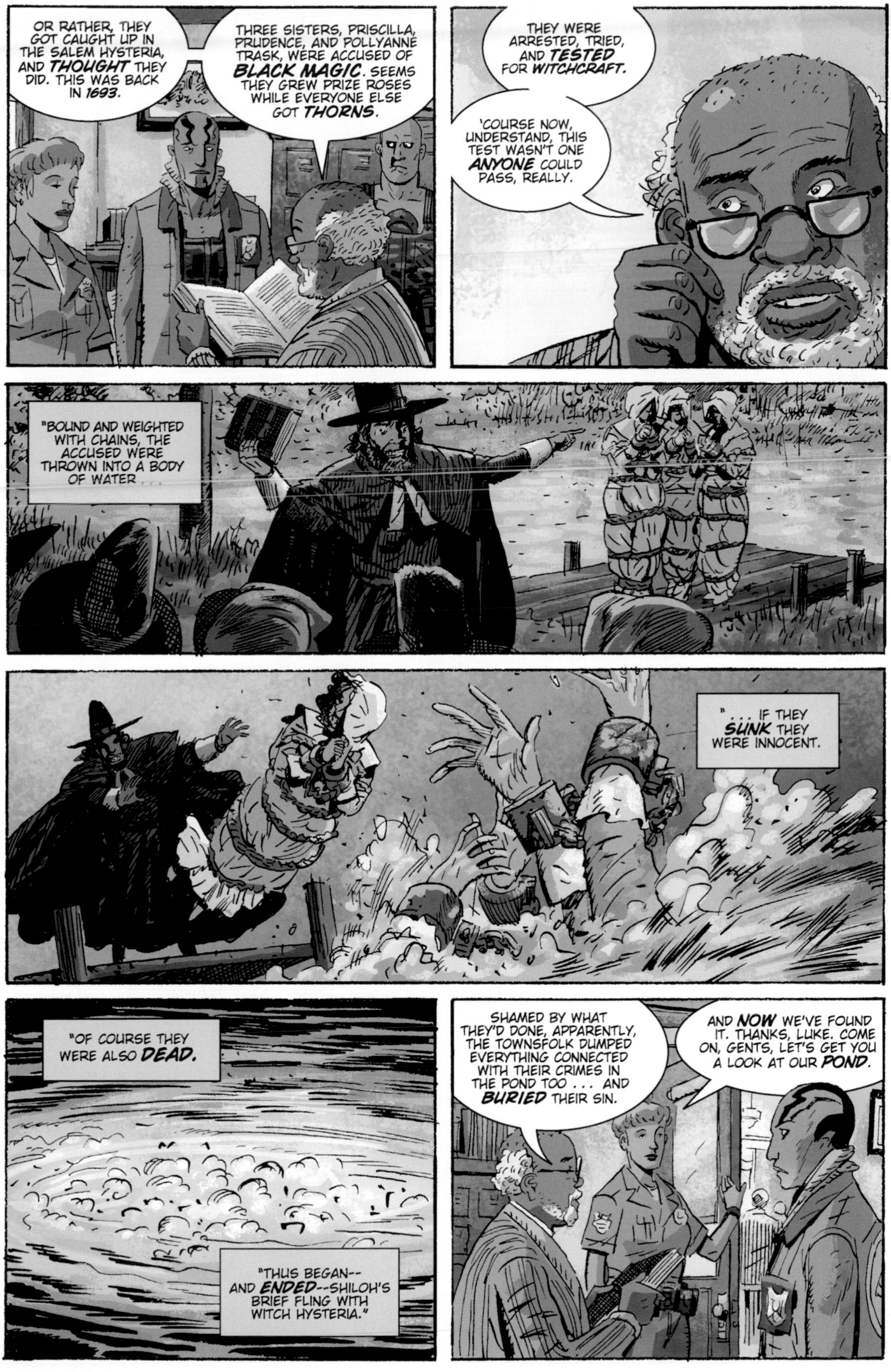
OR RATHER, THEY GOT CAUGHT UP IN THE SALEM HYSTERIA, AND THOUGHT THEY DID. THIS WAS BACK IN 1693.
THREE SISTERS, PRISCILLA, PRUDENCE, AND POLLYANNE TRASK, WERE ACCUSED OF BLACK MAGIC. SEEMS THEY GREW PRIZE ROSES WHILE EVERYONE ELSE GOT THORNS.
THEY WERE ARRESTED, TRIED, AND TESTED FOR WITCHCRAFT.
'COURSE NOW, UNDERSTAND, THIS TEST WASN'T ONE ANYONE COULD PASS, REALLY.
"BOUND AND WEIGHTED WITH CHAINS, THE ACCUSED WERE THROWN INTO A BODY OF WATER . . .
" . . . IF THEY SUNK THEY WERE INNOCENT.
"OF COURSE THEY WERE ALSO DEAD.
"THUS BEGAN-- AND ENDED--SHILOH'S BRIEF FLING WITH WITCH HYSTERIA."
SHAMED BY WHAT THEY'D DONE, APPARENTLY, THE TOWNSFOLK DUMPED EVERYTHING CONNECTED WITH THEIR CRIMES IN THE POND TOO . . . AND BURIED THEIR SIN.
AND NOW WE'VE FOUND IT. THANKS, LUKE. COME ON, GENTS, LET'S GET YOU A LOOK AT OUR POND.

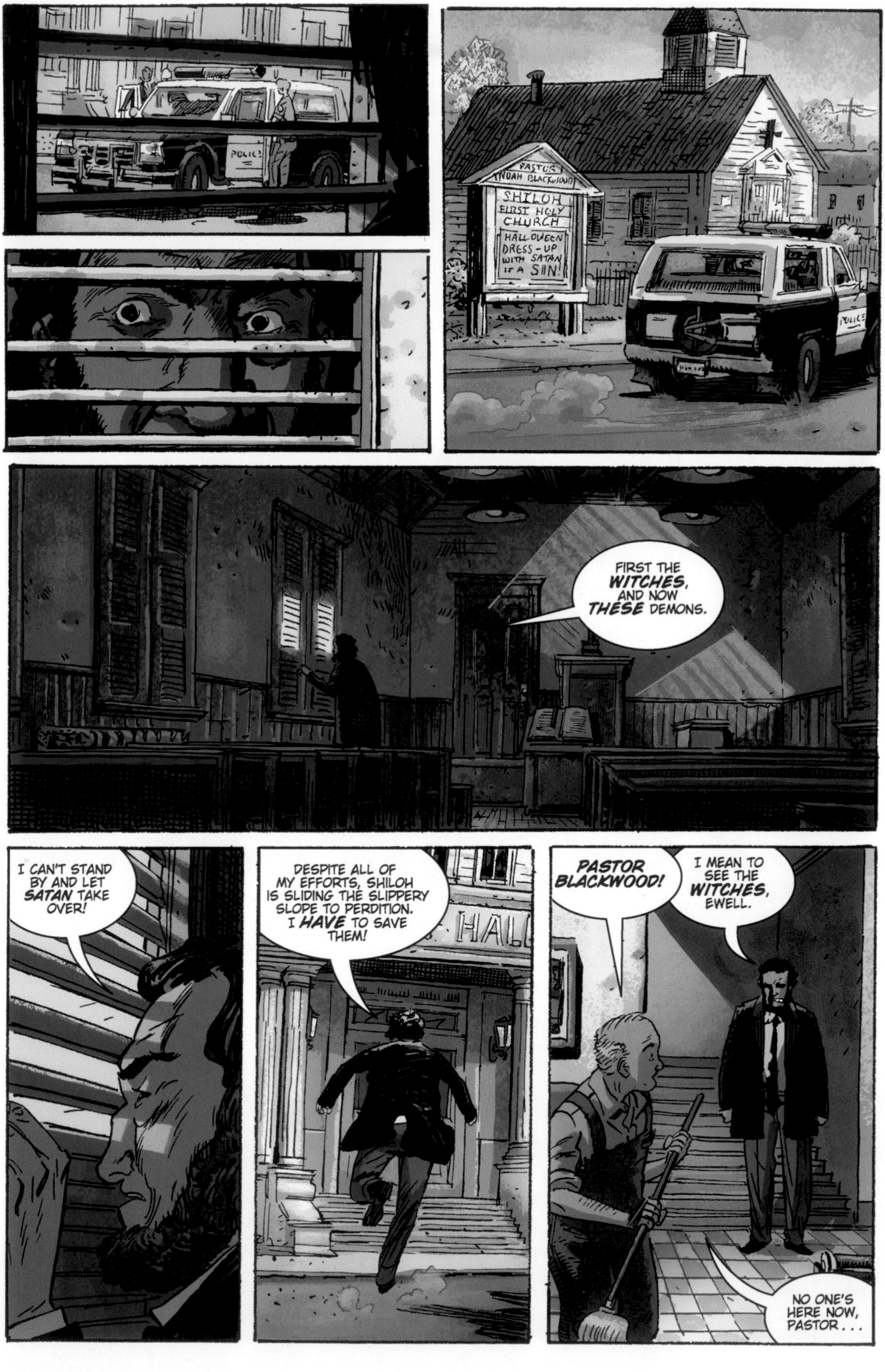
POLICE
PASTOR NOAH BLACKWOOD
SHILOH FIRST HOLY CHURCH
HALLOWEEN DRESS-UP WITH SATAN IS A SIN!
POLICE
FIRST THE WITCHES, AND NOW THESE DEMONS.
I CAN'T STAND BY AND LET SATAN TAKE OVER!
DESPITE ALL OF MY EFFORTS, SHILOH IS SLIDING THE SLIPPERY SLOPE TO PERDITION. I HAVE TO SAVE THEM!
PASTOR BLACKWOOD!
I MEAN TO SEE THE WITCHES, EWELL.
NO ONE'S HERE NOW, PASTOR . . .

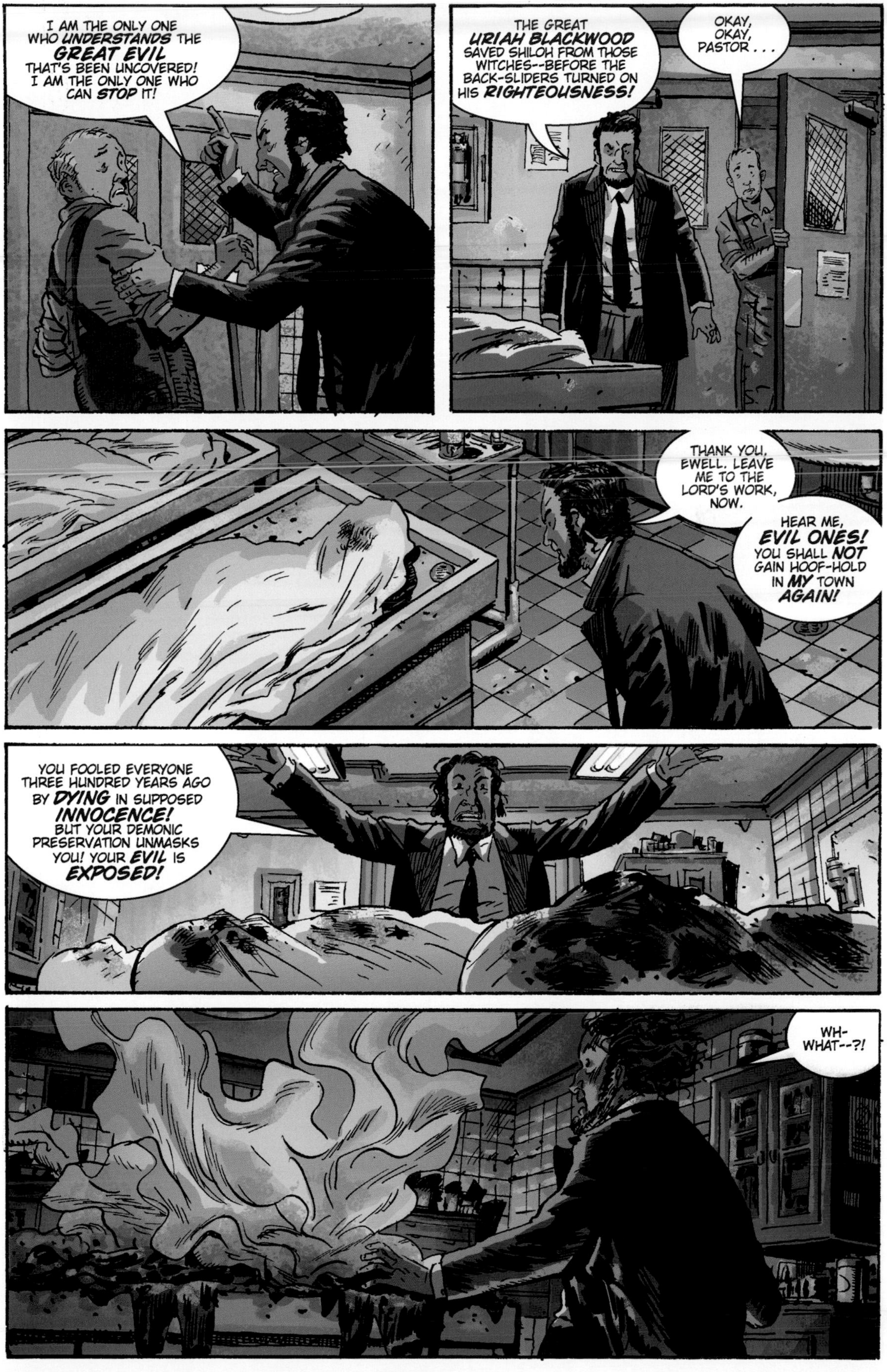
I AM THE ONLY ONE WHO UNDERSTANDS THE GREAT EVIL THAT'S BEEN UNCOVERED! I AM THE ONLY ONE WHO CAN STOP IT!
THE GREAT URIAH BLACKWOOD SAVED SHILOH FROM THOSE WITCHES--BEFORE THE BACK-SLIDERS TURNED ON HIS RIGHTEOUSNESS!
OKAY, OKAY, PASTOR . . .
THANK YOU, EWELL. LEAVE ME TO THE LORD'S WORK, NOW.
HEAR ME, EVIL ONES! YOU SHALL NOT GAIN HOOF-HOLD IN MY TOWN AGAIN!
YOU FOOLED EVERYONE THREE HUNDRED YEARS AGO BY DYING IN SUPPOSED INNOCENCE! BUT YOUR DEMONIC PRESERVATION UNMASKS YOU! YOUR EVIL IS EXPOSED!
WH- WHAT--?!

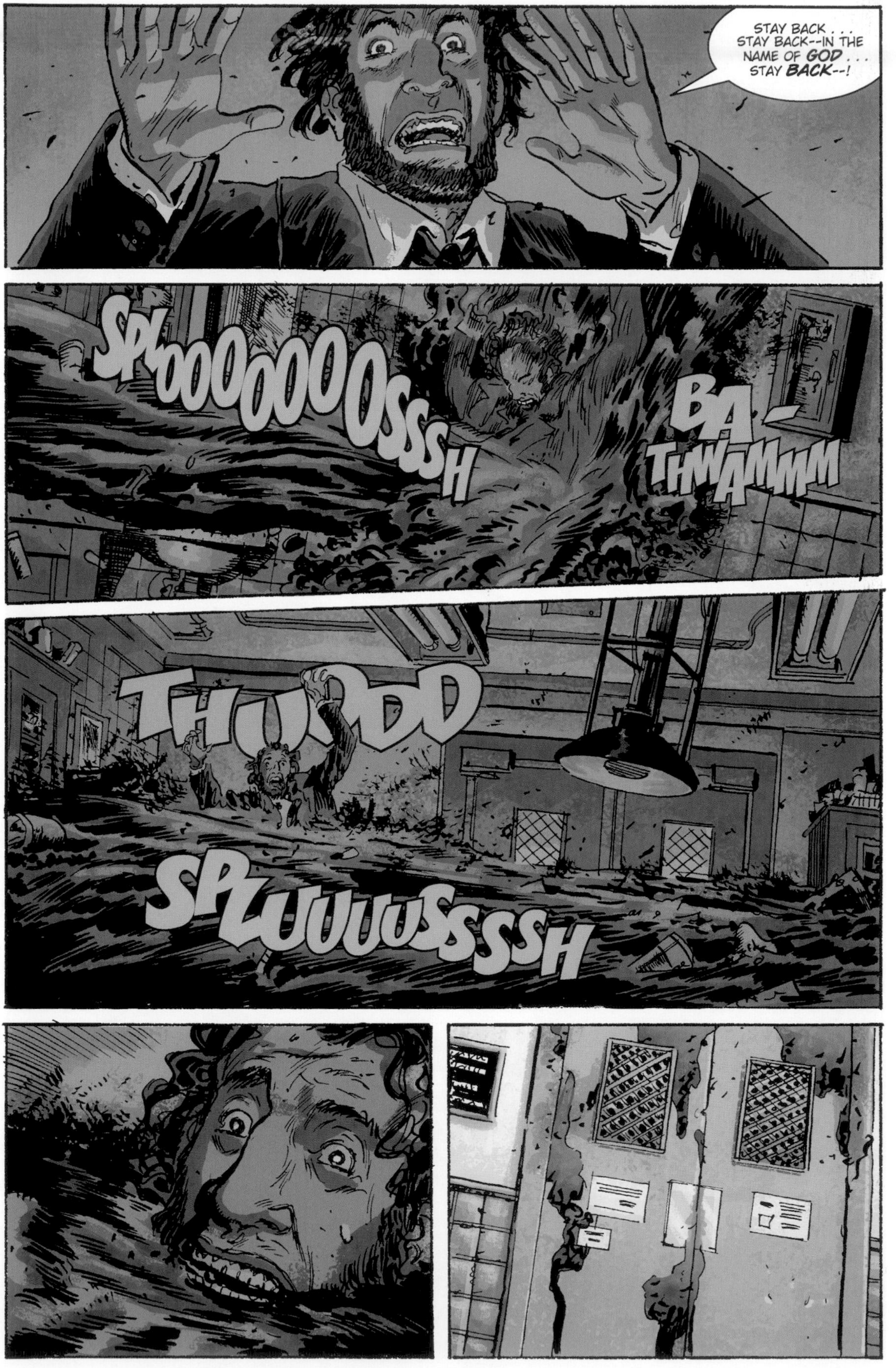

STAY BACK . . . STAY BACK--IN THE NAME OF GOD . . . STAY BACK--!
SPLOOOOOOOSSSSH
BA-THWAMMM
THUDD
SPLUUUUSSSSH

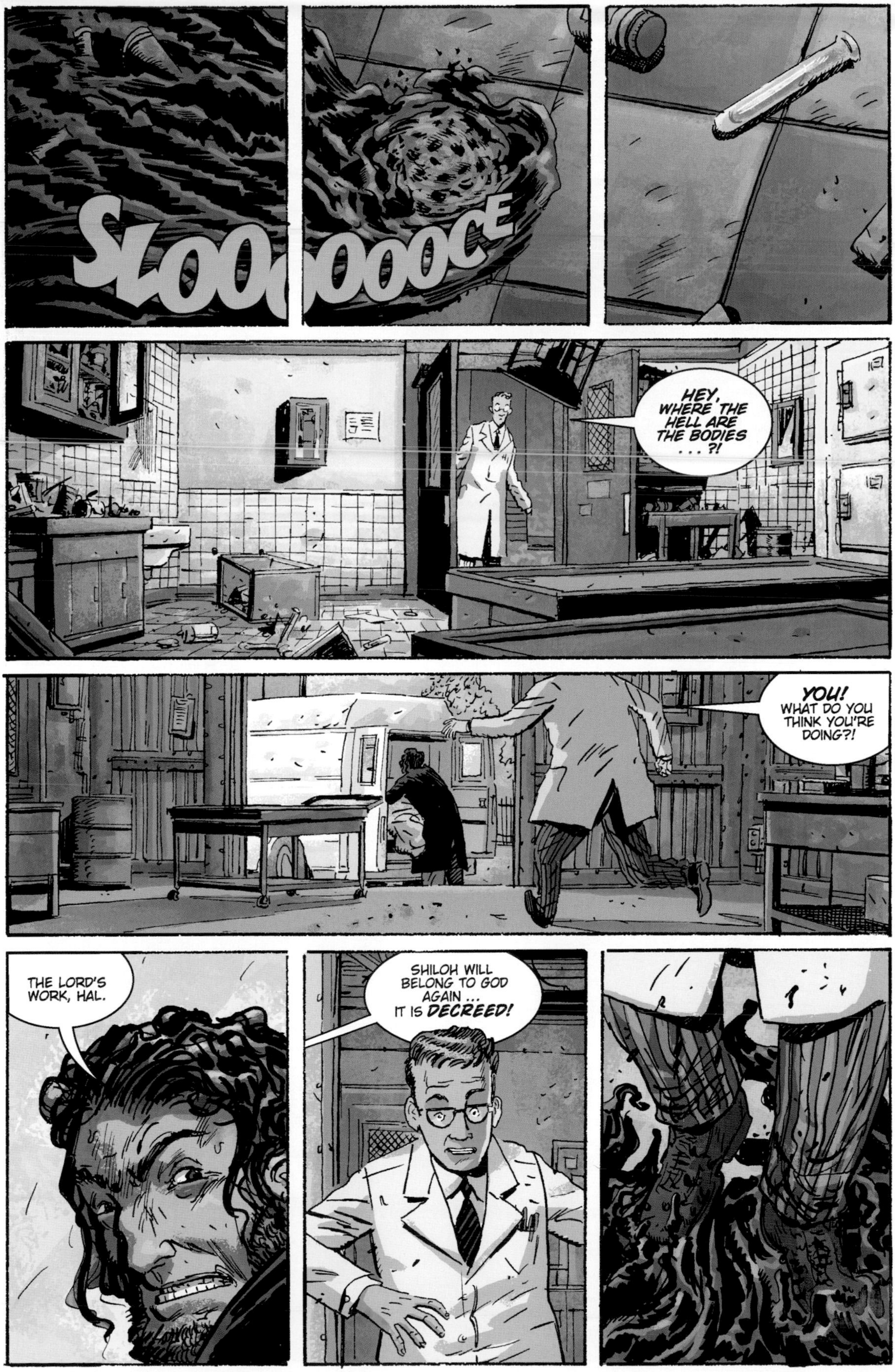
SLOOOOOOCE
HEY, WHERE THE HELL ARE THE BODIES . . . ?!
YOU! WHAT DO YOU THINK YOU'RE DOING?!
THE LORD'S WORK, HAL.
SHILOH WILL BELONG TO GOD AGAIN ... IT IS DECREED!

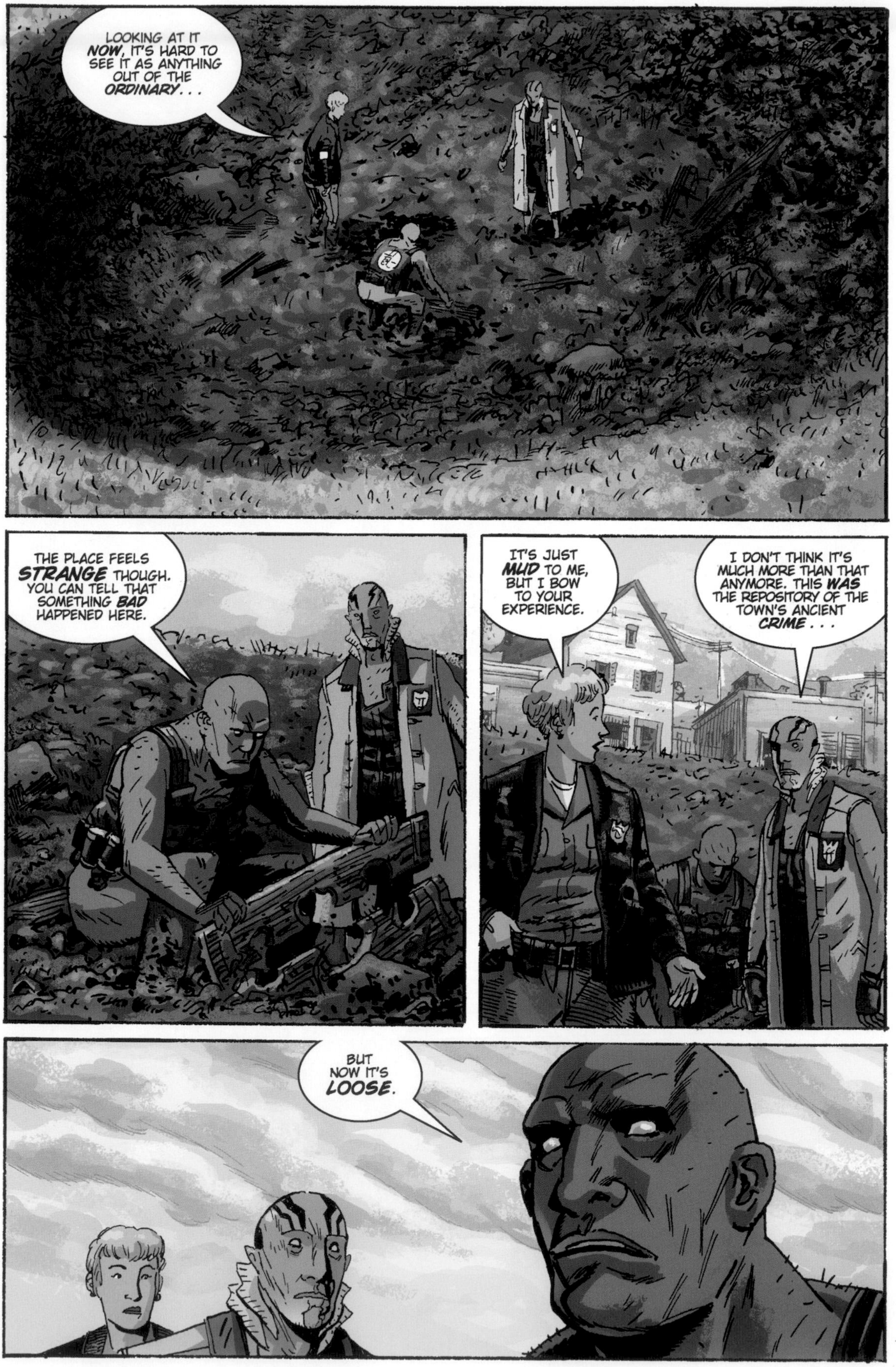
LOOKING AT IT NOW, IT'S HARD TO SEE IT AS ANYTHING OUT OF THE ORDINARY . . .
THE PLACE FEELS STRANGE THOUGH. YOU CAN TELL THAT SOMETHING BAD HAPPENED HERE.
IT'S JUST MUD TO ME, BUT I BOW TO YOUR EXPERIENCE.
I DON'T THINK IT'S MUCH MORE THAN THAT ANYMORE. THIS WAS THE REPOSITORY OF THE TOWN'S ANCIENT CRIME . . .
BUT NOW IT'S LOOSE.

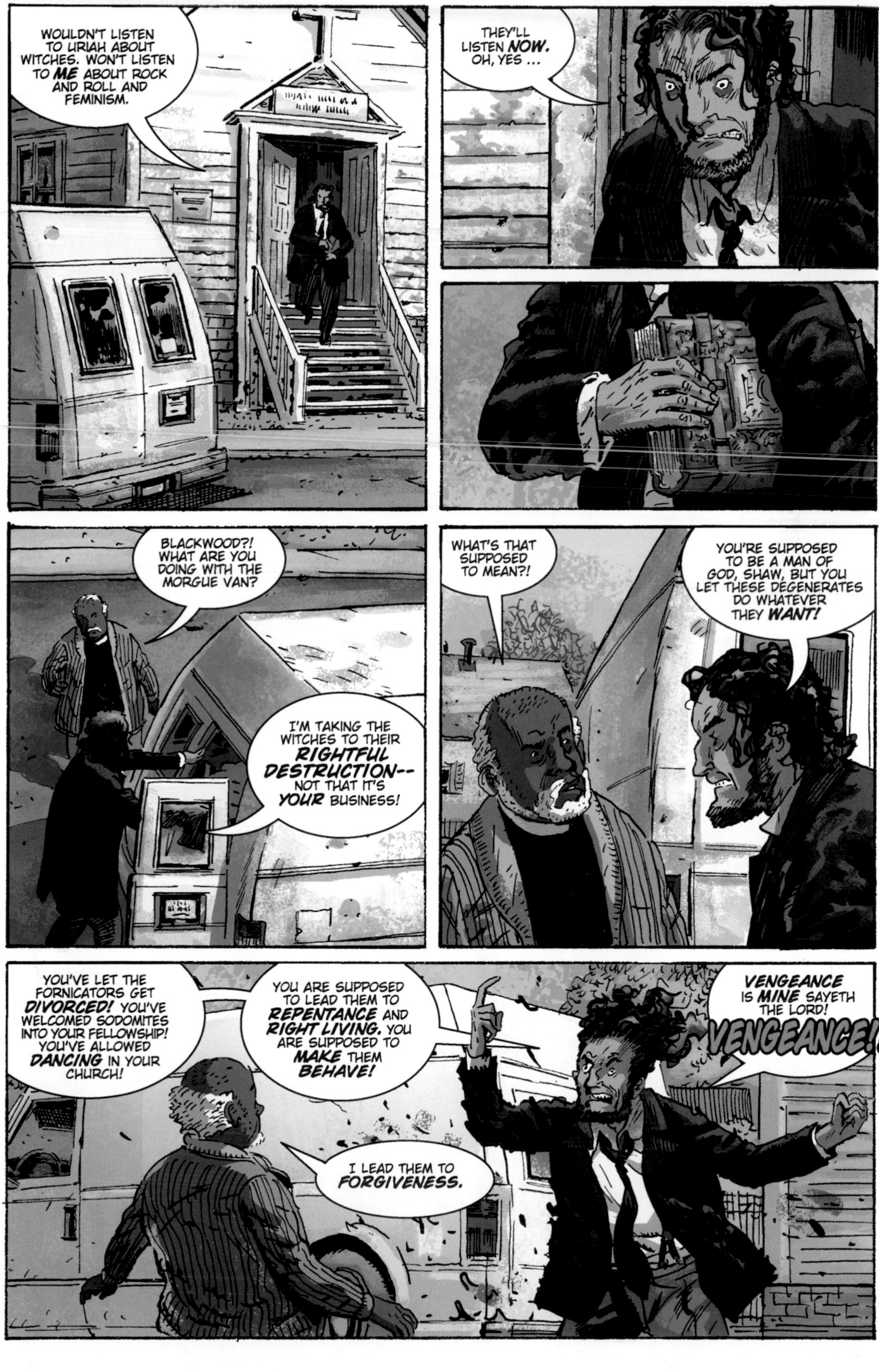
WOULDN'T LISTEN TO URIAH ABOUT WITCHES. WON'T LISTEN TO ME ABOUT ROCK AND ROLL AND FEMINISM.
THEY'LL LISTEN NOW. OH, YES ...
BLACKWOOD?! WHAT ARE YOU DOING WITH THE MORGUE VAN?
I'M TAKING THE WITCHES TO THEIR RIGHTFUL DESTRUCTION-- NOT THAT IT'S YOUR BUSINESS!
WHAT'S THAT SUPPOSED TO MEAN?!
YOU'RE SUPPOSED TO BE A MAN OF GOD, SHAW, BUT YOU LET THESE DEGENERATES DO WHATEVER THEY WANT!
YOU'VE LET THE FORNICATORS GET DIVORCED! YOU'VE WELCOMED SODOMITES INTO YOUR FELLOWSHIP! YOU'VE ALLOWED DANCING IN YOUR CHURCH!
YOU ARE SUPPOSED TO LEAD THEM TO REPENTANCE AND RIGHT LIVING. YOU ARE SUPPOSED TO MAKE THEM BEHAVE!
I LEAD THEM TO FORGIVENESS.
VENGEANCE IS MINE SAYETH THE LORD! VENGEANCE!!

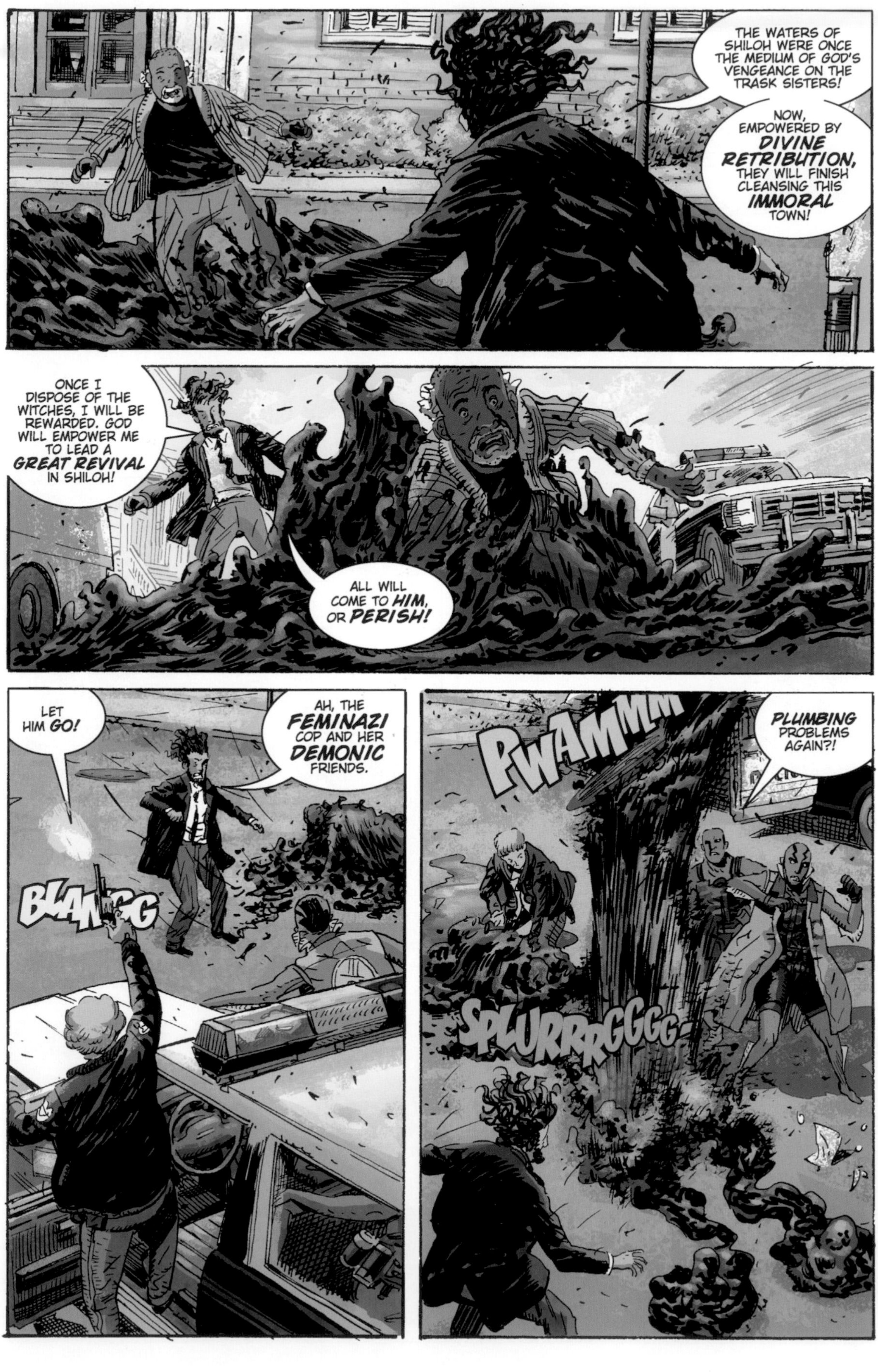

THE WATERS OF SHILOH WERE ONCE THE MEDIUM OF GOD'S VENGEANCE ON THE TRASK SISTERS!
NOW, EMPOWERED BY DIVINE RETRIBUTION, THEY WILL FINISH CLEANSING THIS IMMORAL TOWN!
ONCE I DISPOSE OF THE WITCHES, I WILL BE REWARDED. GOD WILL EMPOWER ME TO LEAD A GREAT REVIVAL IN SHILOH!
ALL WILL COME TO HIM, OR PERISH!
LET HIM GO!
BLAMGG
AH, THE FEMINAZI COP AND HER DEMONIC FRIENDS.
PWAMMM
PLUMBING PROBLEMS AGAIN?!
SPLURRRRGGGG-

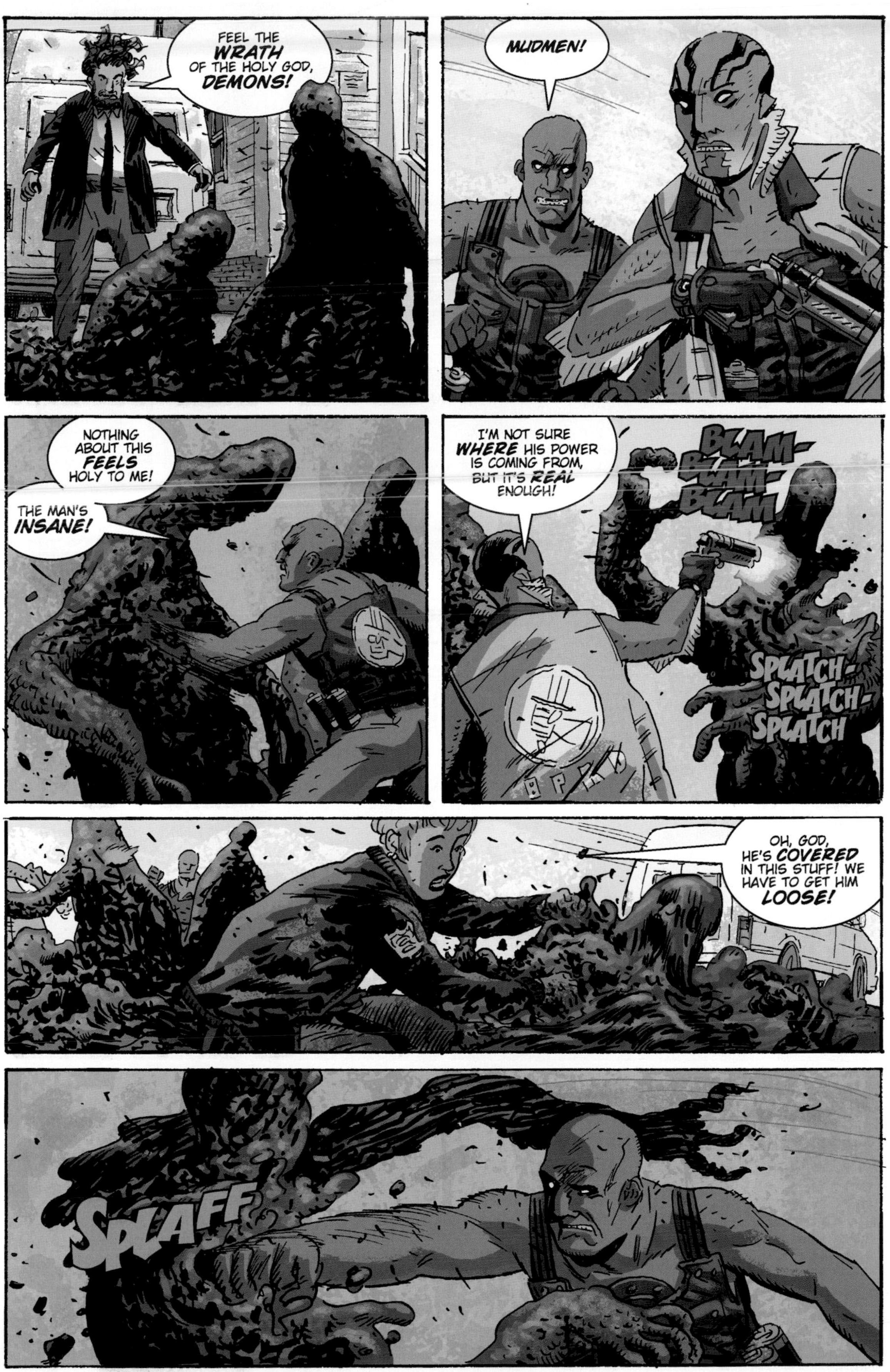
FEEL THE WRATH OF THE HOLY GOD, DEMONS!
MUDMEN!
NOTHING ABOUT THIS FEELS HOLY TO ME!
THE MAN'S INSANE!
I'M NOT SURE WHERE HIS POWER IS COMING FROM, BUT IT'S REAL ENOUGH!
BLAM-BLAM-BLAM
SPLATCH-SPLATCH-SPLATCH
OH, GOD, HE'S COVERED IN THIS STUFF! WE HAVE TO GET HIM LOOSE!
SPLAFF

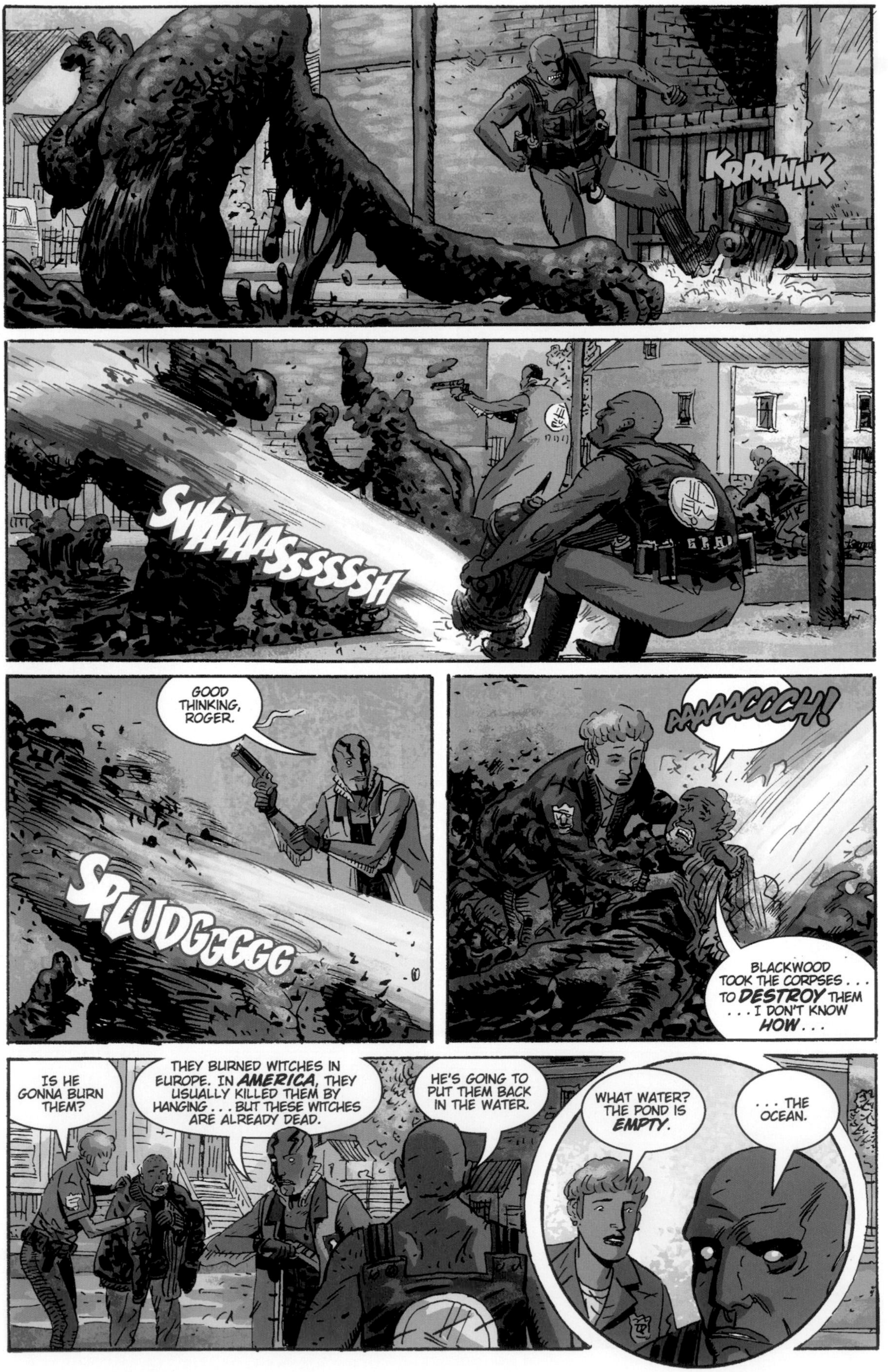
KRRNNNK
SWAAAASSSSSSH
GOOD THINKING, ROGER.
SPLUDGGGGG
PAAAACOOH!
BLACKWOOD TOOK THE CORPSES . . . TO DESTROY THEM . . . I DON'T KNOW HOW . . .
IS HE GONNA BURN THEM?
THEY BURNED WITCHES IN EUROPE. IN AMERICA, THEY USUALLY KILLED THEM BY HANGING . . . BUT THESE WITCHES ARE ALREADY DEAD.
HE'S GOING TO PUT THEM BACK IN THE WATER.
WHAT WATER? THE POND IS EMPTY.
. . . THE OCEAN.

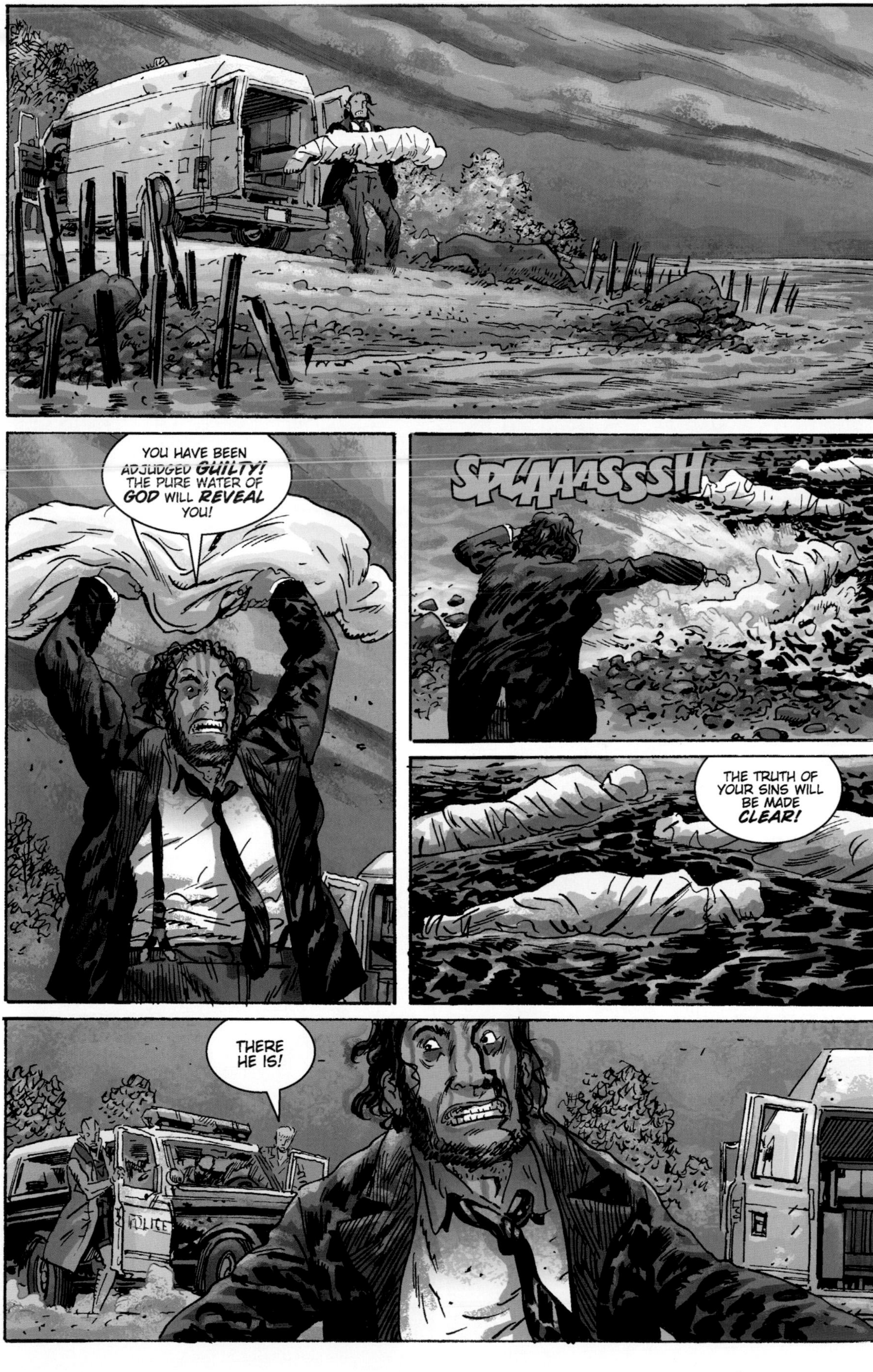
YOU HAVE BEEN ADJUDGED GUILTY! THE PURE WATER OF GOD WILL REVEAL YOU!
SPLAAASSSH
THE TRUTH OF YOUR SINS WILL BE MADE CLEAR!
THERE HE IS!
POLICE

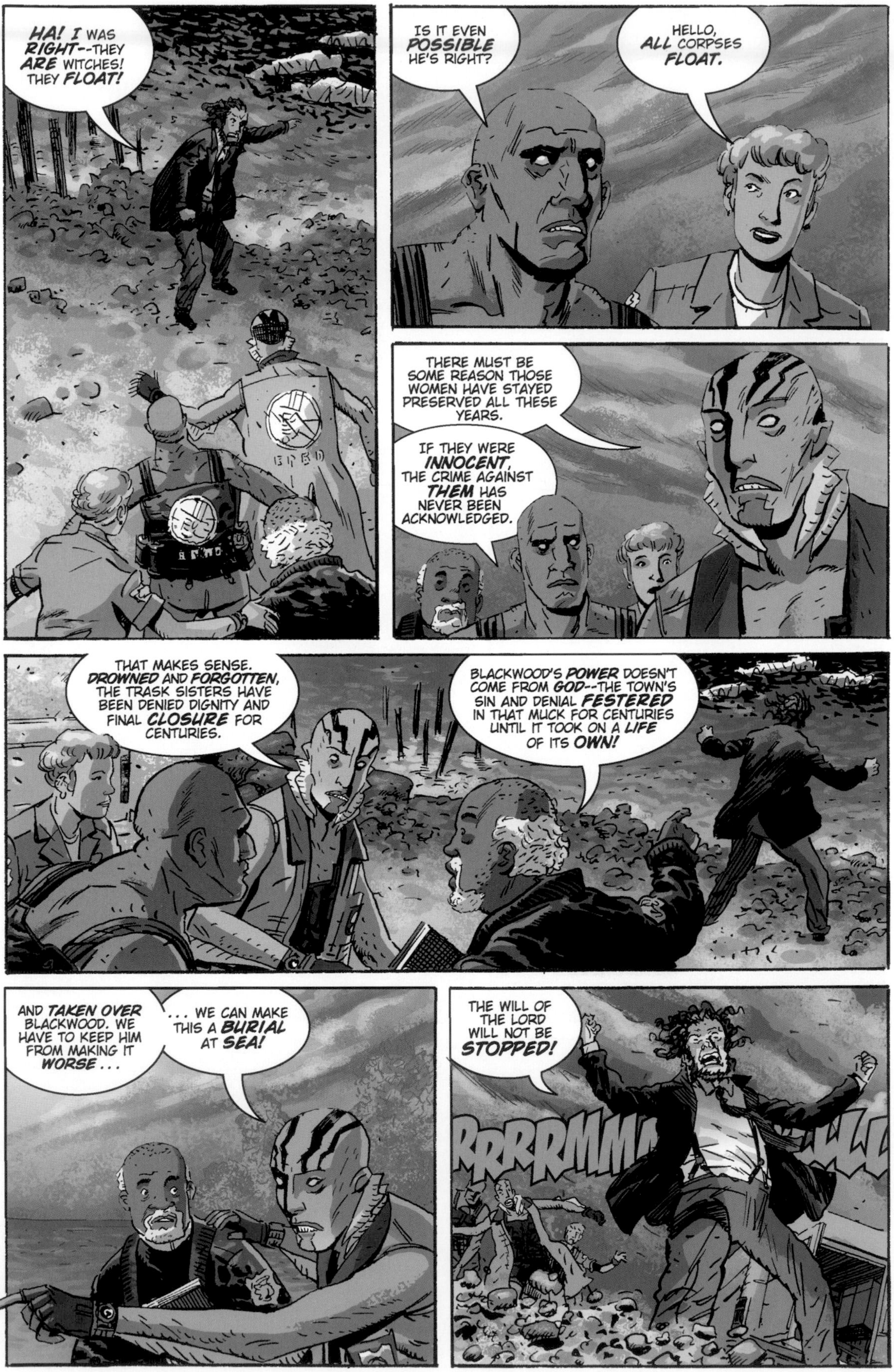
HA! I WAS RIGHT--THEY ARE WITCHES! THEY FLOAT!
IS IT EVEN POSSIBLE HE'S RIGHT?
HELLO, ALL CORPSES FLOAT.
THERE MUST BE SOME REASON THOSE WOMEN HAVE STAYED PRESERVED ALL THESE YEARS.
IF THEY WERE INNOCENT, THE CRIME AGAINST THEM HAS NEVER BEEN ACKNOWLEDGED.
THAT MAKES SENSE. DROWNED AND FORGOTTEN, THE TRASK SISTERS HAVE BEEN DENIED DIGNITY AND FINAL CLOSURE FOR CENTURIES.
BLACKWOOD'S POWER DOESN'T COME FROM GOD--THE TOWN'S SIN AND DENIAL FESTERED IN THAT MUCK FOR CENTURIES UNTIL IT TOOK ON A LIFE OF ITS OWN!
AND TAKEN OVER BLACKWOOD. WE HAVE TO KEEP HIM FROM MAKING IT WORSE . . .
. . . WE CAN MAKE THIS A BURIAL AT SEA!
THE WILL OF THE LORD WILL NOT BE STOPPED!
RRRRMMM

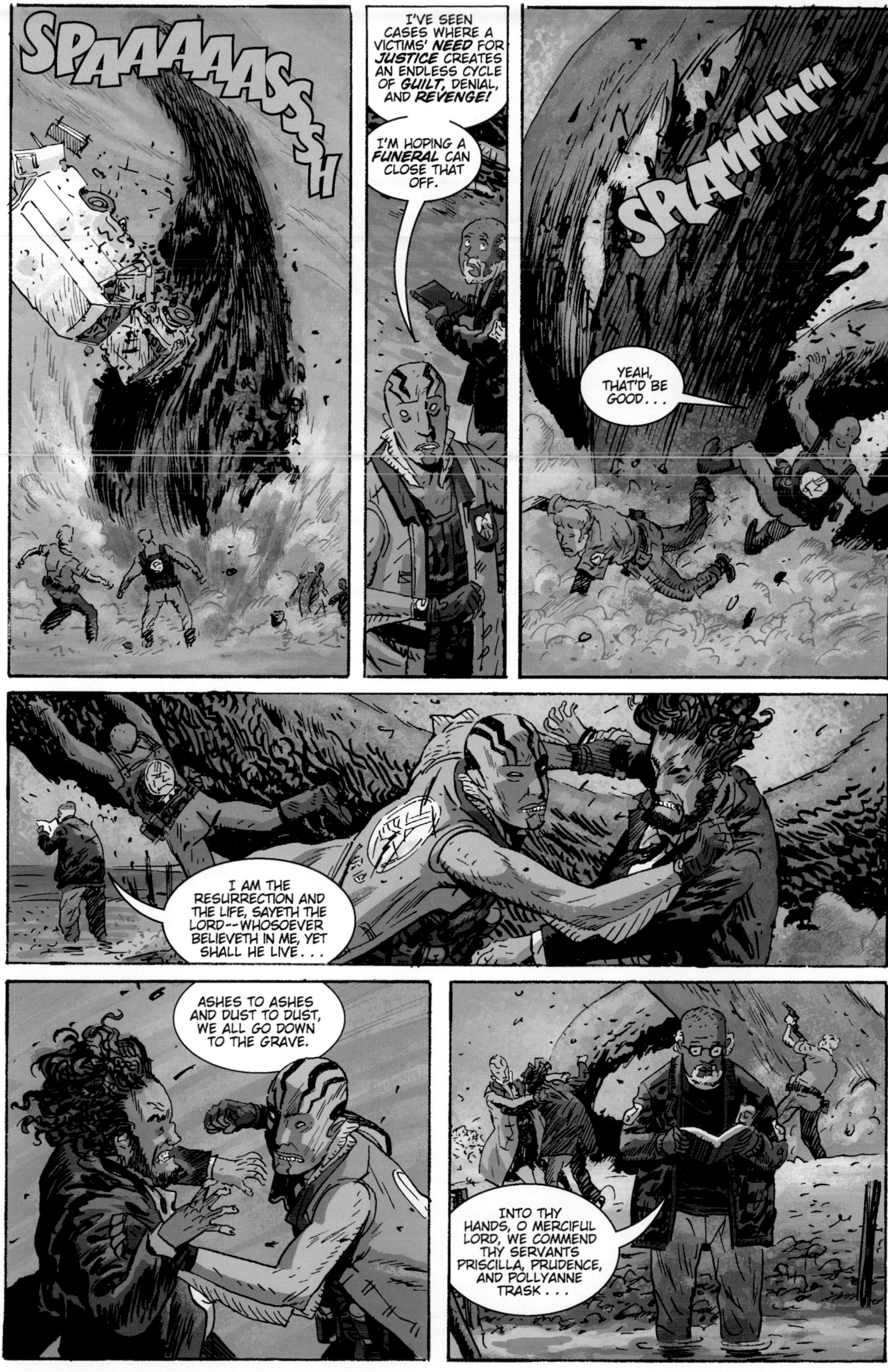
SPAAAAAASSSSH
I'VE SEEN CASES WHERE A VICTIMS' NEED FOR JUSTICE CREATES AN ENDLESS CYCLE OF GUILT, DENIAL, AND REVENGE!
I'M HOPING A FUNERAL CAN CLOSE THAT OFF.
SPLAMMMMM
YEAH, THAT'D BE GOOD . . .
I AM THE RESURRECTION AND THE LIFE, SAYETH THE LORD--WHOSOEVER BELIEVETH IN ME, YET SHALL HE LIVE . . .
ASHES TO ASHES AND DUST TO DUST, WE ALL GO DOWN TO THE GRAVE.
INTO THY HANDS, O MERCIFUL LORD, WE COMMEND THY SERVANTS PRISCILLA, PRUDENCE, AND POLLYANNE TRASK . . .

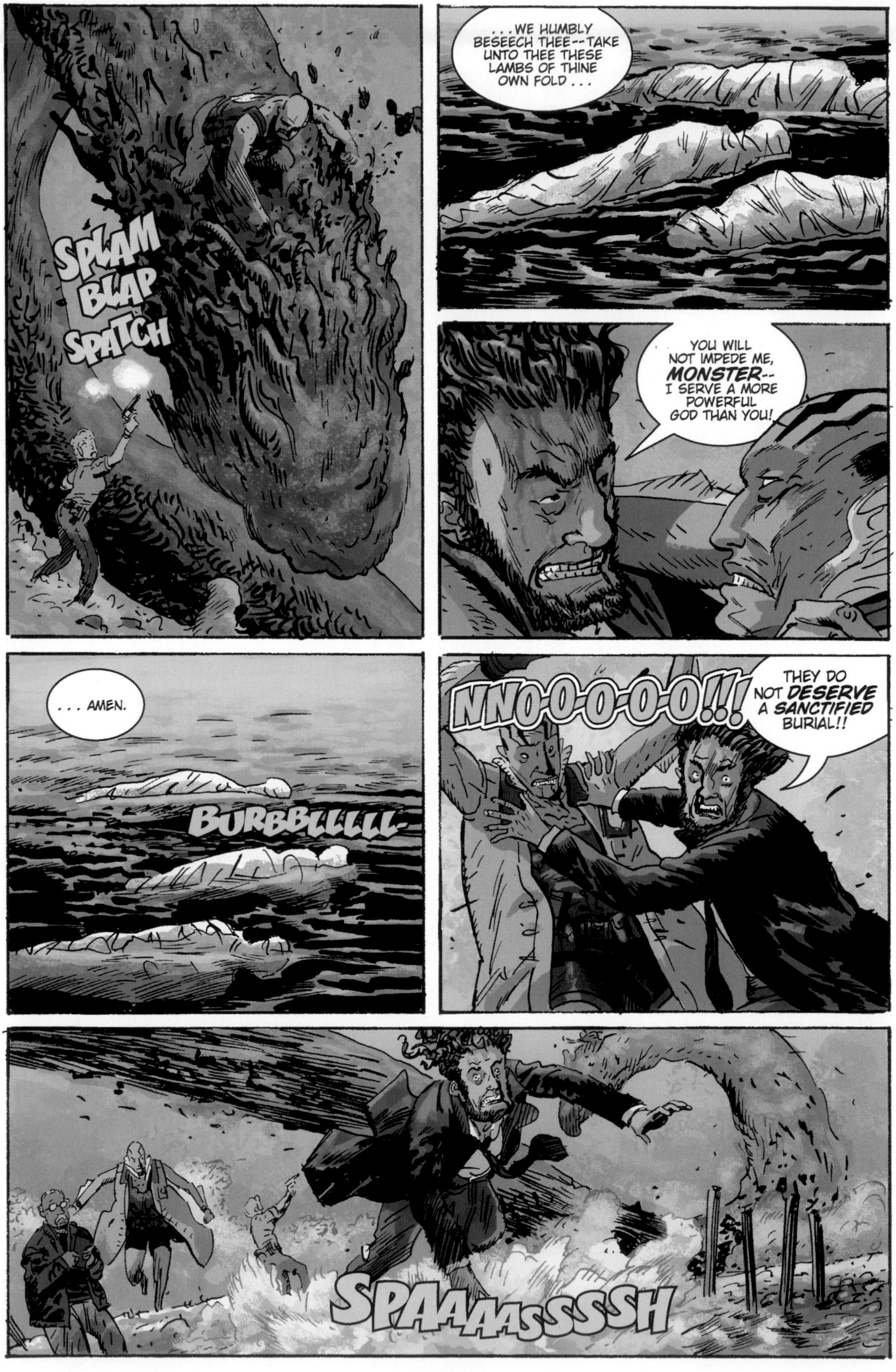
SPLAM
BLAP
SPATCH
. . . WE HUMBLY BESEECH THEE--TAKE UNTO THEE THESE LAMBS OF THINE OWN FOLD . . .
YOU WILL NOT IMPEDE ME, MONSTER-- I SERVE A MORE POWERFUL GOD THAN YOU!
. . . AMEN.
BURBBLLLLL
NNO-O-O-O-O!!!
THEY DO NOT DESERVE A SANCTIFIED BURIAL!!
SPAAAASSSSH

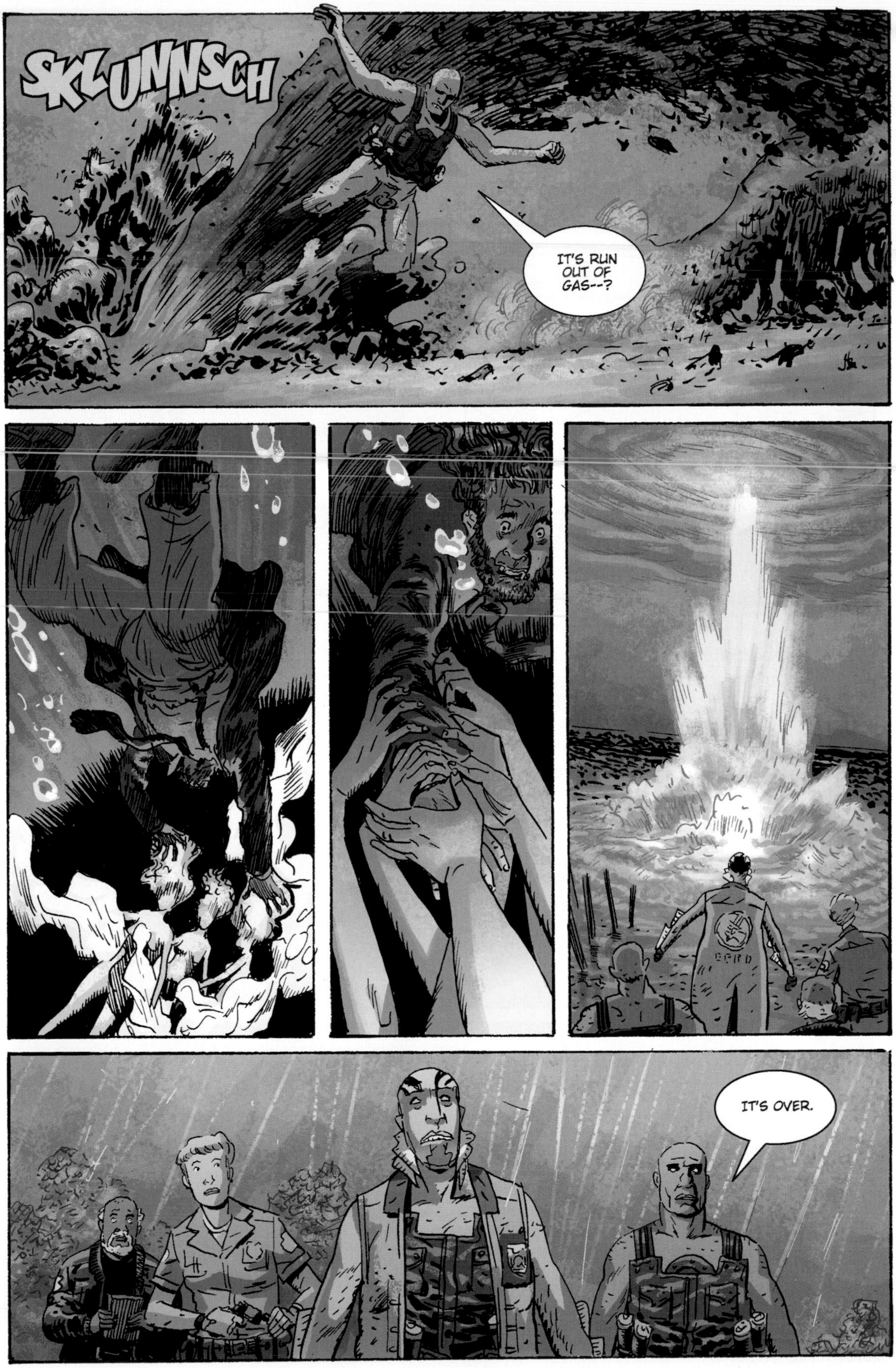
SKLUNNSCH
IT'S RUN OUT OF GAS--?
IT'S OVER.

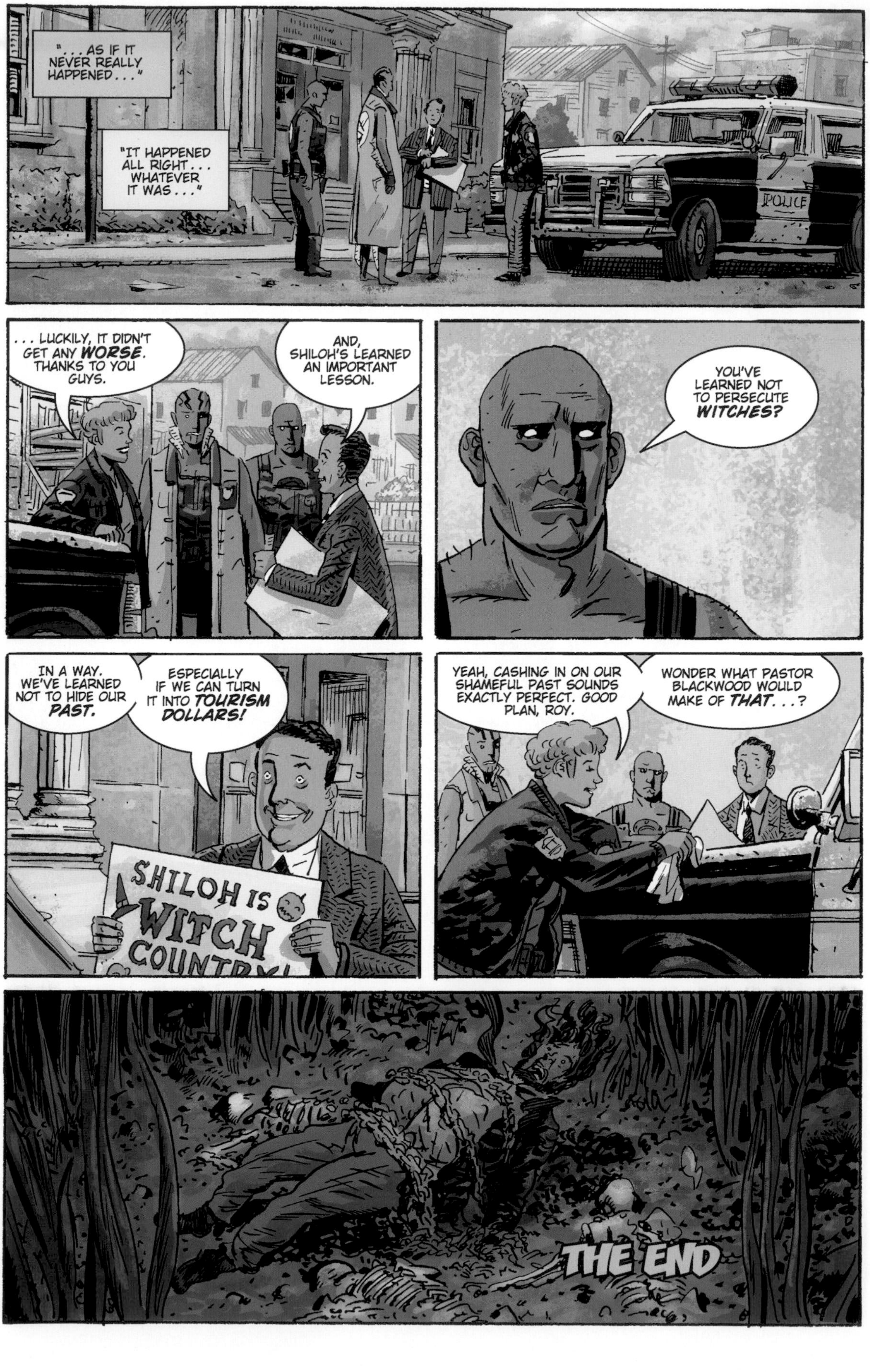

"...AS IF IT NEVER REALLY HAPPENED..."
"IT HAPPENED ALL RIGHT... WHATEVER IT WAS..."
POLICE
...LUCKILY, IT DIDN'T GET ANY WORSE. THANKS TO YOU GUYS.
AND, SHILOH'S LEARNED AN IMPORTANT LESSON.
YOU'VE LEARNED NOT TO PERSECUTE WITCHES?
IN A WAY. WE'VE LEARNED NOT TO HIDE OUR PAST.
ESPECIALLY IF WE CAN TURN IT INTO TOURISM DOLLARS!
SHILOH IS WITCH COUNTRY!
YEAH, CASHING IN ON OUR SHAMEFUL PAST SOUNDS EXACTLY PERFECT. GOOD PLAN, ROY.
WONDER WHAT PASTOR BLACKWOOD WOULD MAKE OF THAT...?
THE END

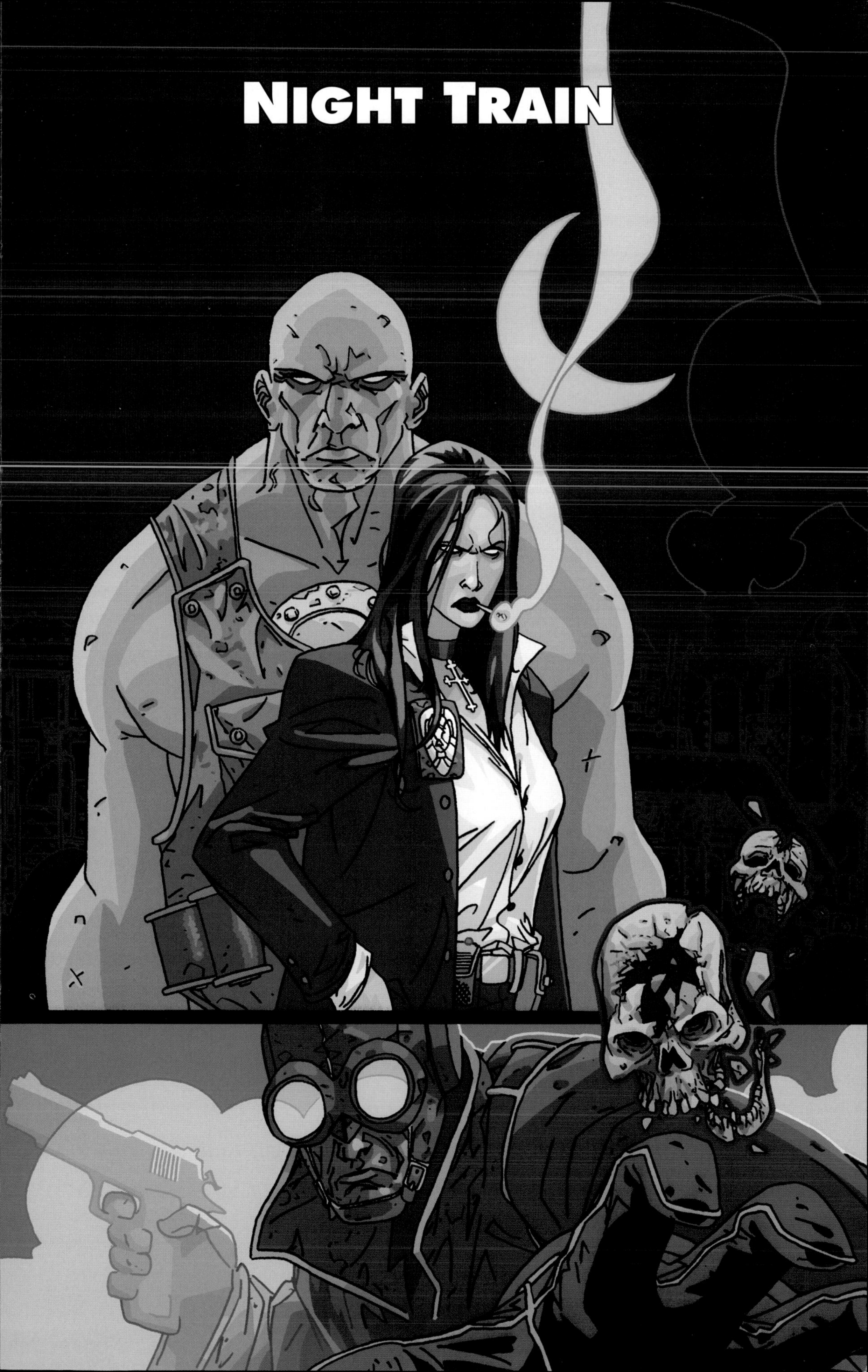
NIGHT TRAIN

NIGHT TRAIN

Story by
GEOFF JOHNS & SCOTT KOLINS

Art by
SCOTT KOLINS & DAVE STEWART

Letters by
PAT BROSSEAU

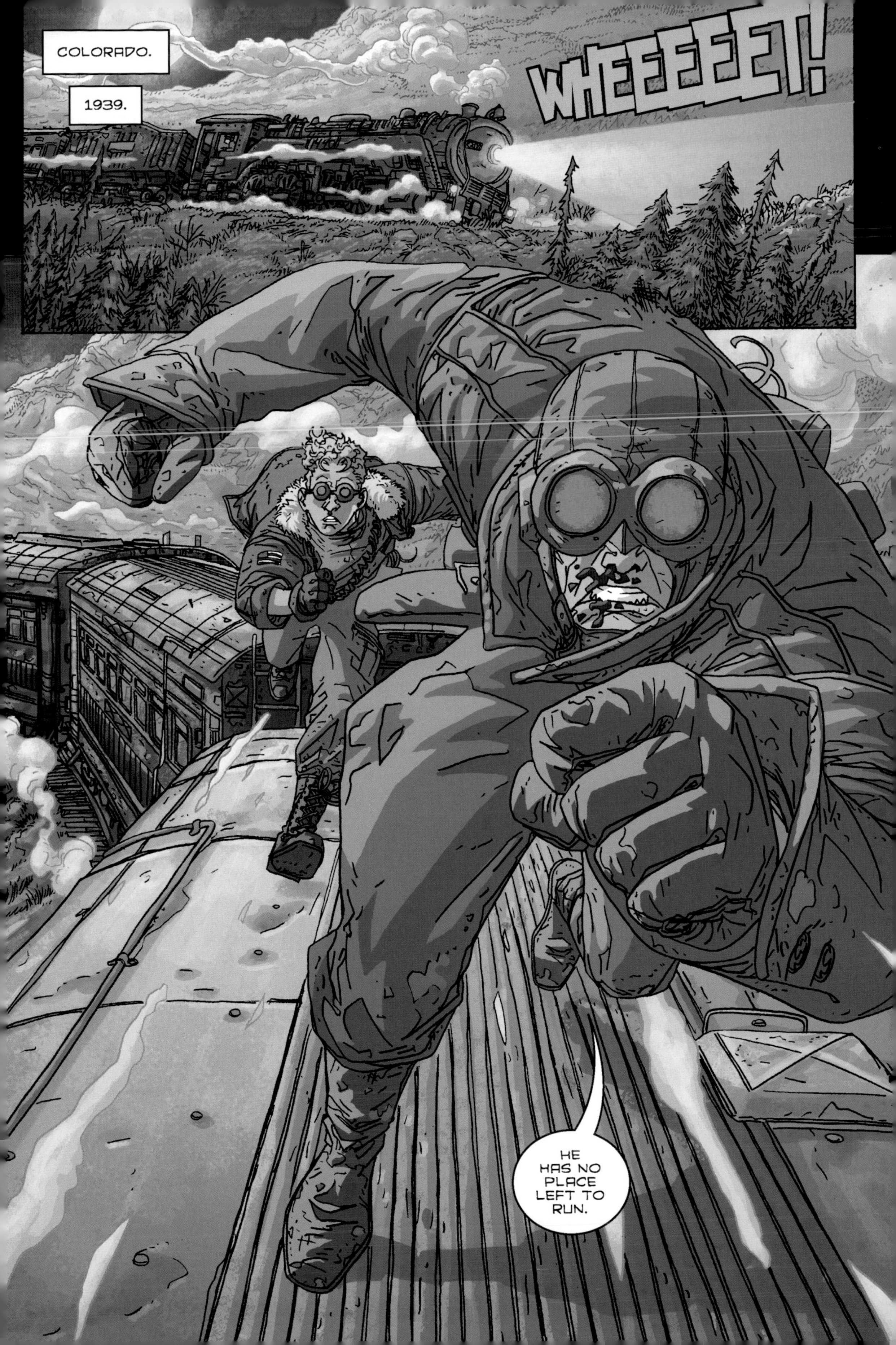
COLORADO.
1939.
WHEEEEET!
HE HAS NO PLACE LEFT TO RUN.

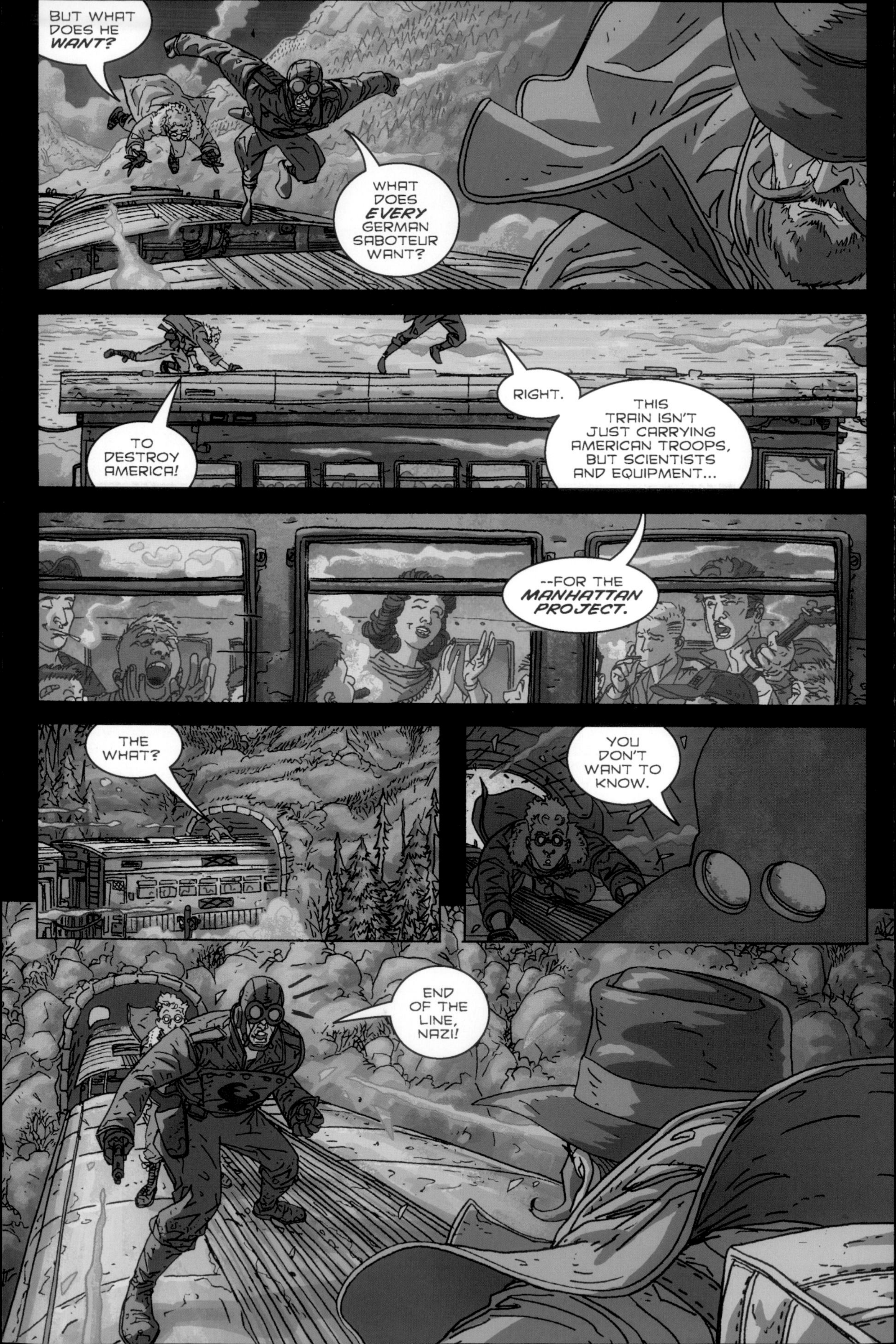
BUT WHAT DOES HE *WANT?*
WHAT DOES *EVERY* GERMAN SABOTEUR WANT?
TO DESTROY AMERICA!
RIGHT.
THIS TRAIN ISN'T JUST CARRYING AMERICAN TROOPS, BUT SCIENTISTS AND EQUIPMENT...
--FOR THE *MANHATTAN PROJECT.*
THE WHAT?
YOU DON'T WANT TO KNOW.
END OF THE LINE, NAZI!

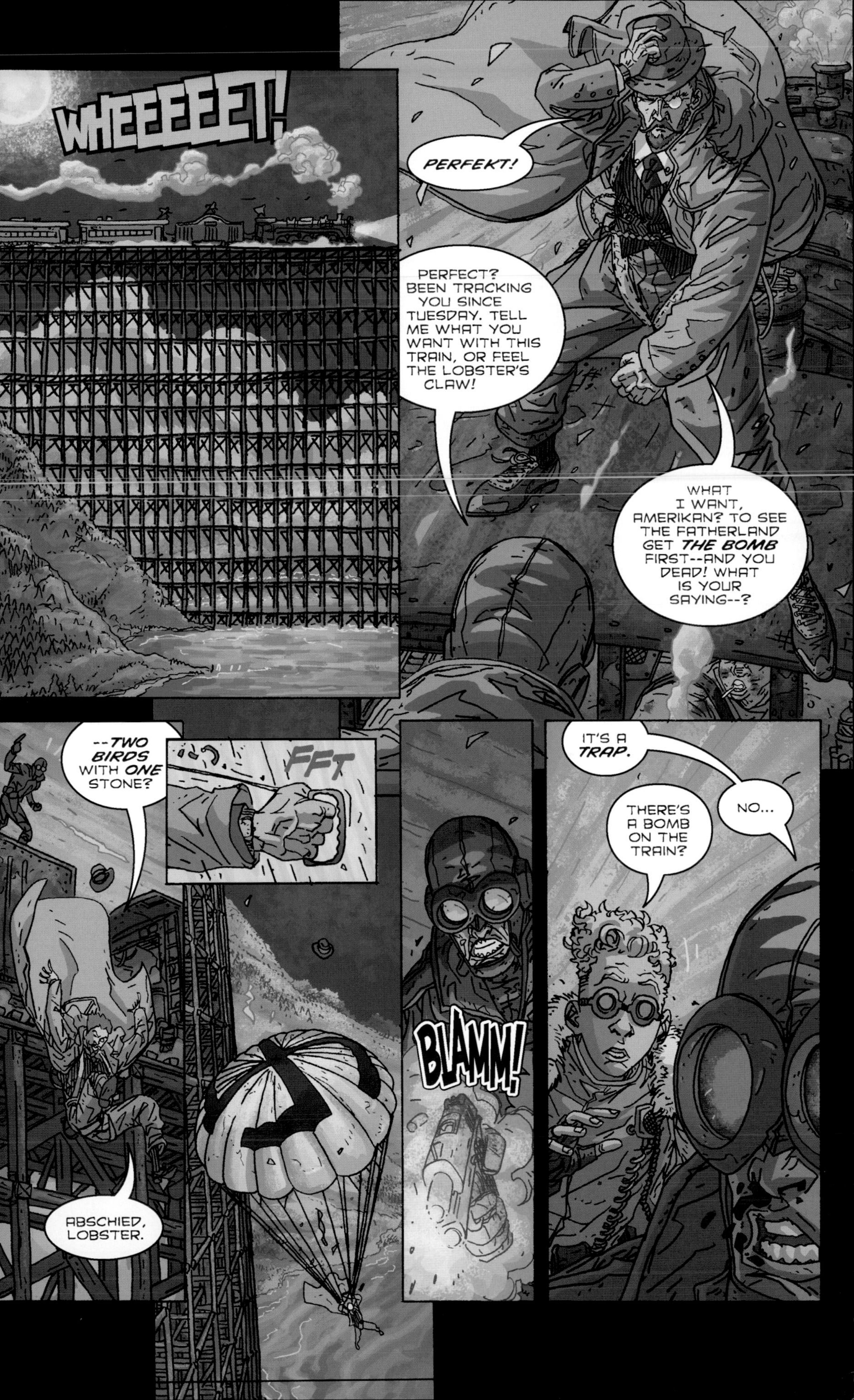
WHEEEEET!
PERFEKT!
PERFECT? BEEN TRACKING YOU SINCE TUESDAY. TELL ME WHAT YOU WANT WITH THIS TRAIN, OR FEEL THE LOBSTER'S CLAW!
WHAT I WANT, AMERIKAN? TO SEE THE FATHERLAND GET THE BOMB FIRST--AND YOU DEAD! WHAT IS YOUR SAYING--?
--TWO BIRDS WITH ONE STONE?
FFT
ABSCHIED, LOBSTER.
BLAMM!
IT'S A TRAP.
NO...
THERE'S A BOMB ON THE TRAIN?

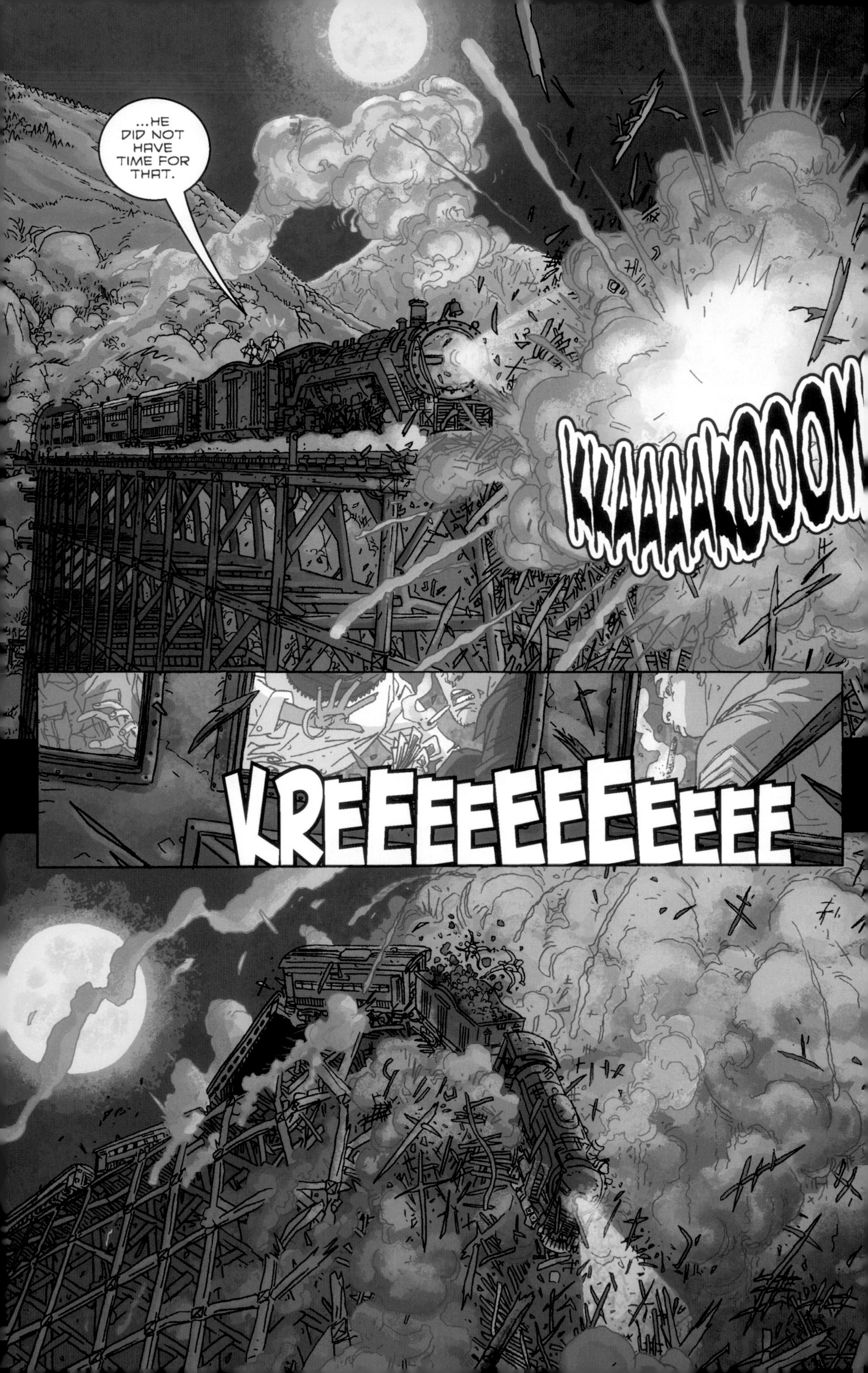
...HE DID NOT HAVE TIME FOR THAT.
KRAAAAKOOOM
KREEEEEEEEEEE

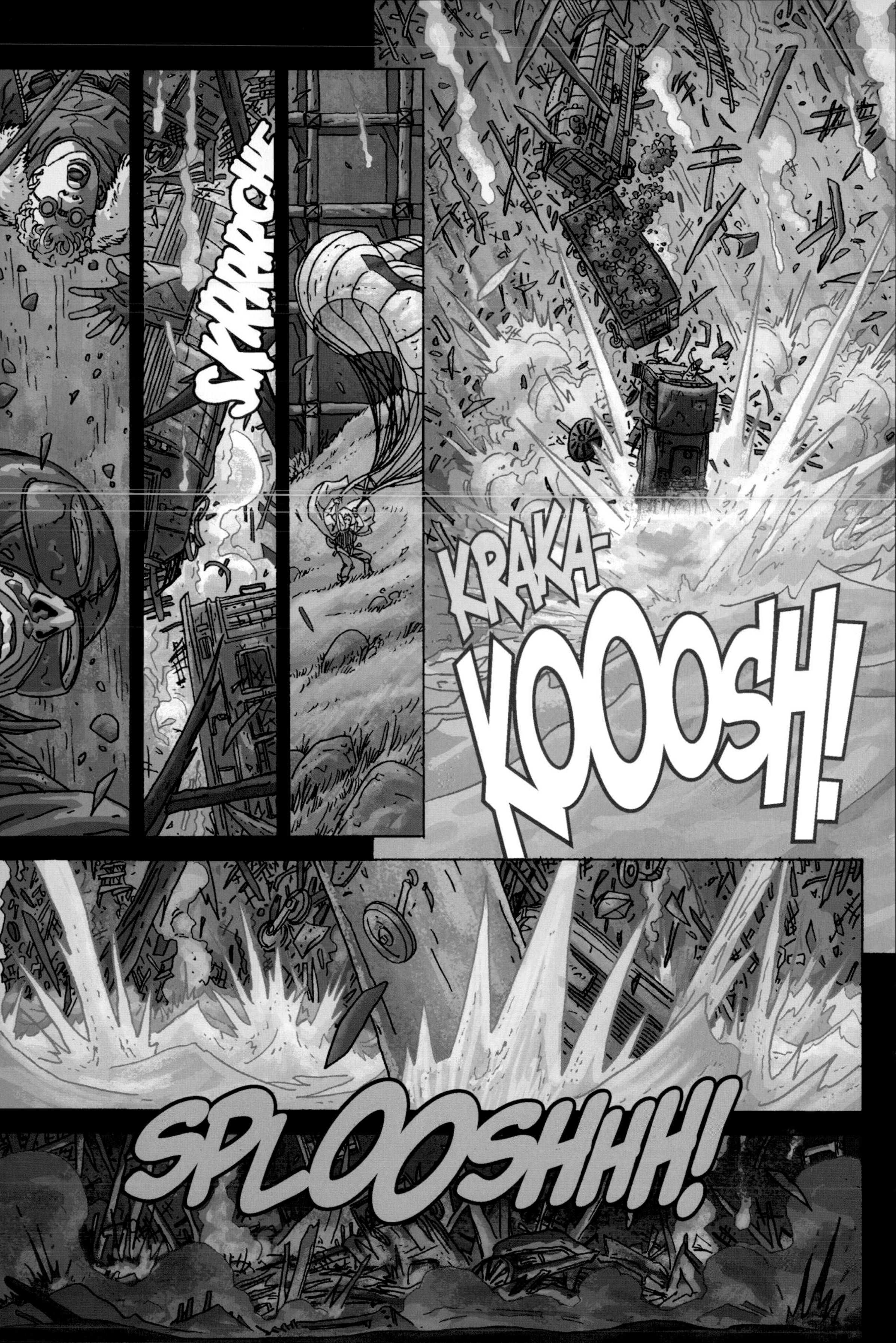
SKRRRCH!
KRAKA-
KOOOSH!
SPLOOSHHH!

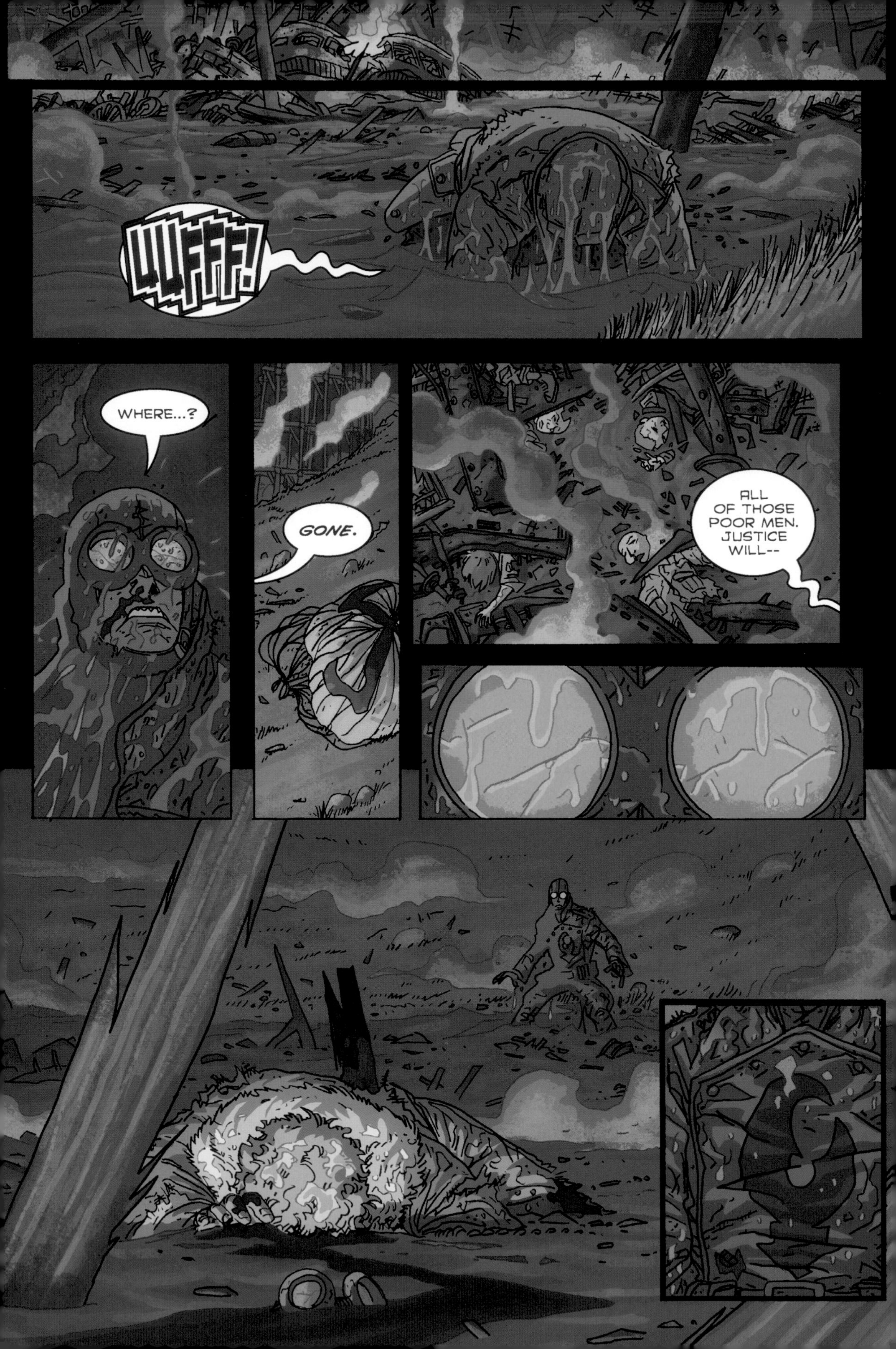
UUFFF!
WHERE...?
GONE.
ALL OF THOSE POOR MEN. JUSTICE WILL--

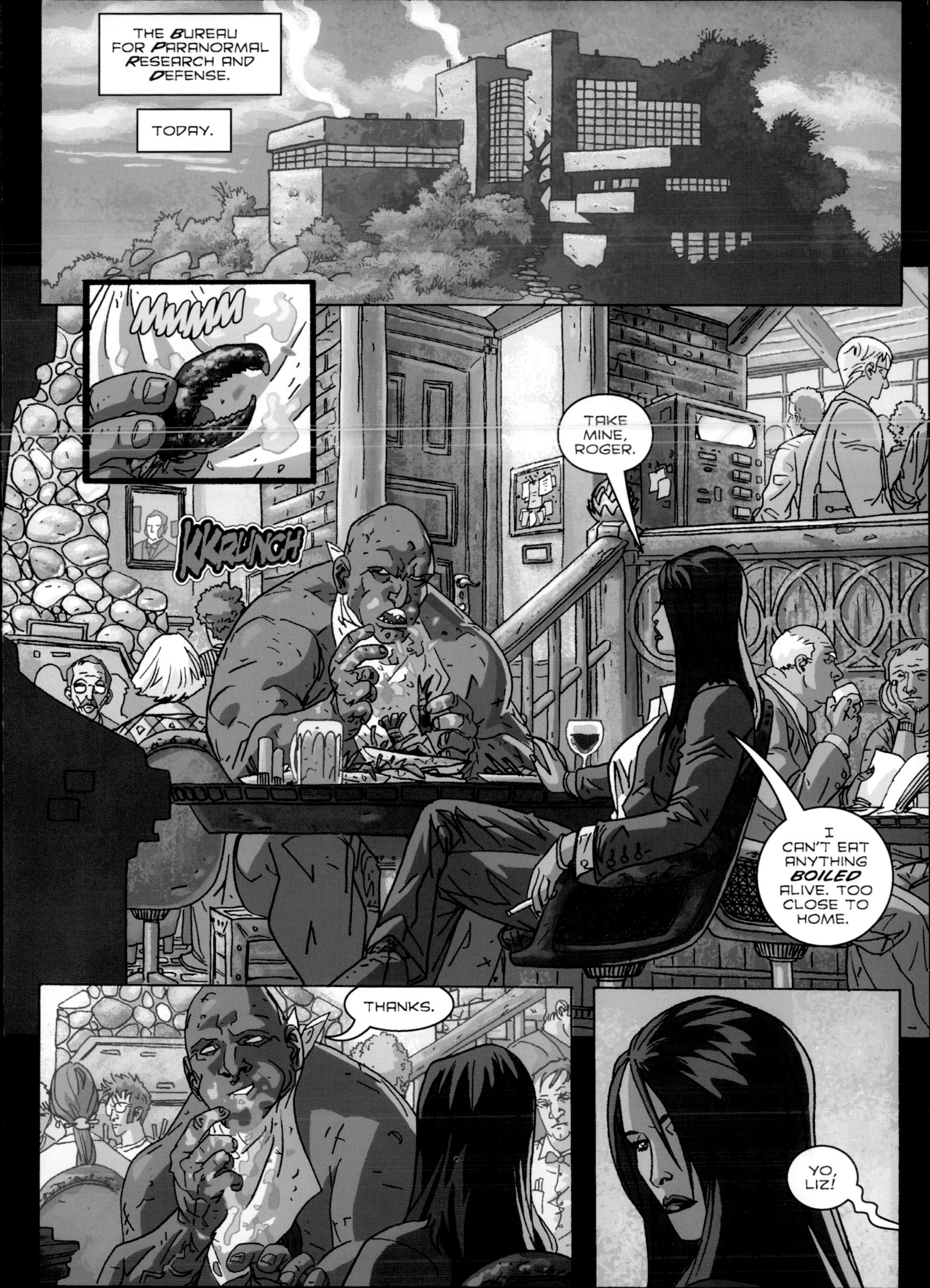
THE BUREAU FOR PARANORMAL RESEARCH AND DEFENSE.
TODAY.
MMMM
KKRUNCH
TAKE MINE, ROGER.
I CAN'T EAT ANYTHING BOILED ALIVE. TOO CLOSE TO HOME.
THANKS.
YO, LIZ!

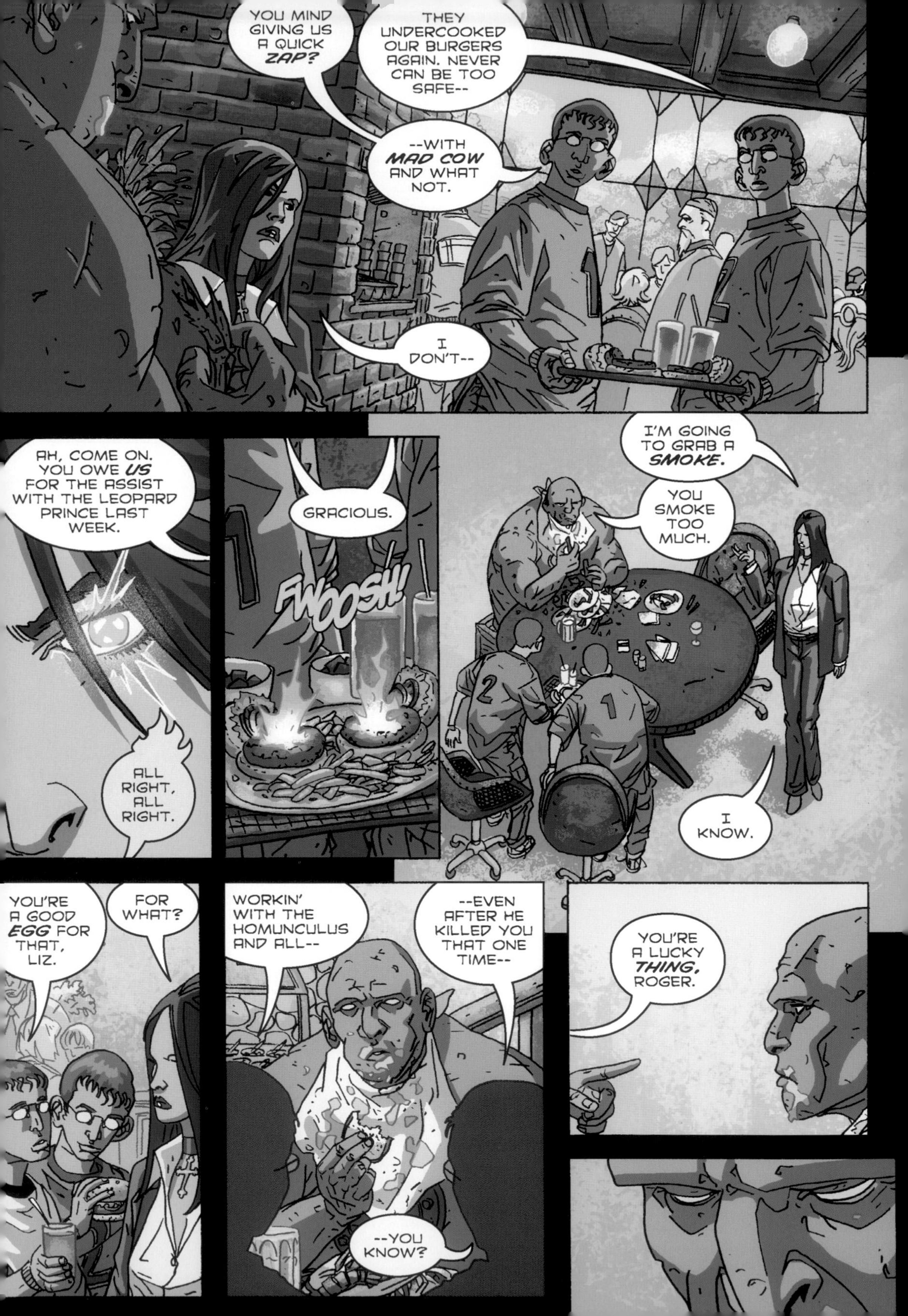
YOU MIND GIVING US A QUICK ZAP?
THEY UNDERCOOKED OUR BURGERS AGAIN. NEVER CAN BE TOO SAFE--
--WITH MAD COW AND WHAT NOT.
I DON'T--
AH, COME ON. YOU OWE US FOR THE ASSIST WITH THE LEOPARD PRINCE LAST WEEK.
ALL RIGHT, ALL RIGHT.
FWOOSH!
GRACIOUS.
I'M GOING TO GRAB A SMOKE.
YOU SMOKE TOO MUCH.
I KNOW.
YOU'RE A GOOD EGG FOR THAT, LIZ.
FOR WHAT?
WORKIN' WITH THE HOMUNCULUS AND ALL--
--EVEN AFTER HE KILLED YOU THAT ONE TIME--
--YOU KNOW?
YOU'RE A LUCKY THING, ROGER.

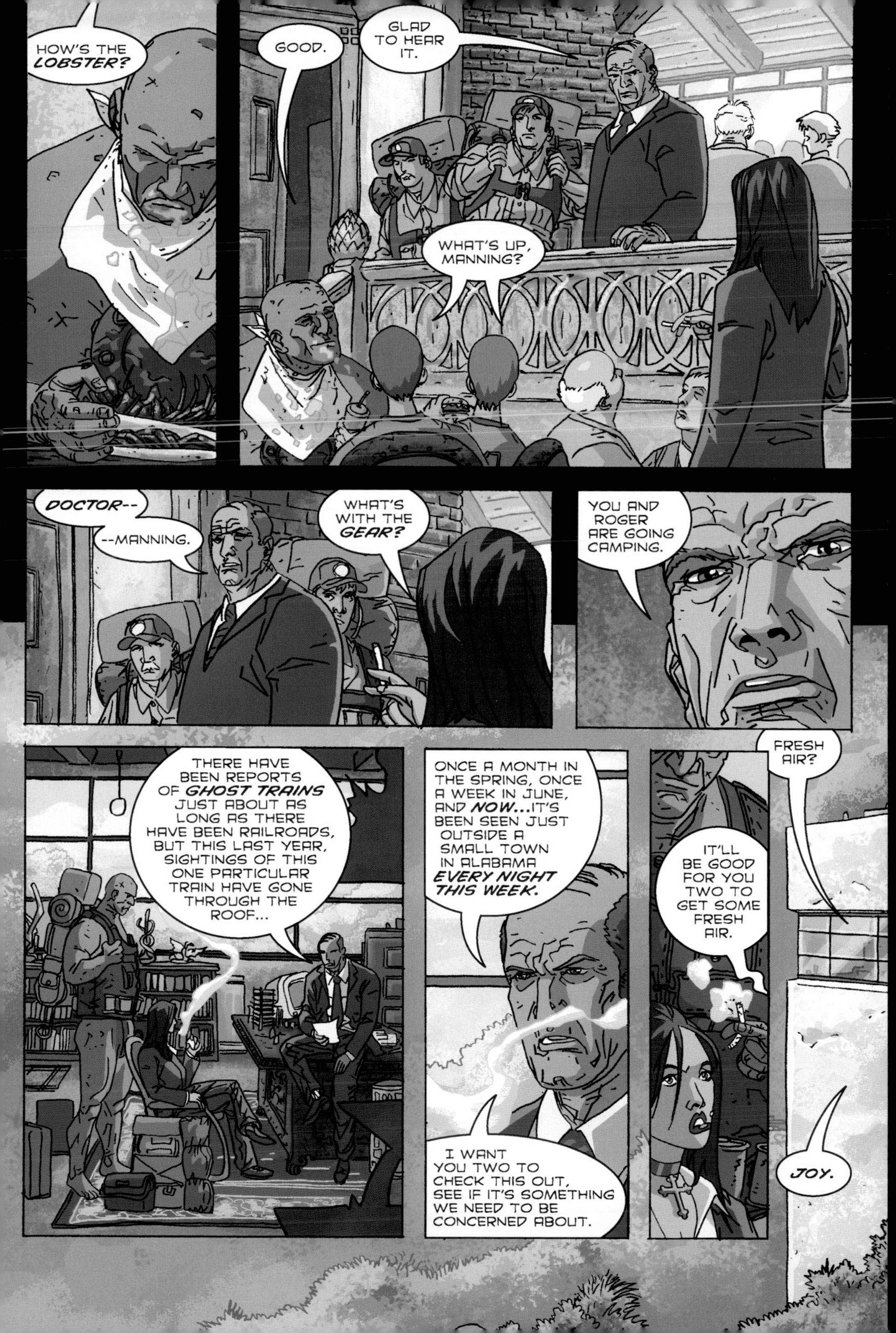
HOW'S THE LOBSTER?
GOOD.
GLAD TO HEAR IT.
WHAT'S UP, MANNING?
DOCTOR--
--MANNING.
WHAT'S WITH THE GEAR?
YOU AND ROGER ARE GOING CAMPING.
THERE HAVE BEEN REPORTS OF GHOST TRAINS JUST ABOUT AS LONG AS THERE HAVE BEEN RAILROADS, BUT THIS LAST YEAR, SIGHTINGS OF THIS ONE PARTICULAR TRAIN HAVE GONE THROUGH THE ROOF...
ONCE A MONTH IN THE SPRING, ONCE A WEEK IN JUNE, AND NOW...IT'S BEEN SEEN JUST OUTSIDE A SMALL TOWN IN ALABAMA EVERY NIGHT THIS WEEK.
I WANT YOU TWO TO CHECK THIS OUT, SEE IF IT'S SOMETHING WE NEED TO BE CONCERNED ABOUT.
FRESH AIR?
IT'LL BE GOOD FOR YOU TWO TO GET SOME FRESH AIR.
JOY.

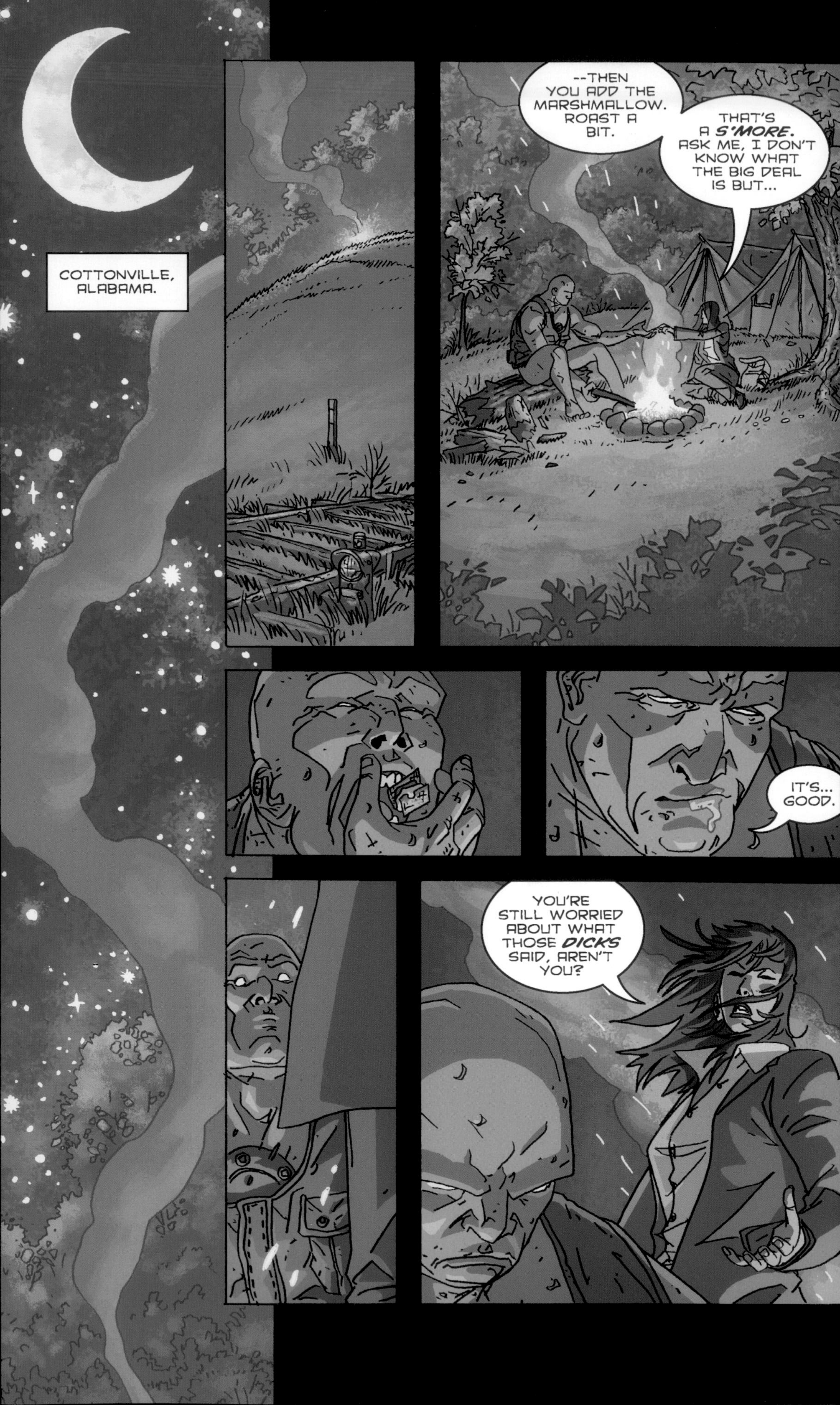

COTTONVILLE, ALABAMA.
--THEN YOU ADD THE MARSHMALLOW. ROAST A BIT.
THAT'S A S'MORE. ASK ME, I DON'T KNOW WHAT THE BIG DEAL IS BUT...
IT'S... GOOD.
YOU'RE STILL WORRIED ABOUT WHAT THOSE DICKS SAID, AREN'T YOU?

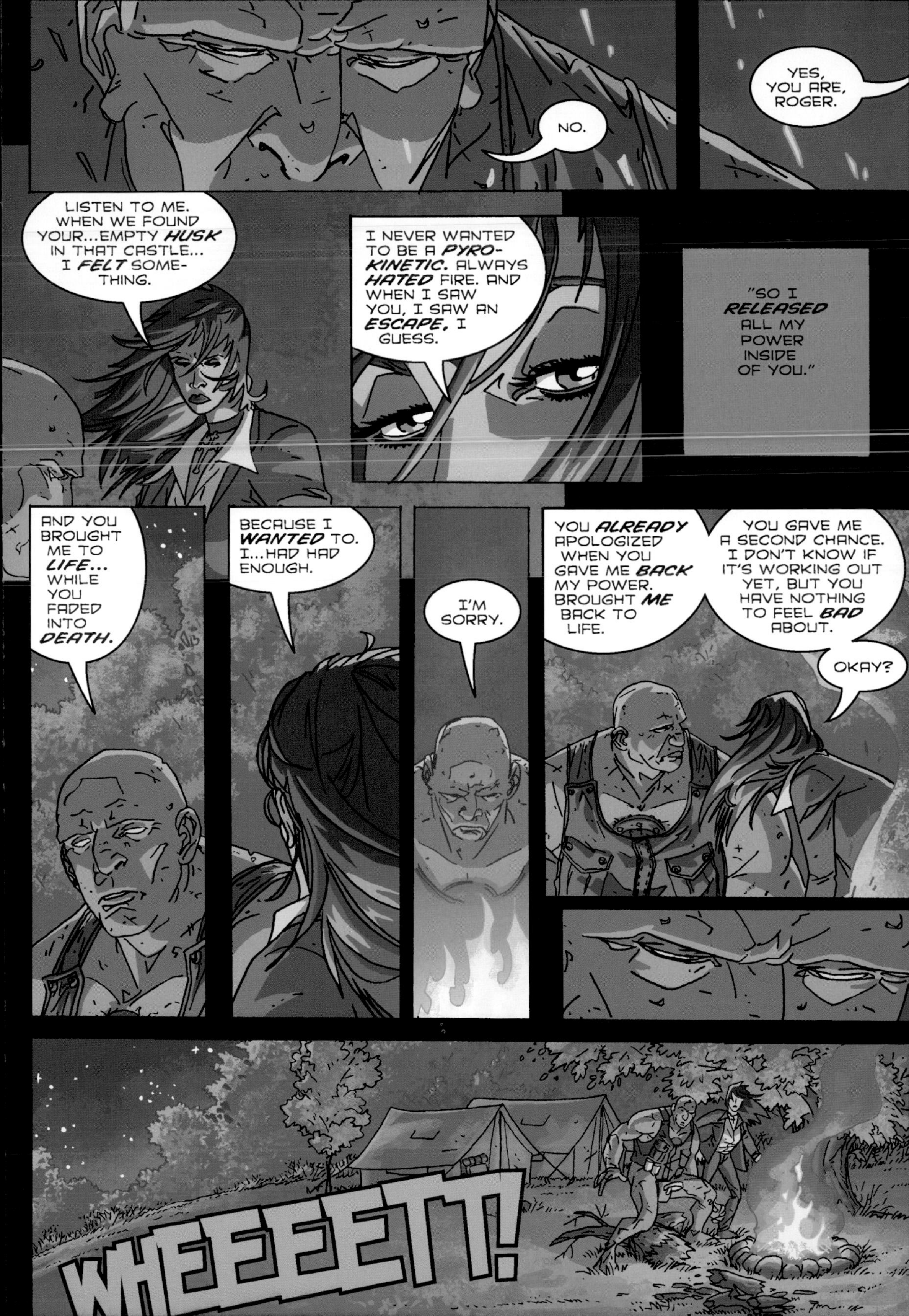

NO.
YES, YOU ARE, ROGER.
LISTEN TO ME. WHEN WE FOUND YOUR...EMPTY HUSK IN THAT CASTLE... I FELT SOMETHING.
I NEVER WANTED TO BE A PYROKINETIC. ALWAYS HATED FIRE. AND WHEN I SAW YOU, I SAW AN ESCAPE, I GUESS.
"SO I RELEASED ALL MY POWER INSIDE OF YOU."
AND YOU BROUGHT ME TO LIFE... WHILE YOU FADED INTO DEATH.
BECAUSE I WANTED TO. I...HAD HAD ENOUGH.
I'M SORRY.
YOU ALREADY APOLOGIZED WHEN YOU GAVE ME BACK MY POWER. BROUGHT ME BACK TO LIFE.
YOU GAVE ME A SECOND CHANCE. I DON'T KNOW IF IT'S WORKING OUT YET, BUT YOU HAVE NOTHING TO FEEL BAD ABOUT.
OKAY?
WHEEEETT!

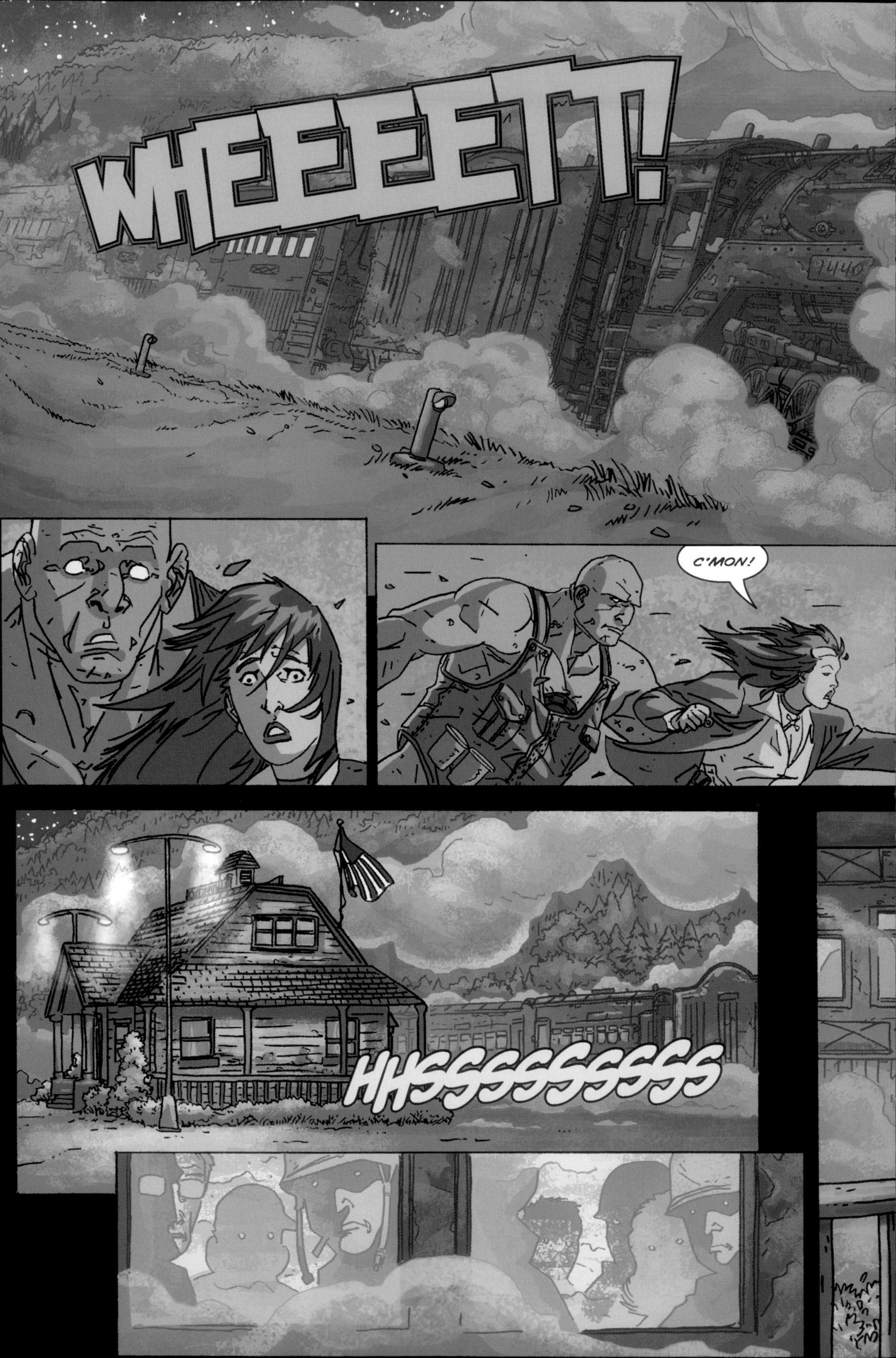
WHEEEETT!
C'MON!
HHSSSSSSSSSS

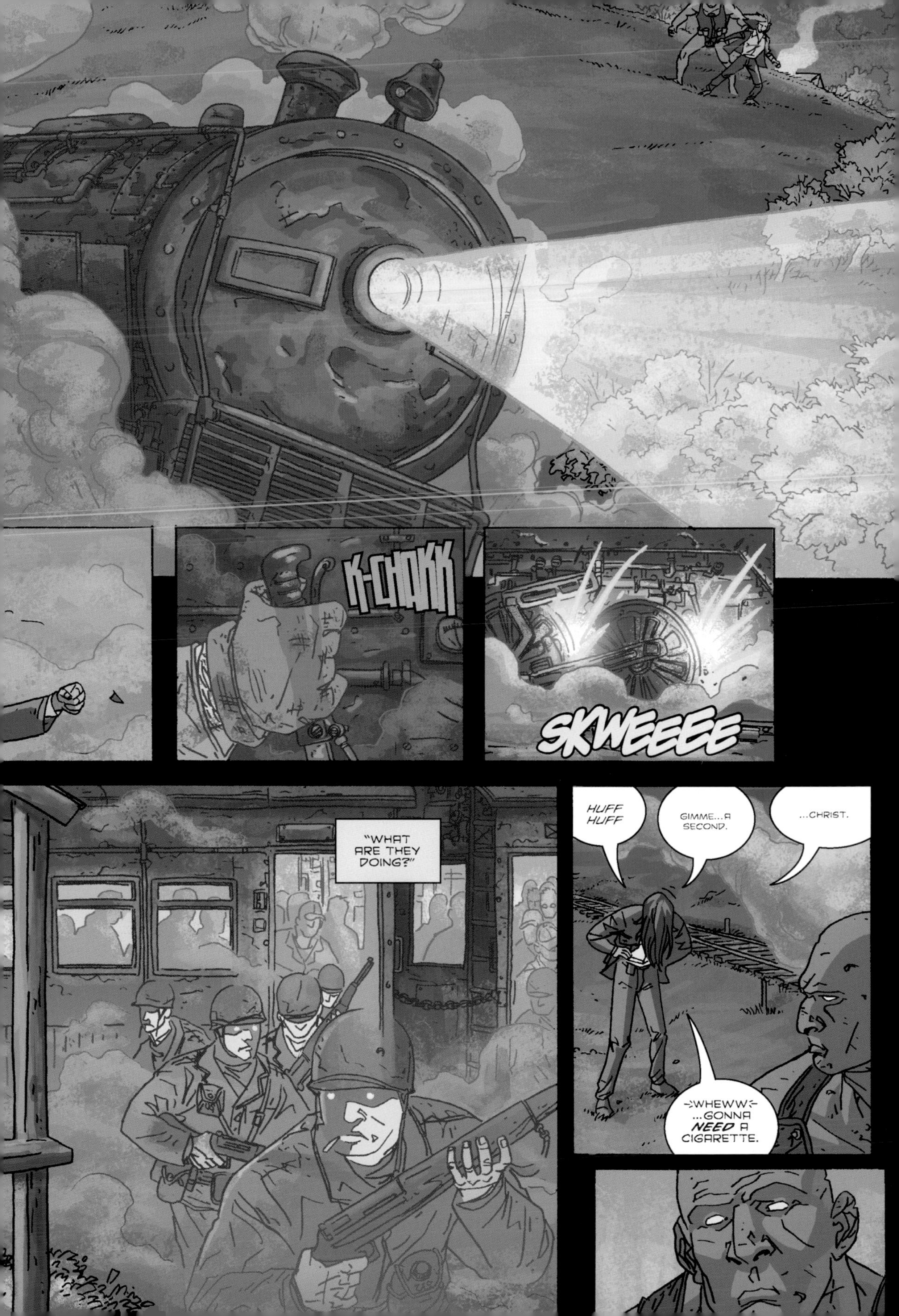
K-CHAKK
SKWEEEE
"WHAT ARE THEY DOING?"
HUFF HUFF
GIMME...A SECOND.
...CHRIST.
-WHEWW-
...GONNA NEED A CIGARETTE.

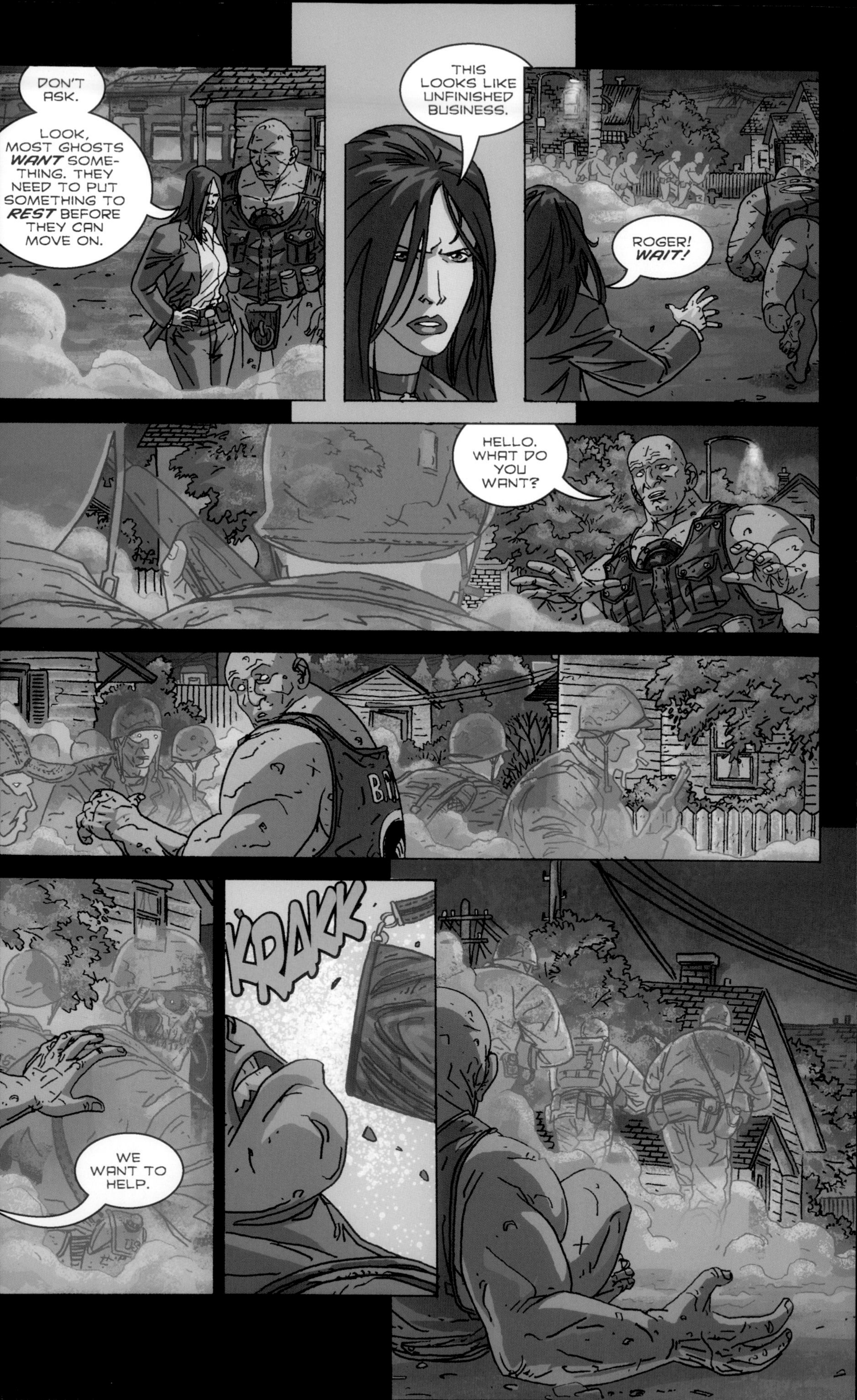
DON'T ASK.
LOOK, MOST GHOSTS WANT SOMETHING. THEY NEED TO PUT SOMETHING TO REST BEFORE THEY CAN MOVE ON.
THIS LOOKS LIKE UNFINISHED BUSINESS.
ROGER! WAIT!
HELLO. WHAT DO YOU WANT?
WE WANT TO HELP.
KRAKK

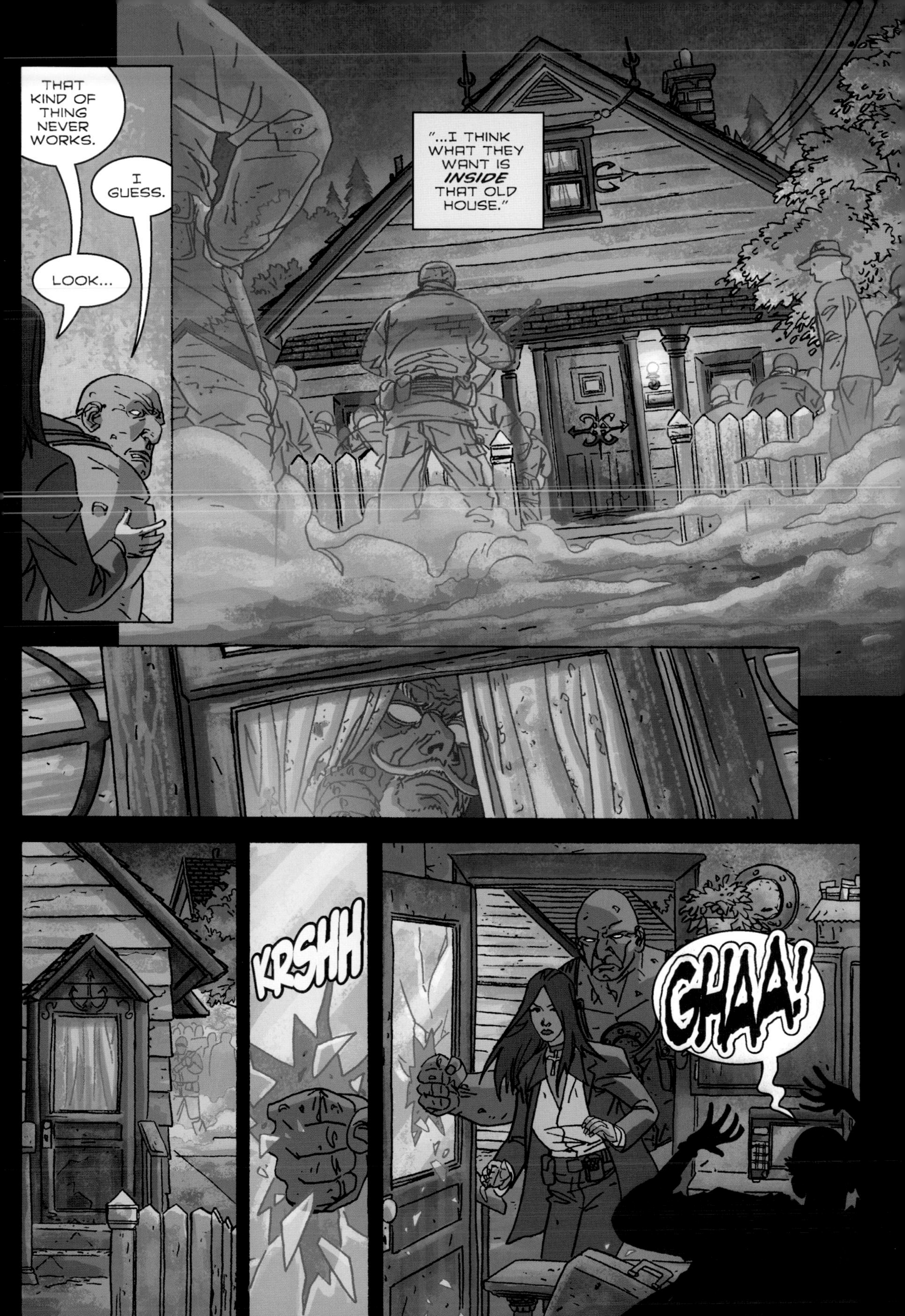
THAT KIND OF THING NEVER WORKS.
I GUESS.
LOOK...
"...I THINK WHAT THEY WANT IS *INSIDE* THAT OLD HOUSE."
KRSHH
GHAA!

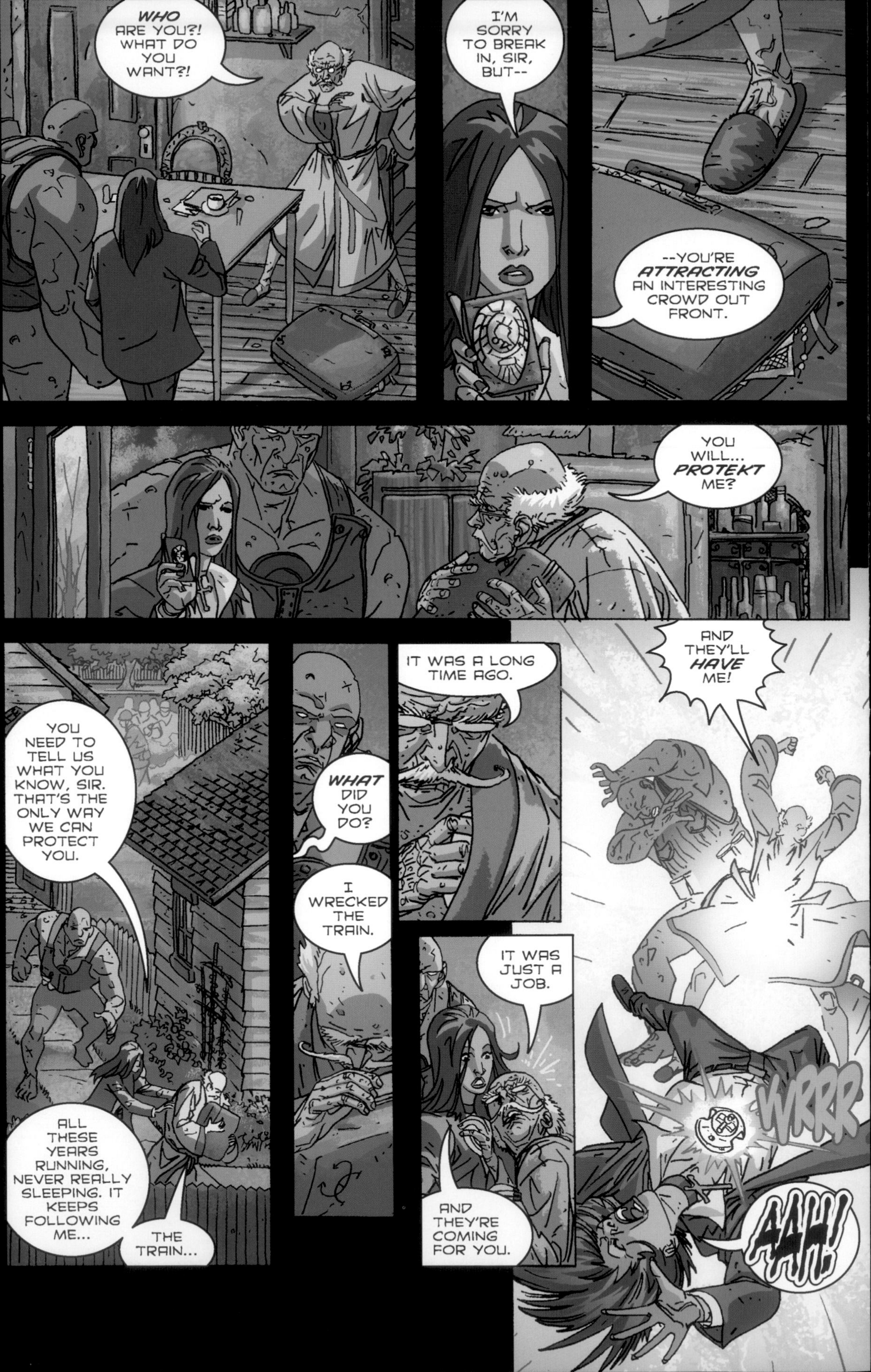
WHO ARE YOU?! WHAT DO YOU WANT?!
I'M SORRY TO BREAK IN, SIR, BUT--
--YOU'RE ATTRACTING AN INTERESTING CROWD OUT FRONT.
YOU WILL... PROTEKT ME?
YOU NEED TO TELL US WHAT YOU KNOW, SIR. THAT'S THE ONLY WAY WE CAN PROTECT YOU.
ALL THESE YEARS RUNNING, NEVER REALLY SLEEPING. IT KEEPS FOLLOWING ME...
THE TRAIN...
WHAT DID YOU DO?
IT WAS A LONG TIME AGO.
I WRECKED THE TRAIN.
IT WAS JUST A JOB.
AND THEY'RE COMING FOR YOU.
AND THEY'LL HAVE ME!
WRRR
AAH!

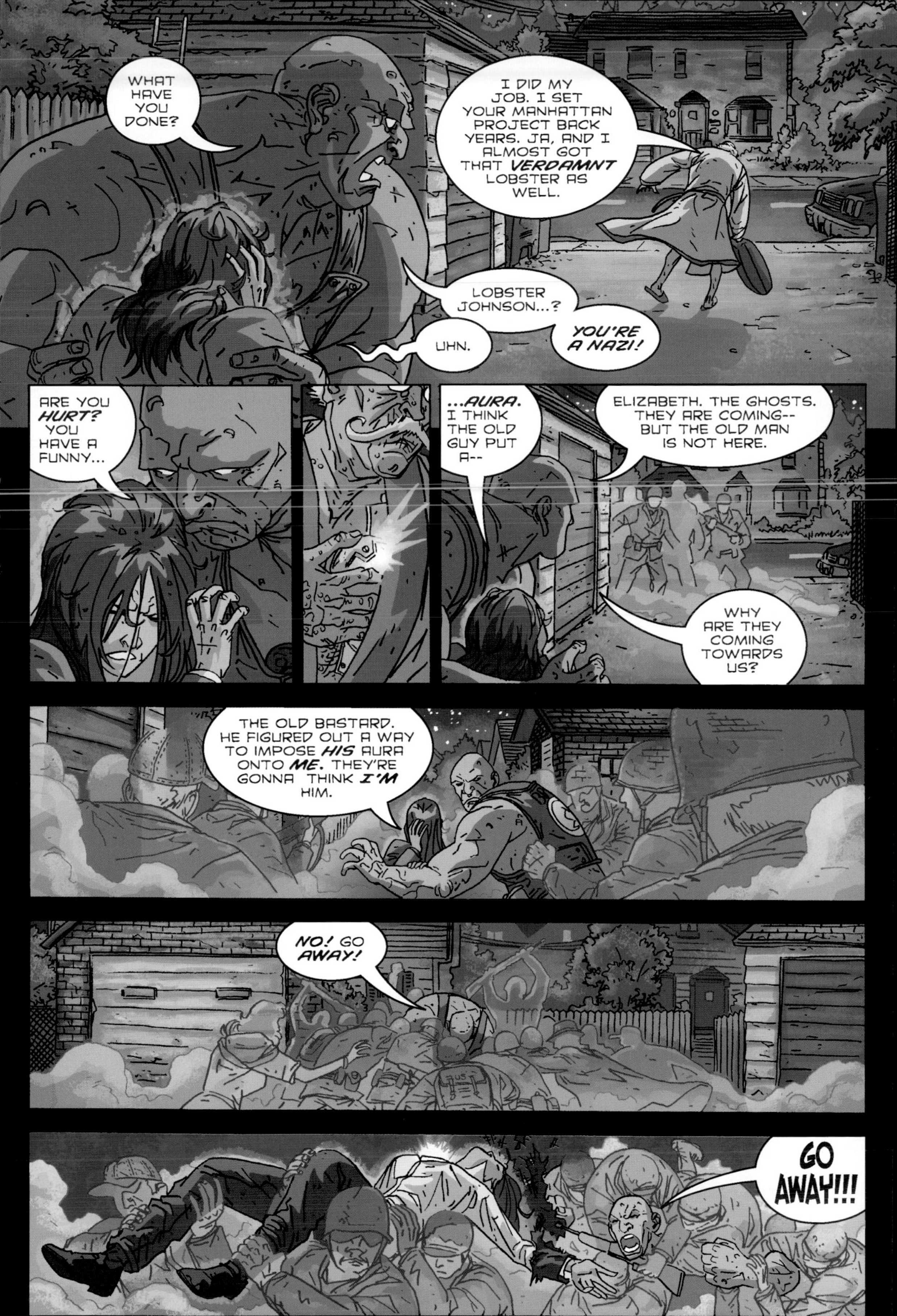

WHAT HAVE YOU DONE?
I DID MY JOB. I SET YOUR MANHATTAN PROJECT BACK YEARS. JA, AND I ALMOST GOT THAT VERDAMNT LOBSTER AS WELL.
LOBSTER JOHNSON...?
UHN.
YOU'RE A NAZI!
ARE YOU HURT? YOU HAVE A FUNNY...
...AURA. I THINK THE OLD GUY PUT A--
ELIZABETH. THE GHOSTS. THEY ARE COMING-- BUT THE OLD MAN IS NOT HERE.
WHY ARE THEY COMING TOWARDS US?
THE OLD BASTARD. HE FIGURED OUT A WAY TO IMPOSE HIS AURA ONTO ME. THEY'RE GONNA THINK I'M HIM.
NO! GO AWAY!
GO AWAY!!!

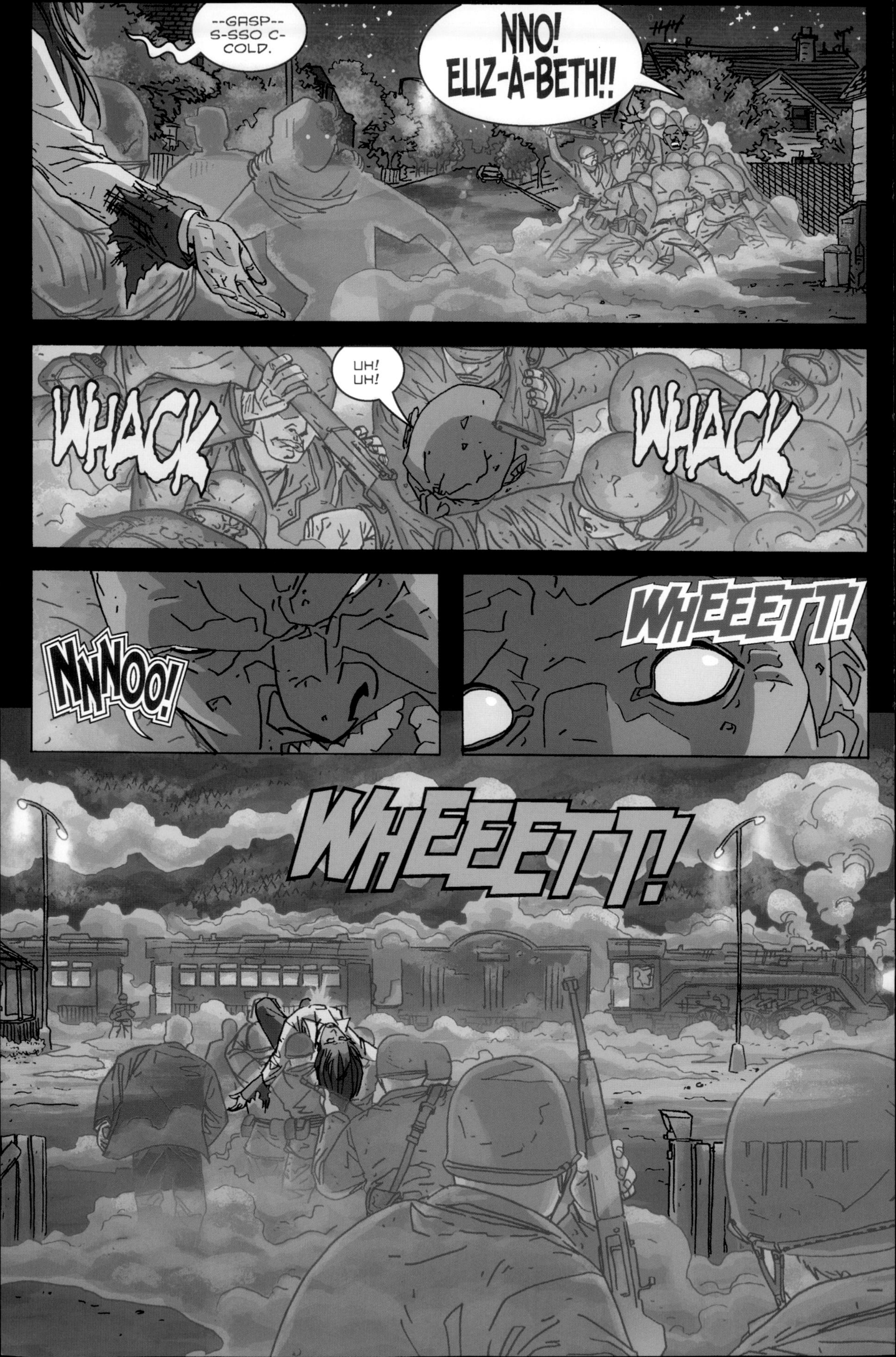
--GASP--
S-SSO C-COLD.
NNO! ELIZ-A-BETH!!
WHACK
UH! UH!
WHACK
NNNOO!
WHEEETT!
WHEEETT!

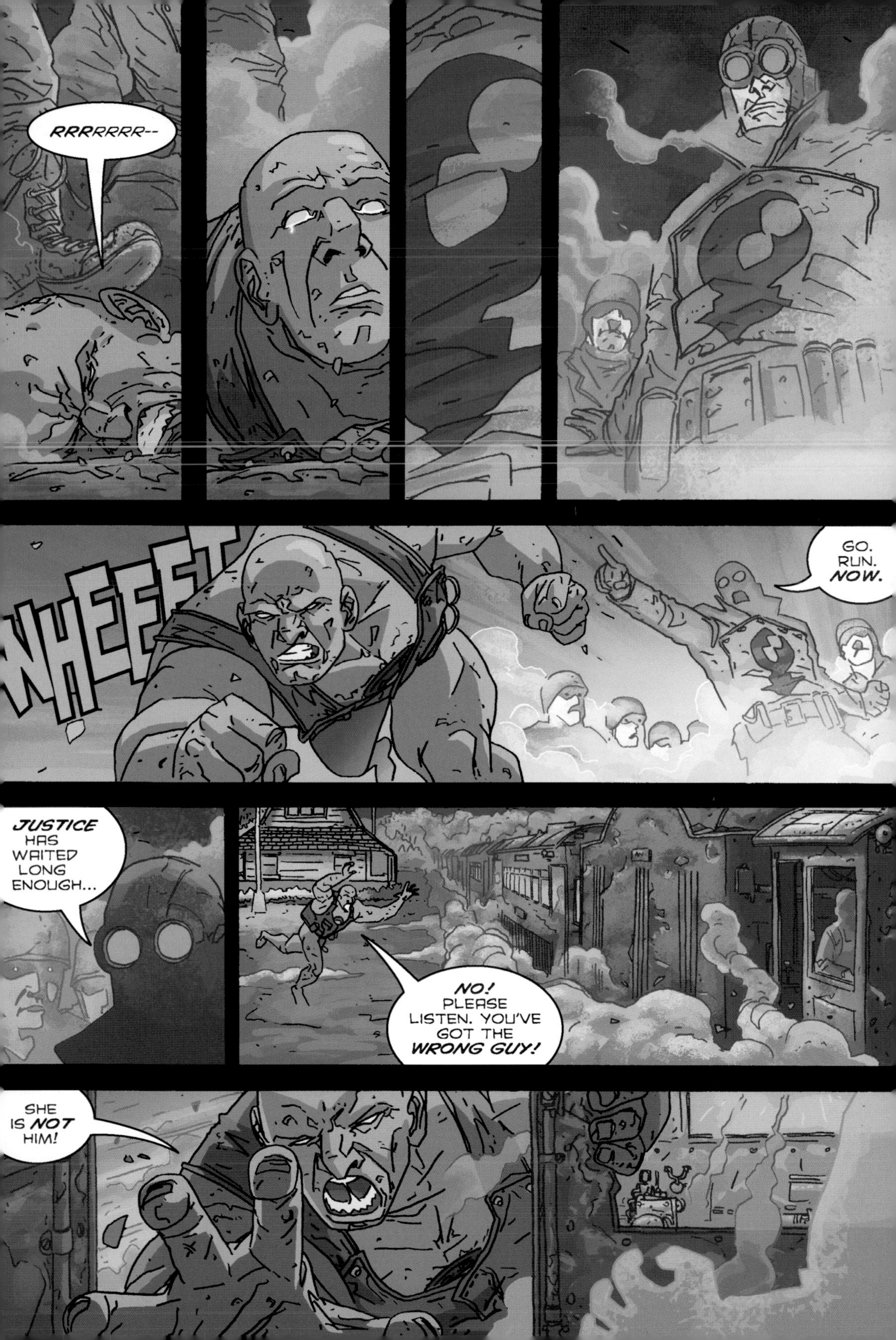
RRRRRRR--
WHEEET
GO. RUN. NOW.
JUSTICE HAS WAITED LONG ENOUGH...
NO! PLEASE LISTEN. YOU'VE GOT THE WRONG GUY!
SHE IS NOT HIM!

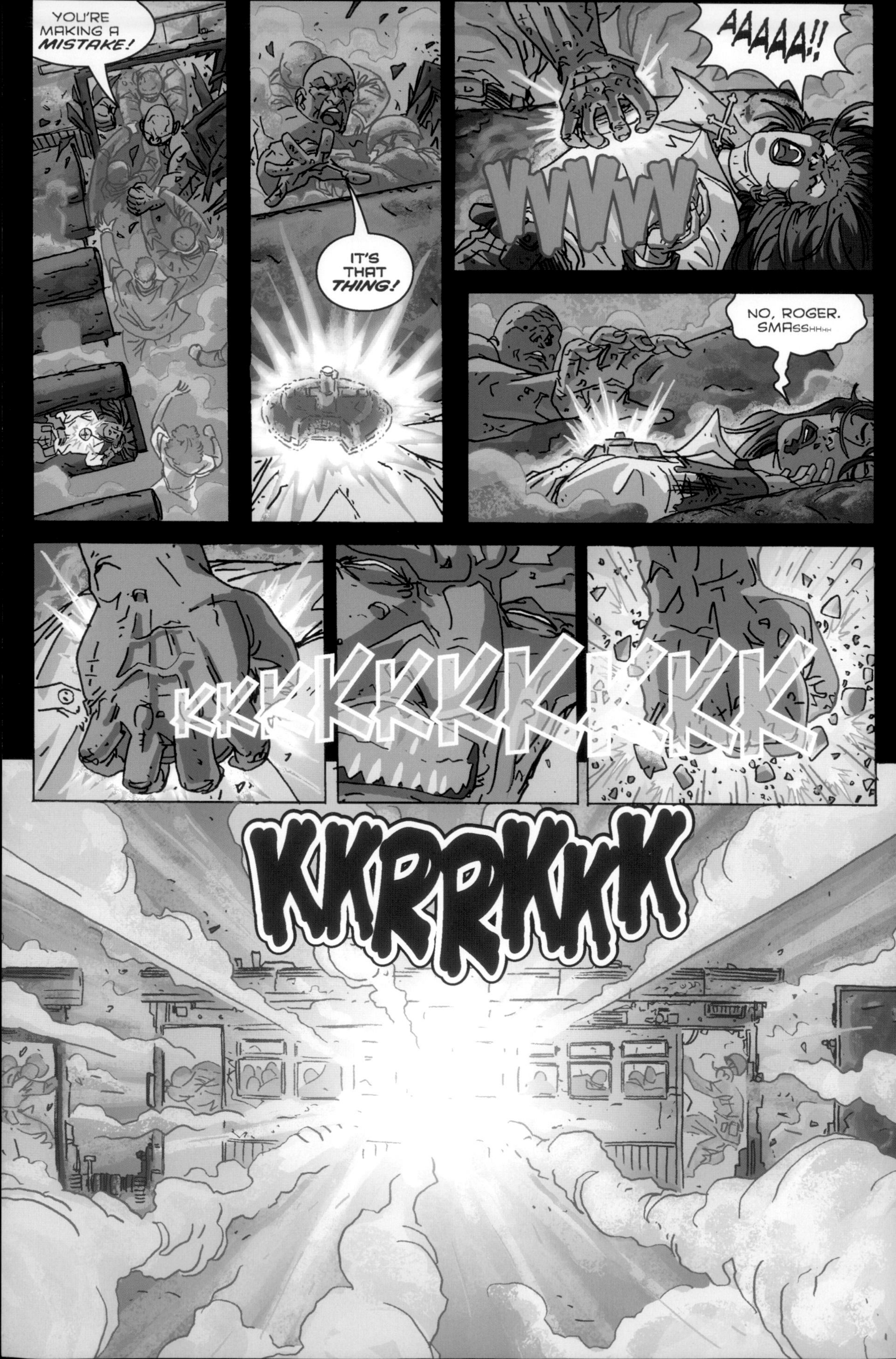

YOU'RE MAKING A MISTAKE!
IT'S THAT THING!
AAAAA!!
VVVVV
NO, ROGER. SMASSHHHH
KKKKKKKKKKK
KKRRKKKK

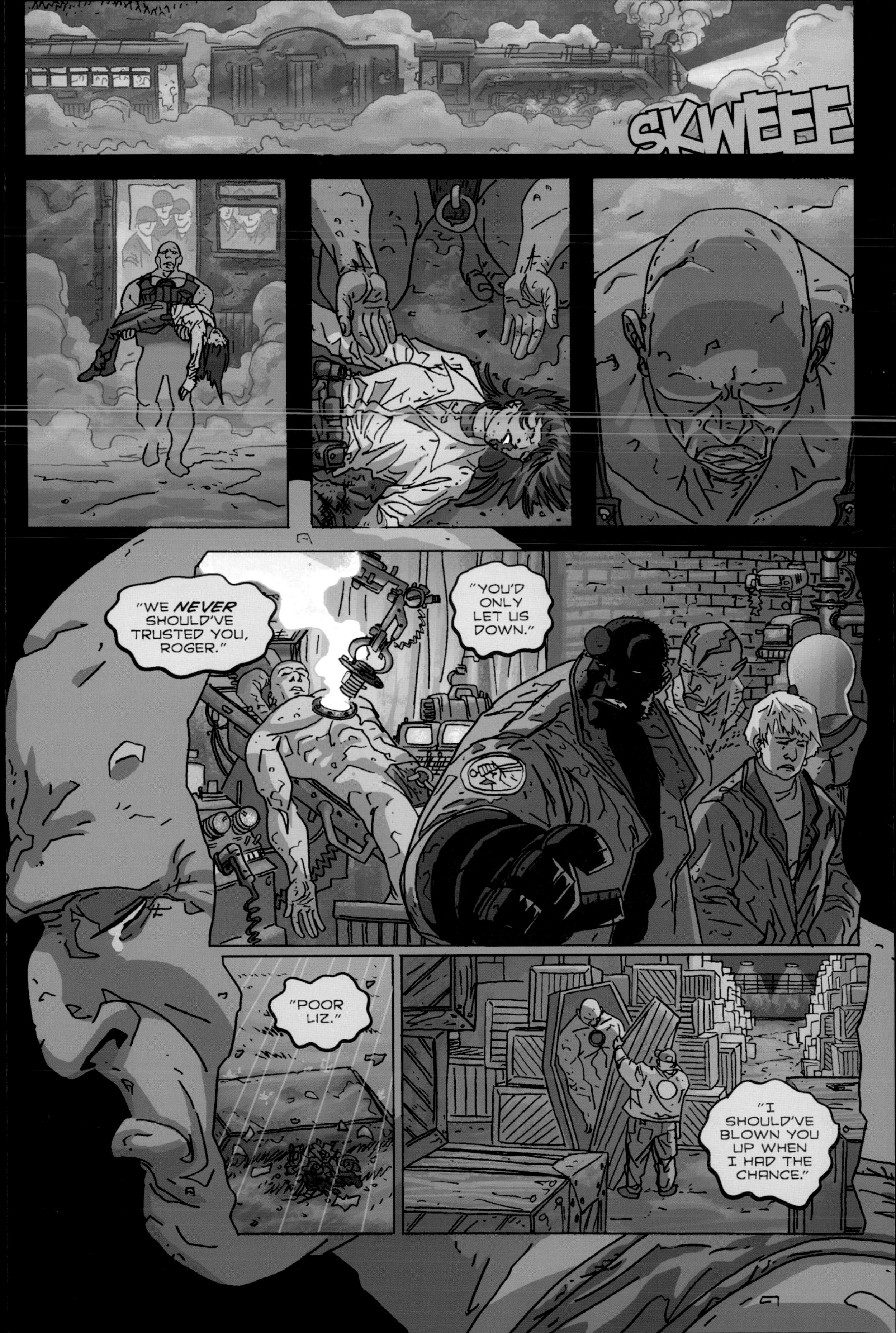
SKWEEE
"WE NEVER SHOULD'VE TRUSTED YOU, ROGER."
"YOU'D ONLY LET US DOWN."
"POOR LIZ."
"I SHOULD'VE BLOWN YOU UP WHEN I HAD THE CHANCE."

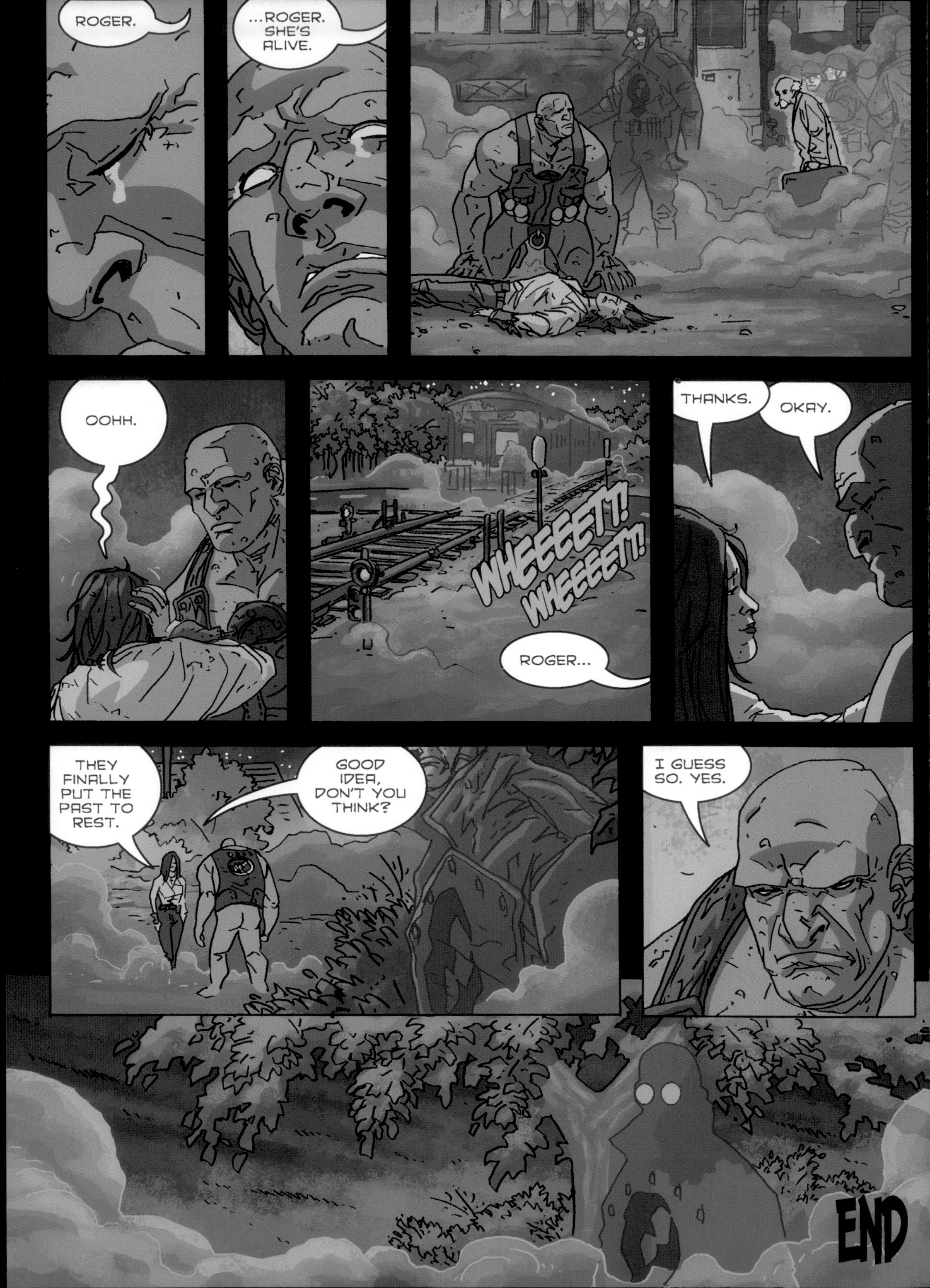
ROGER.
...ROGER. SHE'S ALIVE.
OOHH.
WHEEEEETT! WHEEEEETT!
ROGER...
THANKS.
OKAY.
THEY FINALLY PUT THE PAST TO REST.
GOOD IDEA, DON'T YOU THINK?
I GUESS SO. YES.
END

There's Something Under My Bed

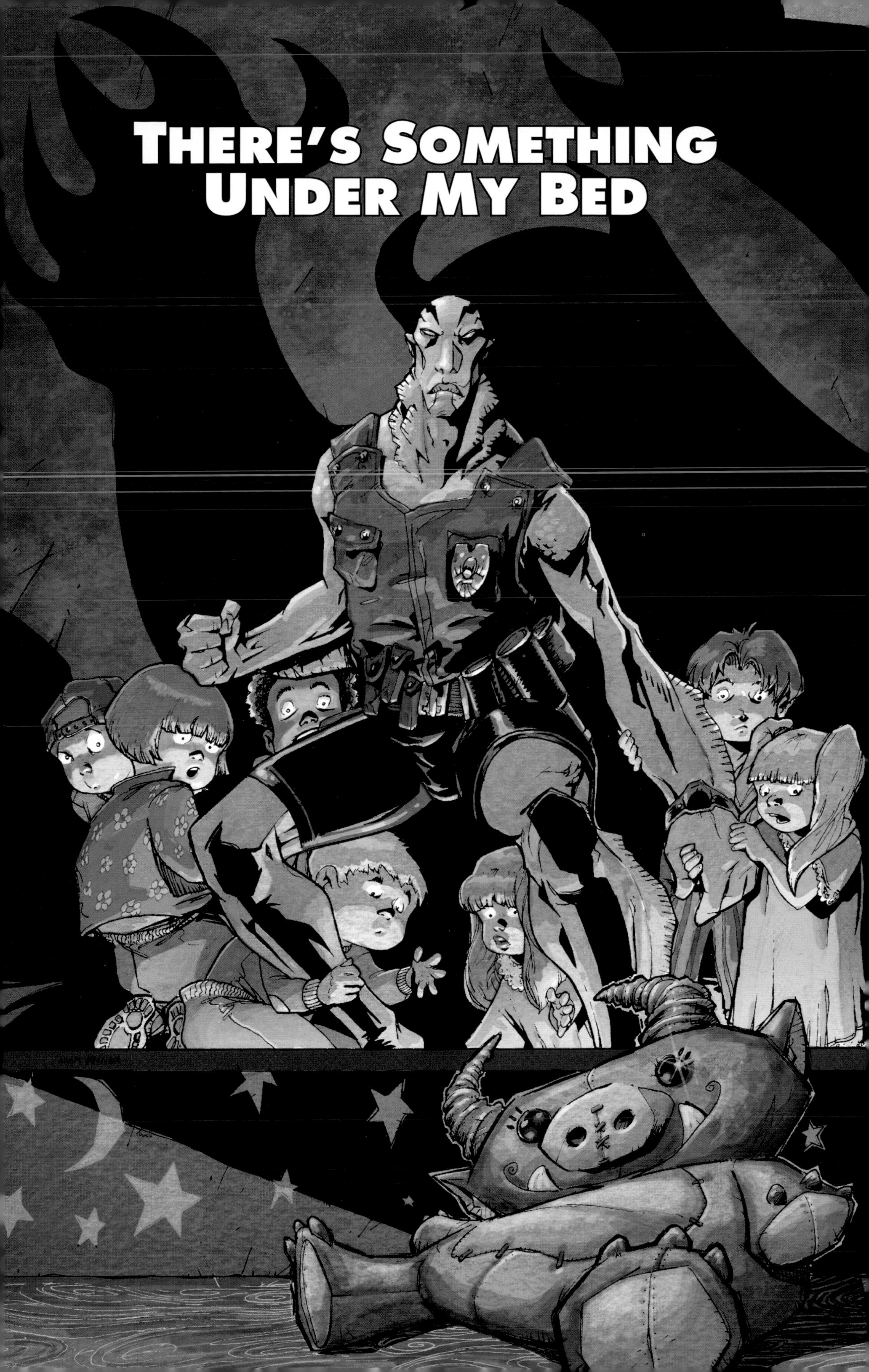

There's Something Under My Bed

Story by
Joe Harris

Pencils by
Adam Pollina

Inks by
Guillermo Zubiaga

Colors by
Lee Loughridge

Letters by
Pat Brosseau

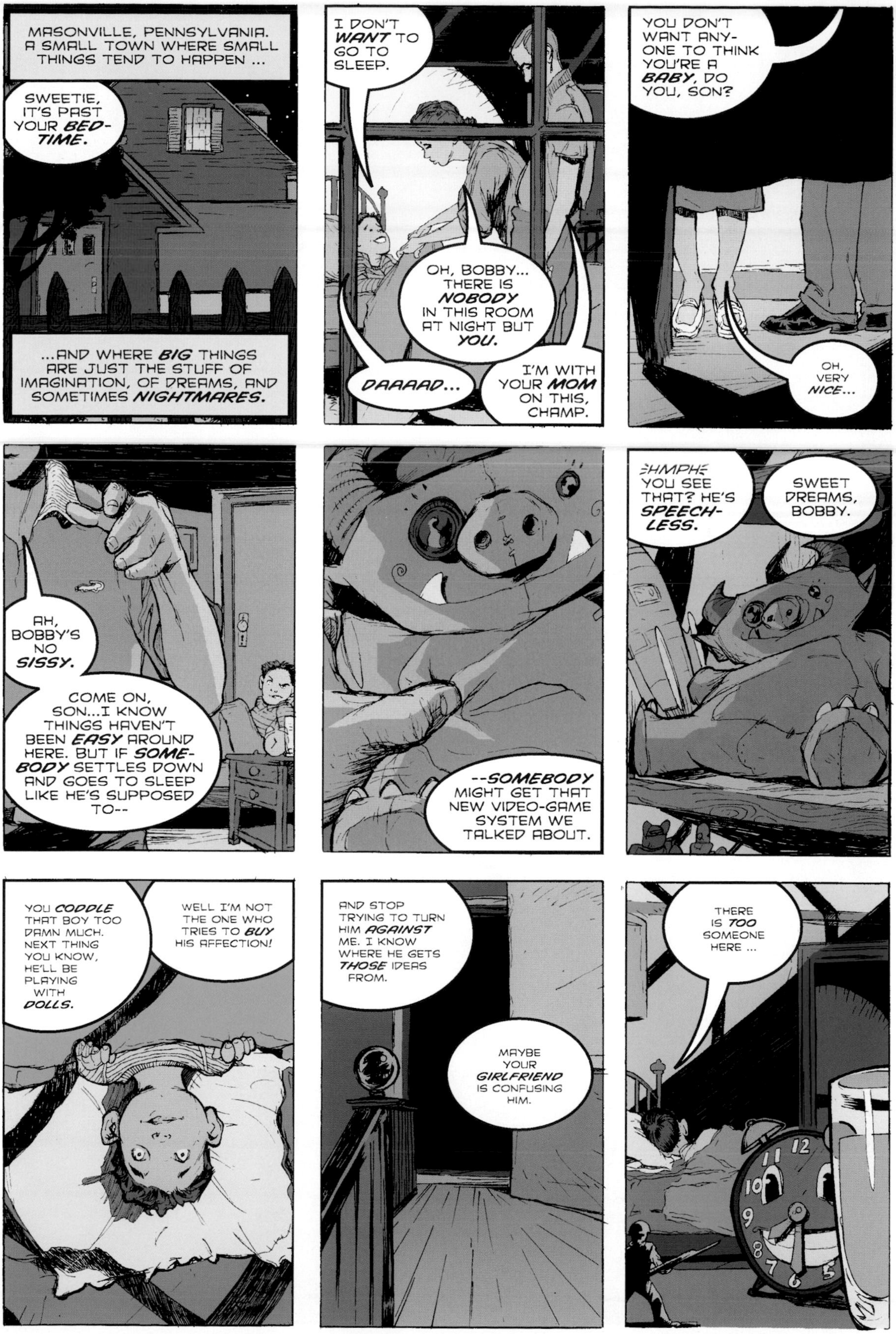
MASONVILLE, PENNSYLVANIA. A SMALL TOWN WHERE SMALL THINGS TEND TO HAPPEN ...
SWEETIE, IT'S PAST YOUR BED-TIME.
...AND WHERE BIG THINGS ARE JUST THE STUFF OF IMAGINATION, OF DREAMS, AND SOMETIMES NIGHTMARES.
I DON'T WANT TO GO TO SLEEP.
OH, BOBBY... THERE IS NOBODY IN THIS ROOM AT NIGHT BUT YOU.
DAAAAD...
I'M WITH YOUR MOM ON THIS, CHAMP.
YOU DON'T WANT ANY-ONE TO THINK YOU'RE A BABY, DO YOU, SON?
OH, VERY NICE...
AH, BOBBY'S NO SISSY.
COME ON, SON...I KNOW THINGS HAVEN'T BEEN EASY AROUND HERE. BUT IF SOME-BODY SETTLES DOWN AND GOES TO SLEEP LIKE HE'S SUPPOSED TO--
--SOMEBODY MIGHT GET THAT NEW VIDEO-GAME SYSTEM WE TALKED ABOUT.
HMPH YOU SEE THAT? HE'S SPEECH-LESS.
SWEET DREAMS, BOBBY.
YOU CODDLE THAT BOY TOO DAMN MUCH. NEXT THING YOU KNOW, HE'LL BE PLAYING WITH DOLLS.
WELL I'M NOT THE ONE WHO TRIES TO BUY HIS AFFECTION!
AND STOP TRYING TO TURN HIM AGAINST ME. I KNOW WHERE HE GETS THOSE IDEAS FROM.
MAYBE YOUR GIRLFRIEND IS CONFUSING HIM.
THERE IS TOO SOMEONE HERE ...

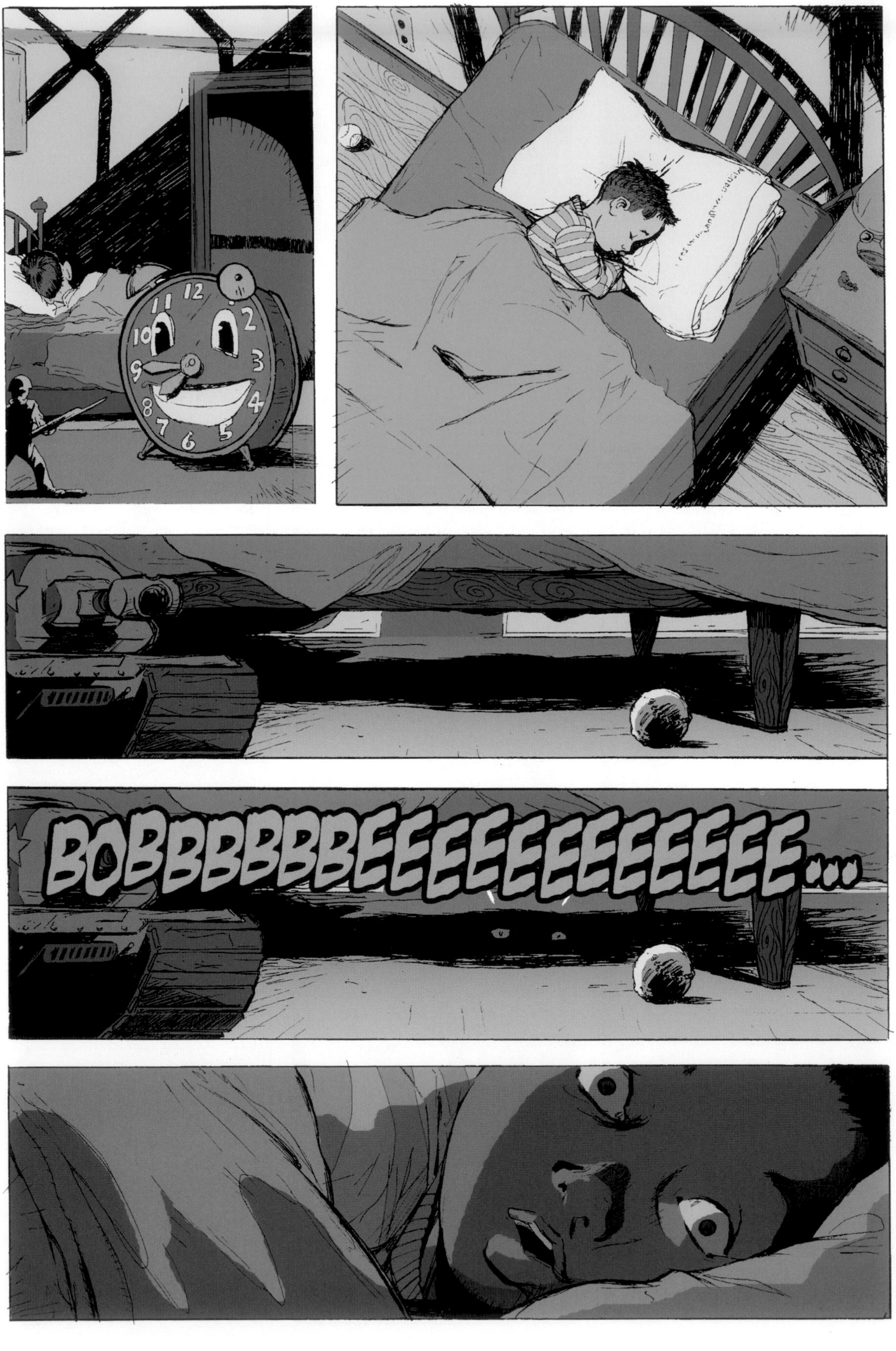

BOBBBBBBEEEEEEEEEEEE...

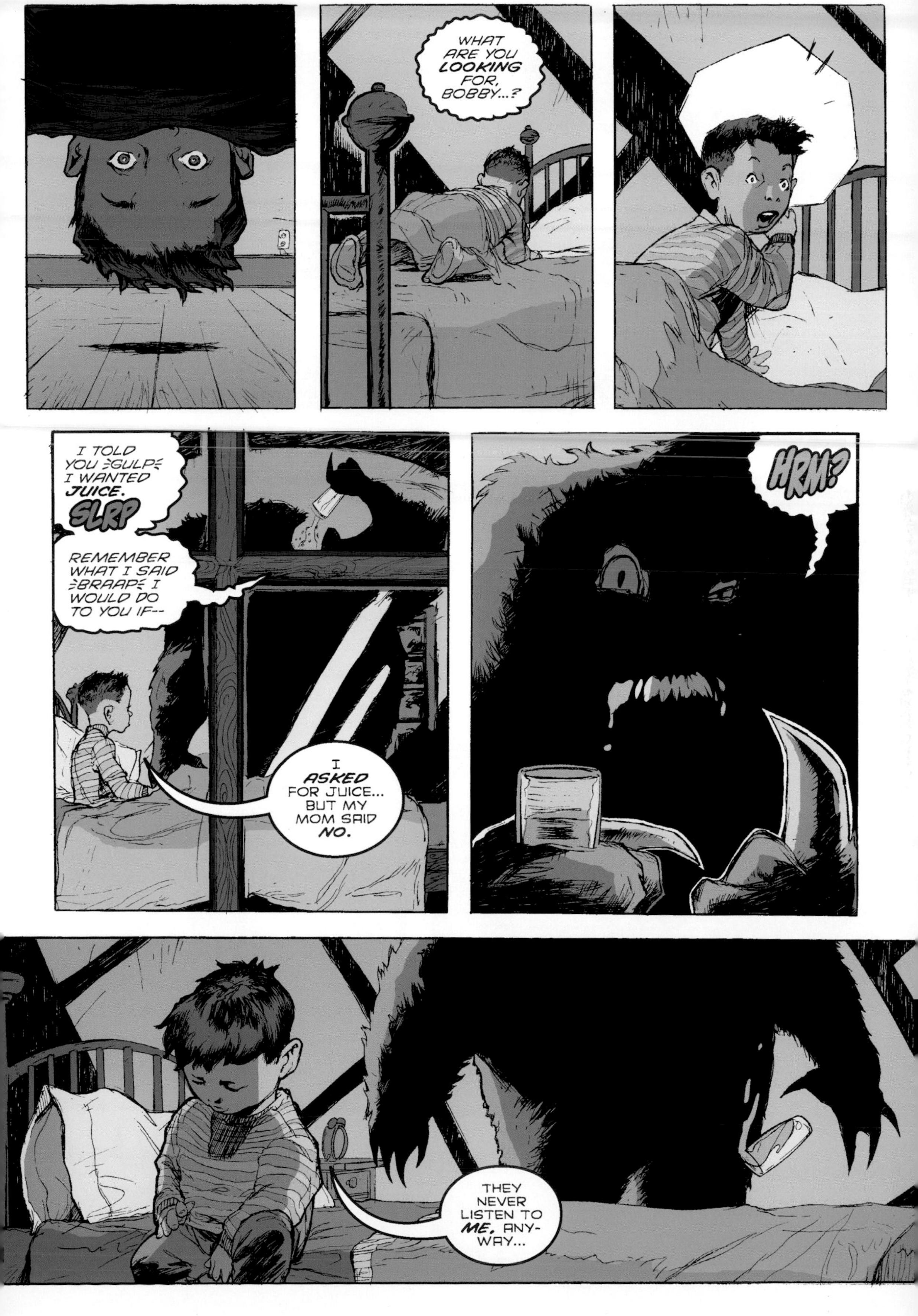
WHAT ARE YOU LOOKING FOR, BOBBY...?
I TOLD YOU ≥GULP≤ I WANTED JUICE.
SLRP
REMEMBER WHAT I SAID ≥BRAAP≤ I WOULD DO TO YOU IF--
I ASKED FOR JUICE... BUT MY MOM SAID NO.
HRM?
THEY NEVER LISTEN TO ME, ANYWAY...

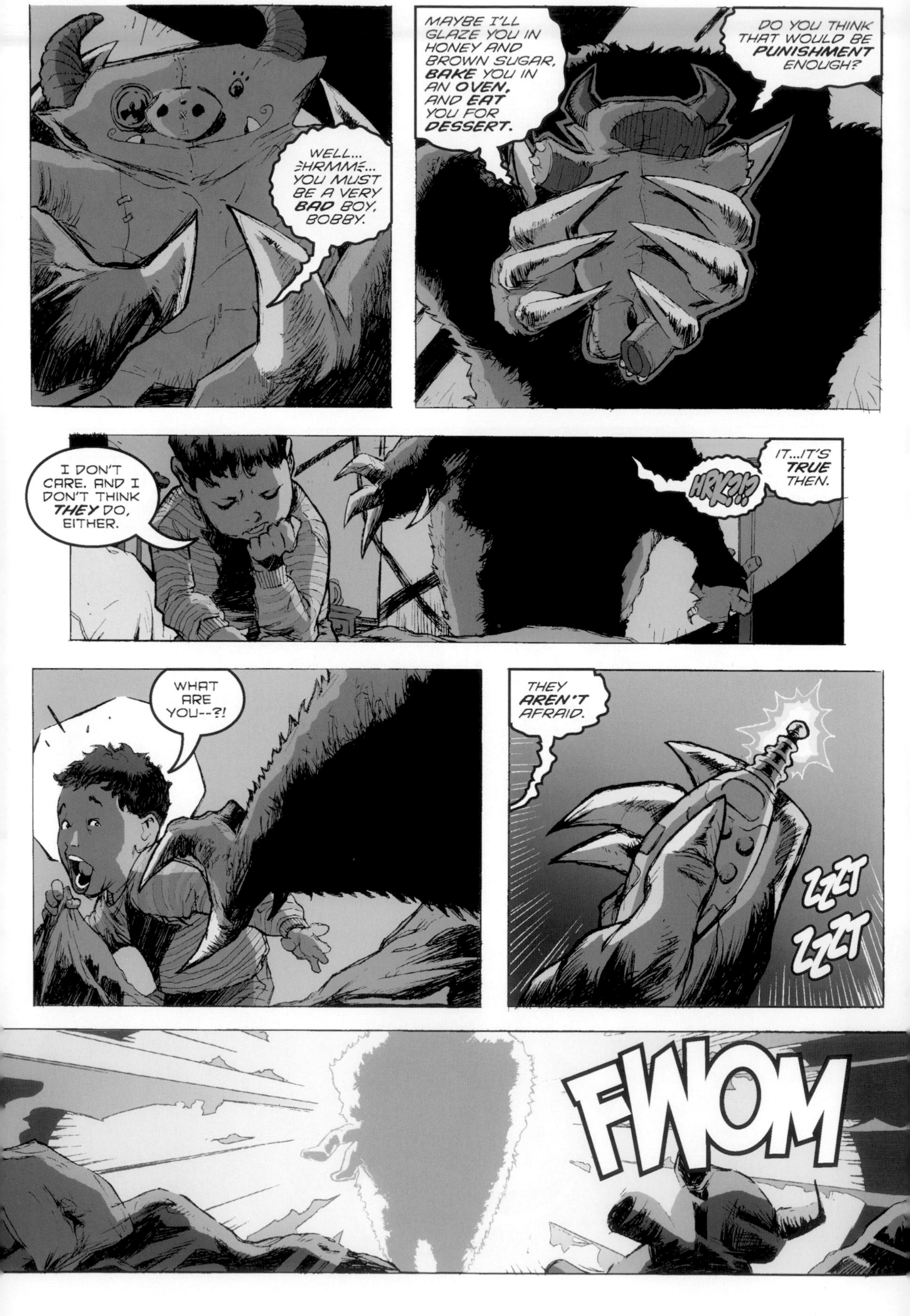
WELL... =HRMM=... YOU MUST BE A VERY BAD BOY, BOBBY.
MAYBE I'LL GLAZE YOU IN HONEY AND BROWN SUGAR, BAKE YOU IN AN OVEN, AND EAT YOU FOR DESSERT.
DO YOU THINK THAT WOULD BE PUNISHMENT ENOUGH?
I DON'T CARE. AND I DON'T THINK THEY DO, EITHER.
HRK?!?
IT...IT'S TRUE THEN.
WHAT ARE YOU--?!
THEY AREN'T AFRAID.
ZZZT
ZZZT
FWOM

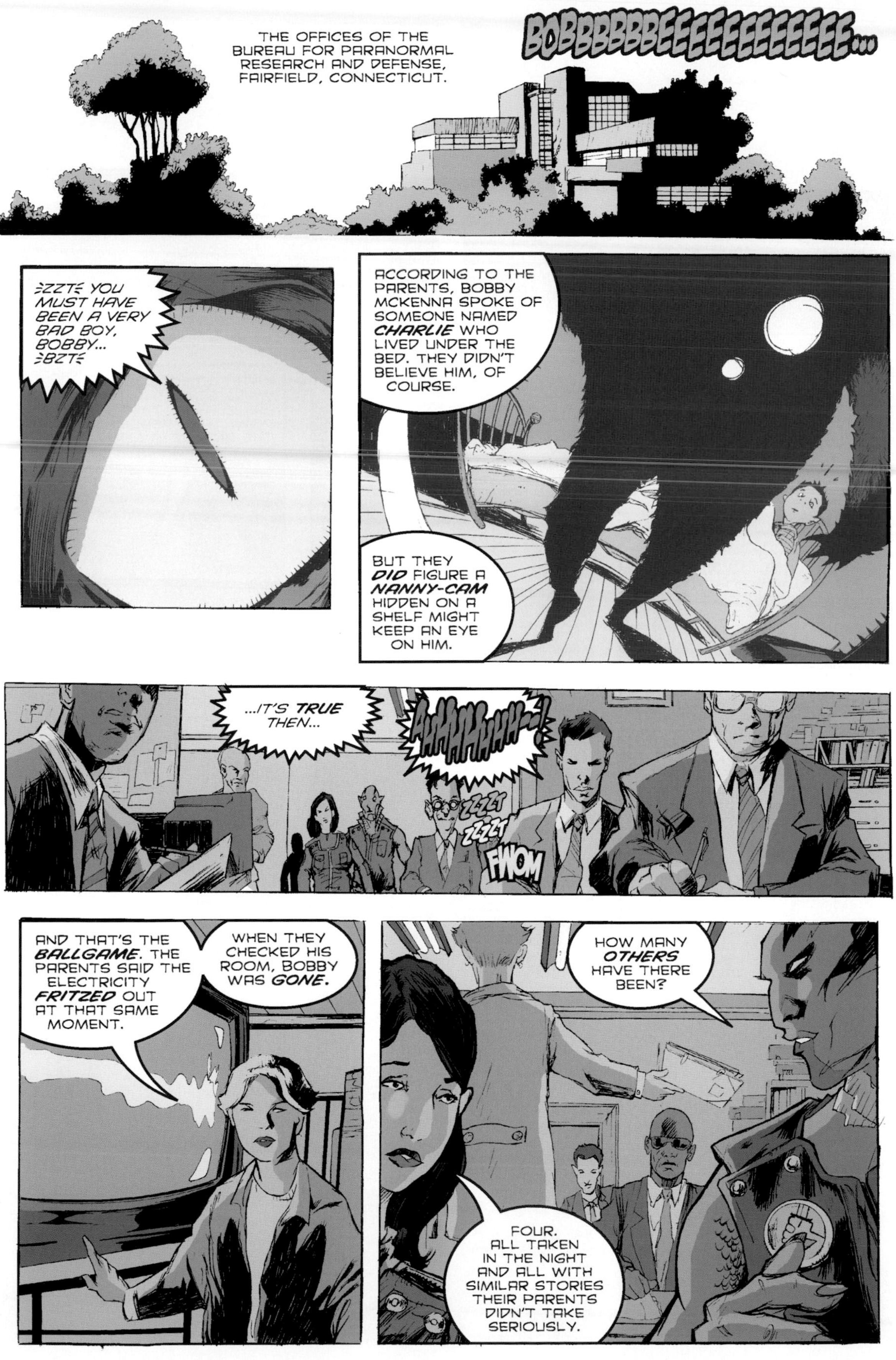
BOBBBBBBEEEEEEEEEEEE...
THE OFFICES OF THE BUREAU FOR PARANORMAL RESEARCH AND DEFENSE, FAIRFIELD, CONNECTICUT.
ZZZT YOU MUST HAVE BEEN A VERY BAD BOY, BOBBY... BZT
ACCORDING TO THE PARENTS, BOBBY McKENNA SPOKE OF SOMEONE NAMED CHARLIE WHO LIVED UNDER THE BED. THEY DIDN'T BELIEVE HIM, OF COURSE.
BUT THEY DID FIGURE A NANNY-CAM HIDDEN ON A SHELF MIGHT KEEP AN EYE ON HIM.
...IT'S TRUE THEN...
AAAAAAAHHH--!
ZZZZT
ZZZZT
FWOM
AND THAT'S THE BALLGAME. THE PARENTS SAID THE ELECTRICITY FRITZED OUT AT THAT SAME MOMENT.
WHEN THEY CHECKED HIS ROOM, BOBBY WAS GONE.
HOW MANY OTHERS HAVE THERE BEEN?
FOUR. ALL TAKEN IN THE NIGHT AND ALL WITH SIMILAR STORIES THEIR PARENTS DIDN'T TAKE SERIOUSLY.

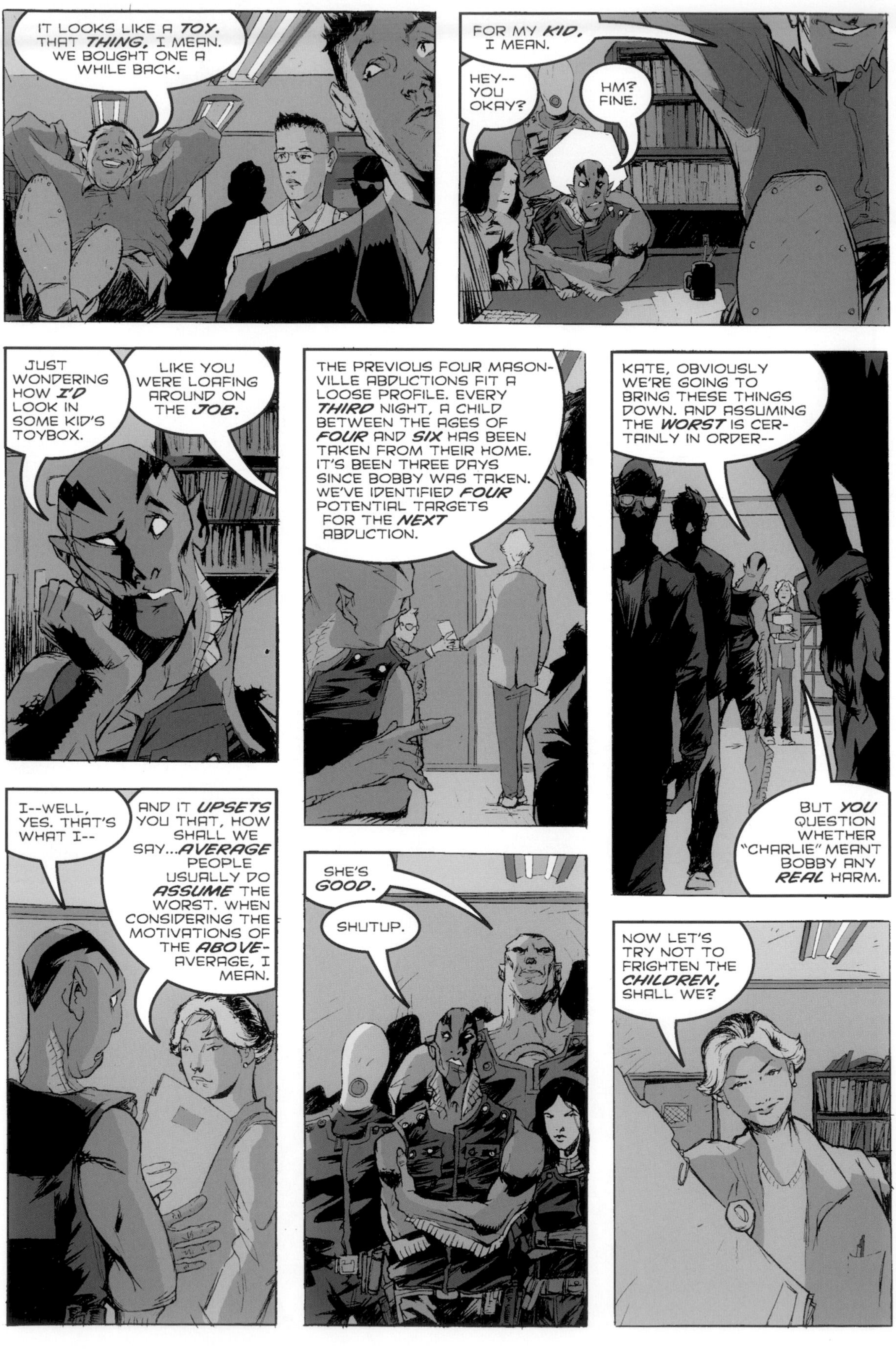
IT LOOKS LIKE A TOY. THAT THING, I MEAN. WE BOUGHT ONE A WHILE BACK.
FOR MY KID, I MEAN.
HEY-- YOU OKAY?
HM? FINE.
JUST WONDERING HOW I'D LOOK IN SOME KID'S TOYBOX.
LIKE YOU WERE LOAFING AROUND ON THE JOB.
THE PREVIOUS FOUR MASONVILLE ABDUCTIONS FIT A LOOSE PROFILE. EVERY THIRD NIGHT, A CHILD BETWEEN THE AGES OF FOUR AND SIX HAS BEEN TAKEN FROM THEIR HOME. IT'S BEEN THREE DAYS SINCE BOBBY WAS TAKEN. WE'VE IDENTIFIED FOUR POTENTIAL TARGETS FOR THE NEXT ABDUCTION.
KATE, OBVIOUSLY WE'RE GOING TO BRING THESE THINGS DOWN. AND ASSUMING THE WORST IS CERTAINLY IN ORDER--
BUT YOU QUESTION WHETHER "CHARLIE" MEANT BOBBY ANY REAL HARM.
I--WELL, YES. THAT'S WHAT I--
AND IT UPSETS YOU THAT, HOW SHALL WE SAY...AVERAGE PEOPLE USUALLY DO ASSUME THE WORST. WHEN CONSIDERING THE MOTIVATIONS OF THE ABOVE-AVERAGE, I MEAN.
SHE'S GOOD.
SHUTUP.
NOW LET'S TRY NOT TO FRIGHTEN THE CHILDREN, SHALL WE?

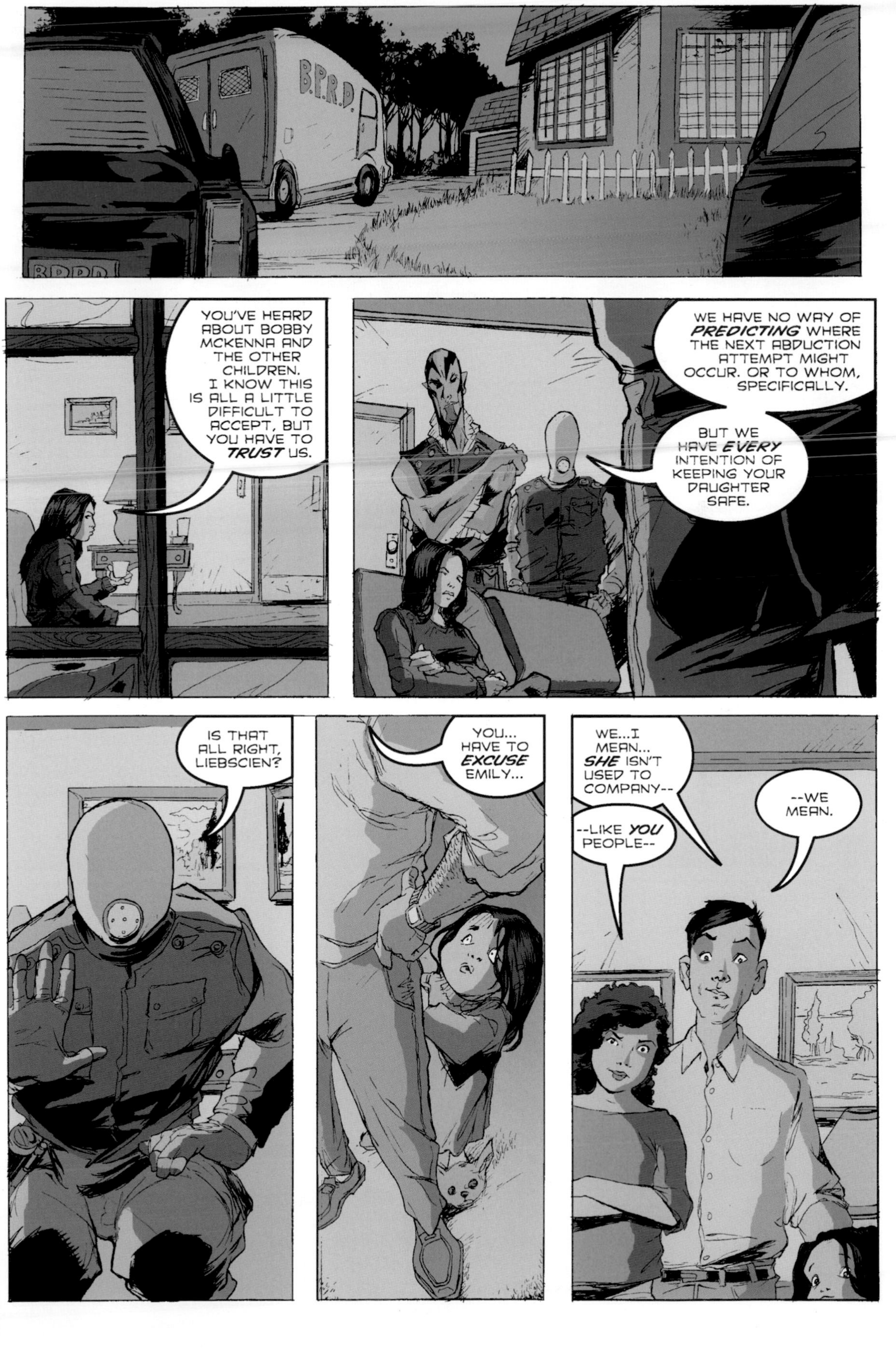
B.P.R.D.
BPRD
YOU'VE HEARD ABOUT BOBBY MCKENNA AND THE OTHER CHILDREN. I KNOW THIS IS ALL A LITTLE DIFFICULT TO ACCEPT, BUT YOU HAVE TO TRUST US.
WE HAVE NO WAY OF PREDICTING WHERE THE NEXT ABDUCTION ATTEMPT MIGHT OCCUR. OR TO WHOM, SPECIFICALLY.
BUT WE HAVE EVERY INTENTION OF KEEPING YOUR DAUGHTER SAFE.
IS THAT ALL RIGHT, LIEBSCIEN?
YOU... HAVE TO EXCUSE EMILY...
WE...I MEAN... SHE ISN'T USED TO COMPANY--
--LIKE YOU PEOPLE--
--WE MEAN.

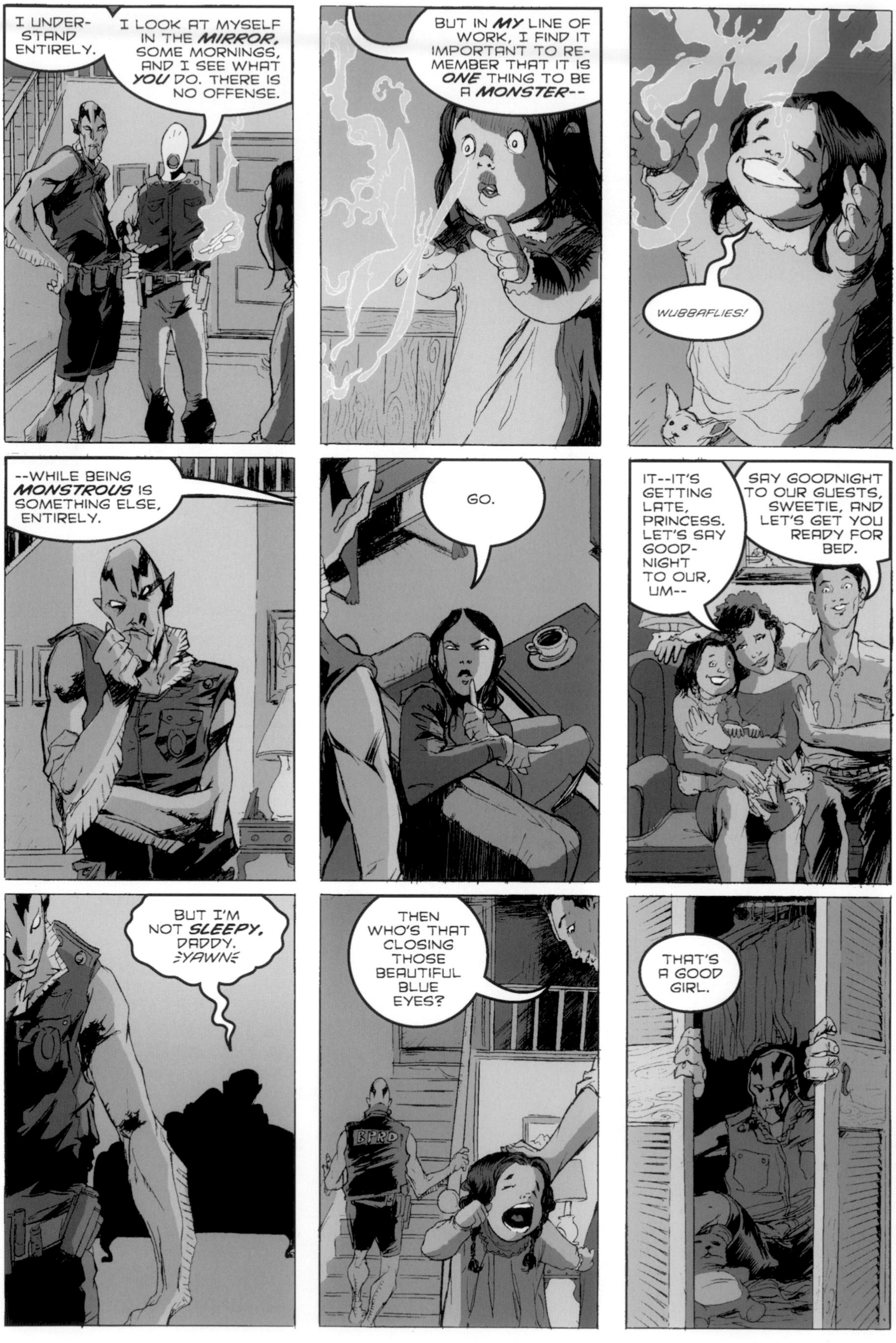
I UNDER-STAND ENTIRELY.
I LOOK AT MYSELF IN THE MIRROR, SOME MORNINGS, AND I SEE WHAT YOU DO. THERE IS NO OFFENSE.
BUT IN MY LINE OF WORK, I FIND IT IMPORTANT TO RE-MEMBER THAT IT IS ONE THING TO BE A MONSTER--
WUBBAFLIES!
--WHILE BEING MONSTROUS IS SOMETHING ELSE, ENTIRELY.
GO.
IT--IT'S GETTING LATE, PRINCESS. LET'S SAY GOOD-NIGHT TO OUR, UM--
SAY GOODNIGHT TO OUR GUESTS, SWEETIE, AND LET'S GET YOU READY FOR BED.
BUT I'M NOT SLEEPY, DADDY. YAWN
THEN WHO'S THAT CLOSING THOSE BEAUTIFUL BLUE EYES?
THAT'S A GOOD GIRL.

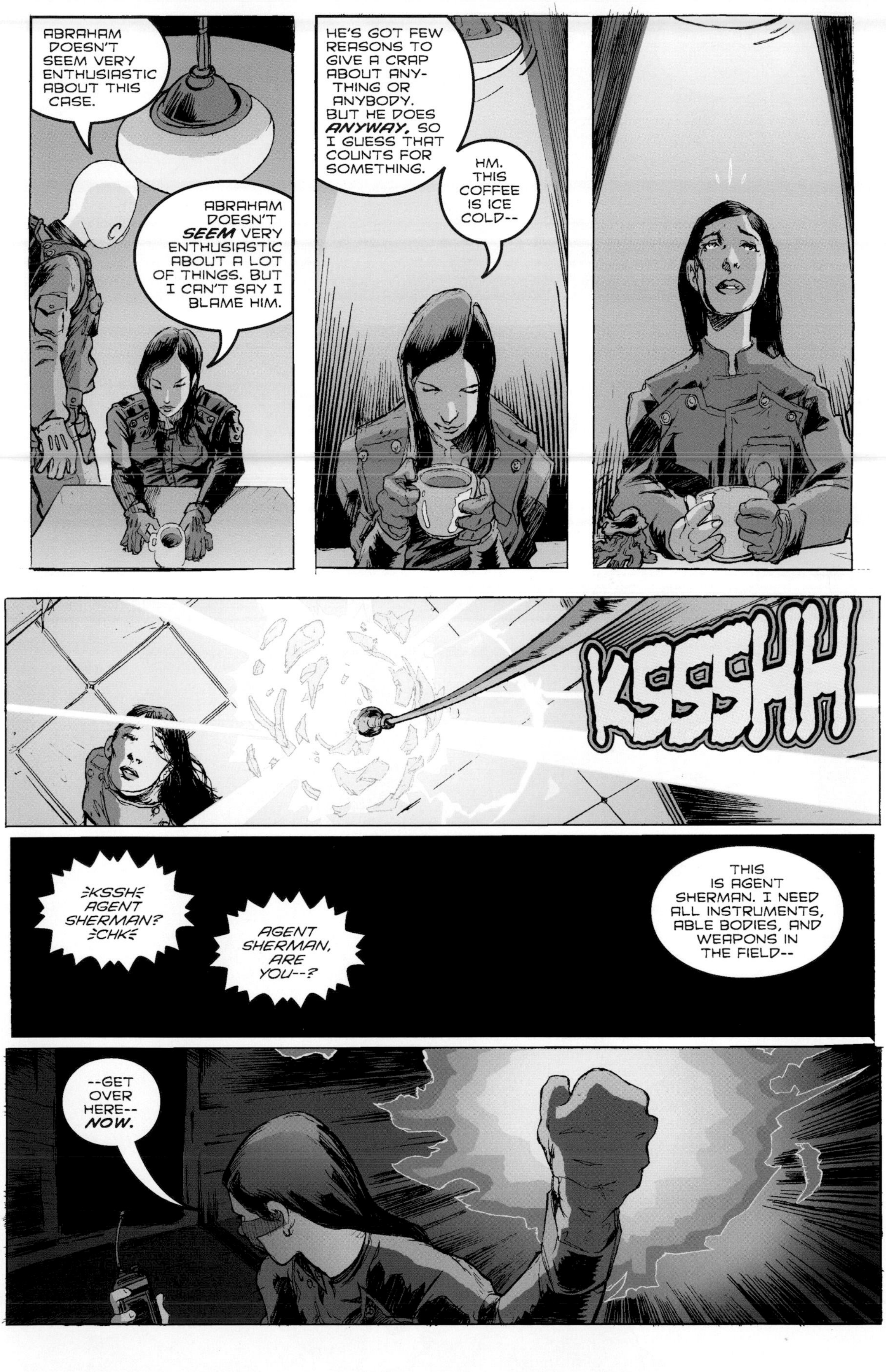
ABRAHAM DOESN'T SEEM VERY ENTHUSIASTIC ABOUT THIS CASE.
ABRAHAM DOESN'T **SEEM** VERY ENTHUSIASTIC ABOUT A LOT OF THINGS. BUT I CAN'T SAY I BLAME HIM.
HE'S GOT FEW REASONS TO GIVE A CRAP ABOUT ANY-THING OR ANYBODY. BUT HE DOES ***ANYWAY,*** SO I GUESS THAT COUNTS FOR SOMETHING.
HM. THIS COFFEE IS ICE COLD--
KSSSHH
KSSH AGENT SHERMAN? CHK
AGENT SHERMAN, ARE YOU--?
THIS IS AGENT SHERMAN. I NEED ALL INSTRUMENTS, ABLE BODIES, AND WEAPONS IN THE FIELD--
--GET OVER HERE-- ***NOW.***

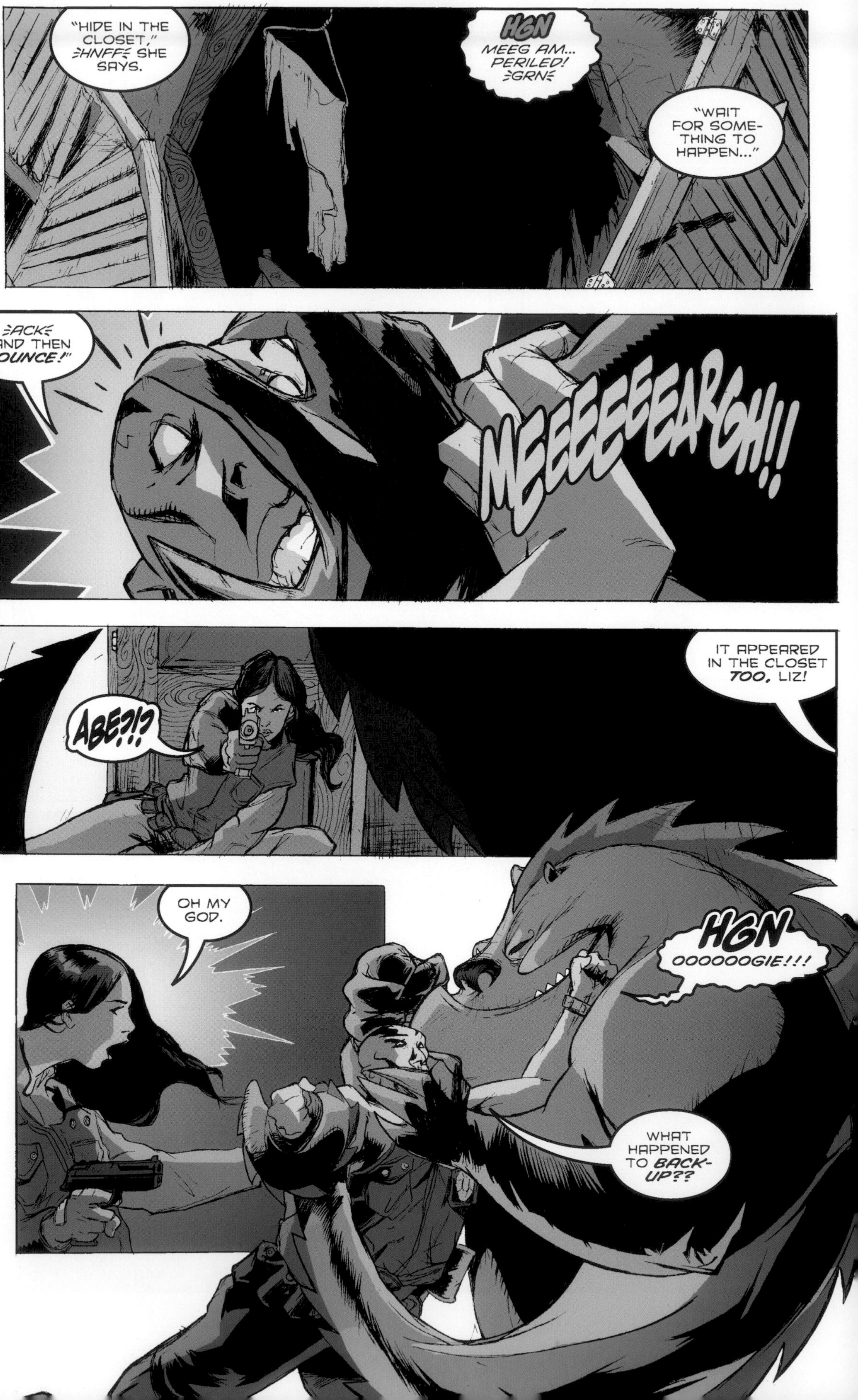
"HIDE IN THE CLOSET," HNFF SHE SAYS.
HGN MEEG AM... PERILED! GRN
"WAIT FOR SOME-THING TO HAPPEN..."
ACK "AND THEN POUNCE!"
MEEEEEEARGH!!
ABE?!?
IT APPEARED IN THE CLOSET TOO, LIZ!
OH MY GOD.
HGN OOOOOOGIE!!!
WHAT HAPPENED TO BACK-UP??

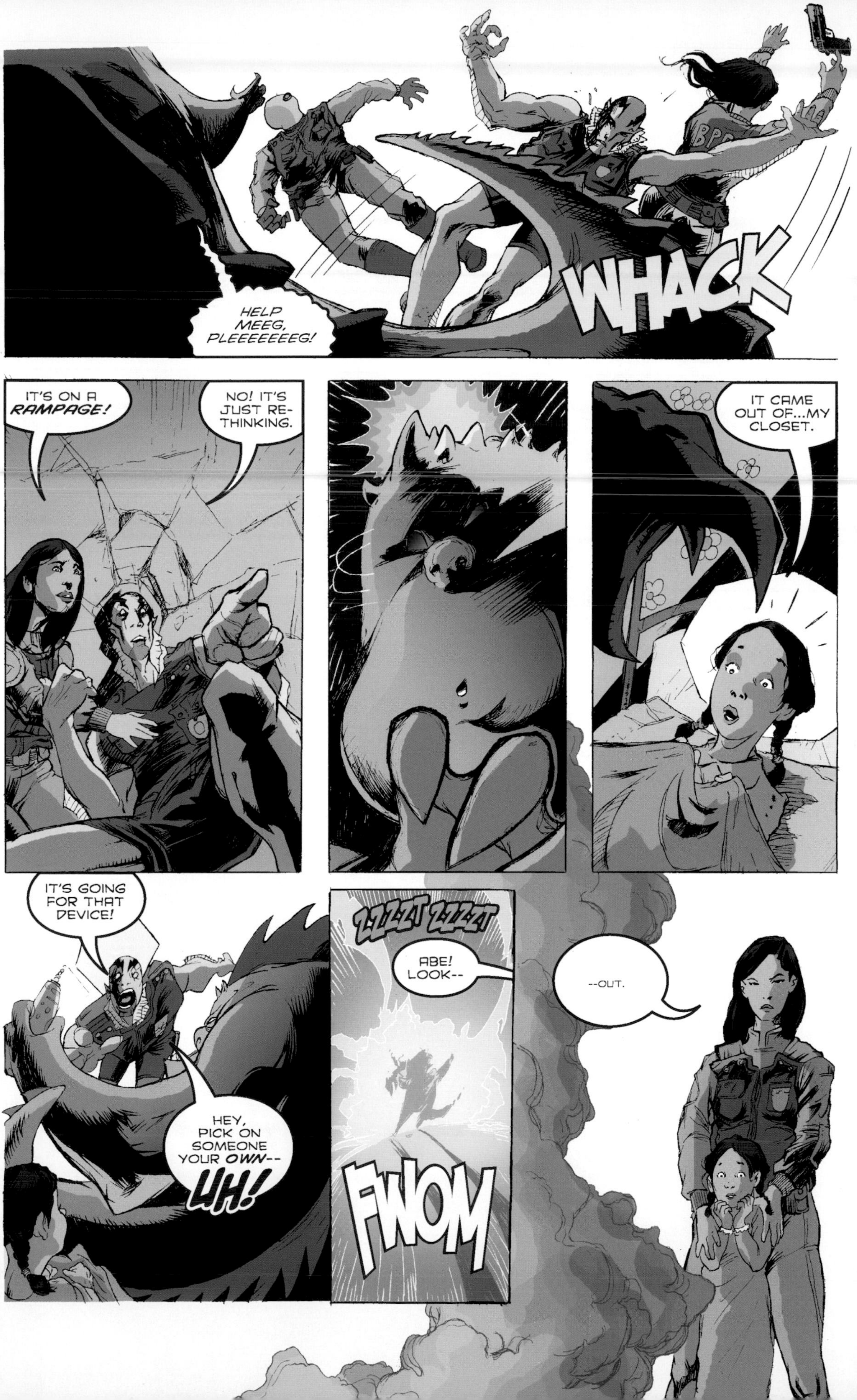

HELP MEEG, PLEEEEEEEG!
WHACK
IT'S ON A RAMPAGE!
NO! IT'S JUST RE-THINKING.
IT CAME OUT OF...MY CLOSET.
IT'S GOING FOR THAT DEVICE!
HEY, PICK ON SOMEONE YOUR OWN--
UH!
ZZZZT ZZZZT
ABE! LOOK--
FWOM
--OUT.

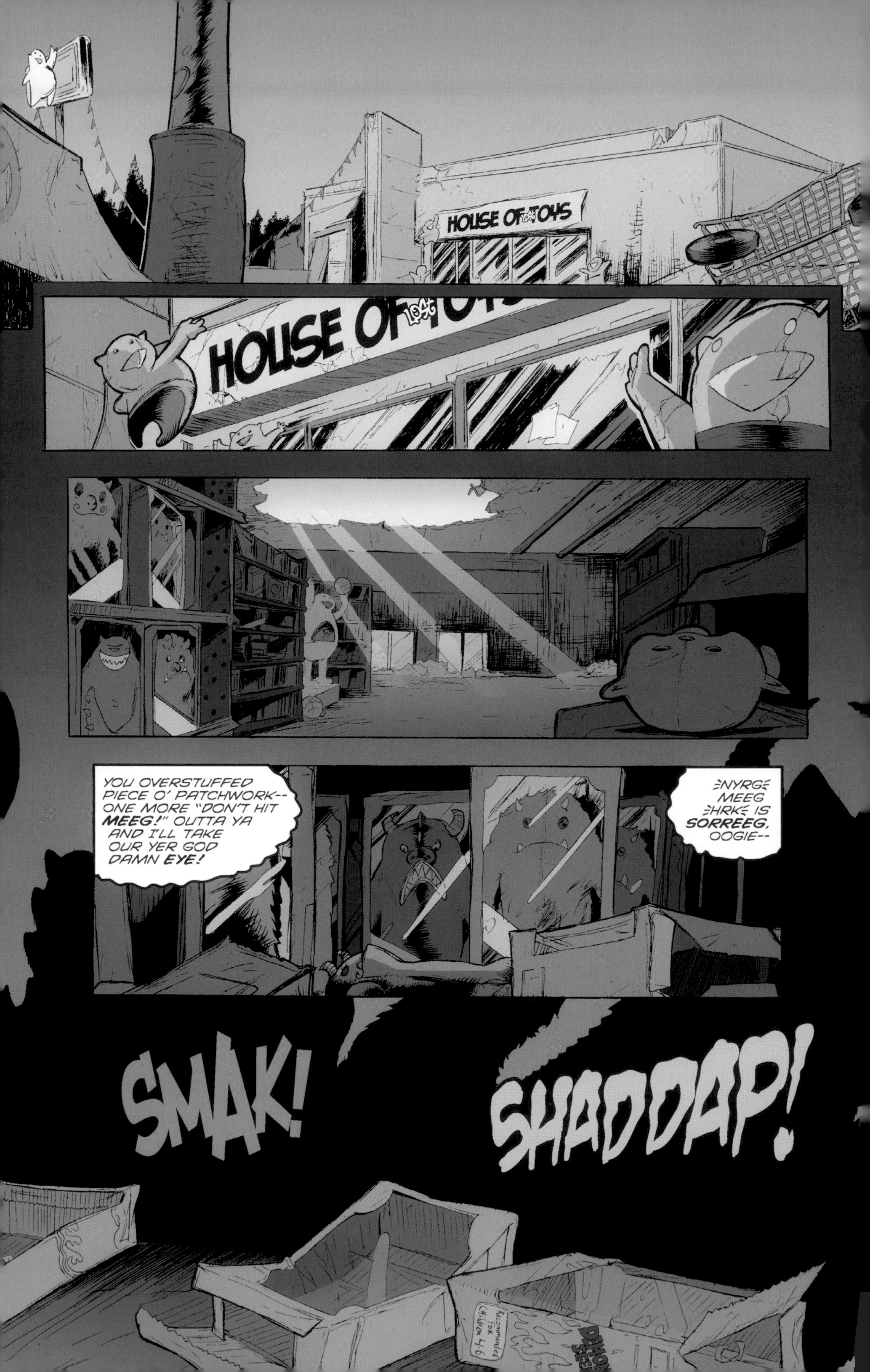

HOUSE OF LOST TOYS
HOUSE OF LOST TOYS
YOU OVERSTUFFED PIECE O' PATCHWORK-- ONE MORE "DON'T HIT MEEG!" OUTTA YA AND I'LL TAKE OUR YER GOD DAMN EYE!
NYRG MEEG HRK IS SORREEG, OOGIE--
SMAK!
SHADDAP!

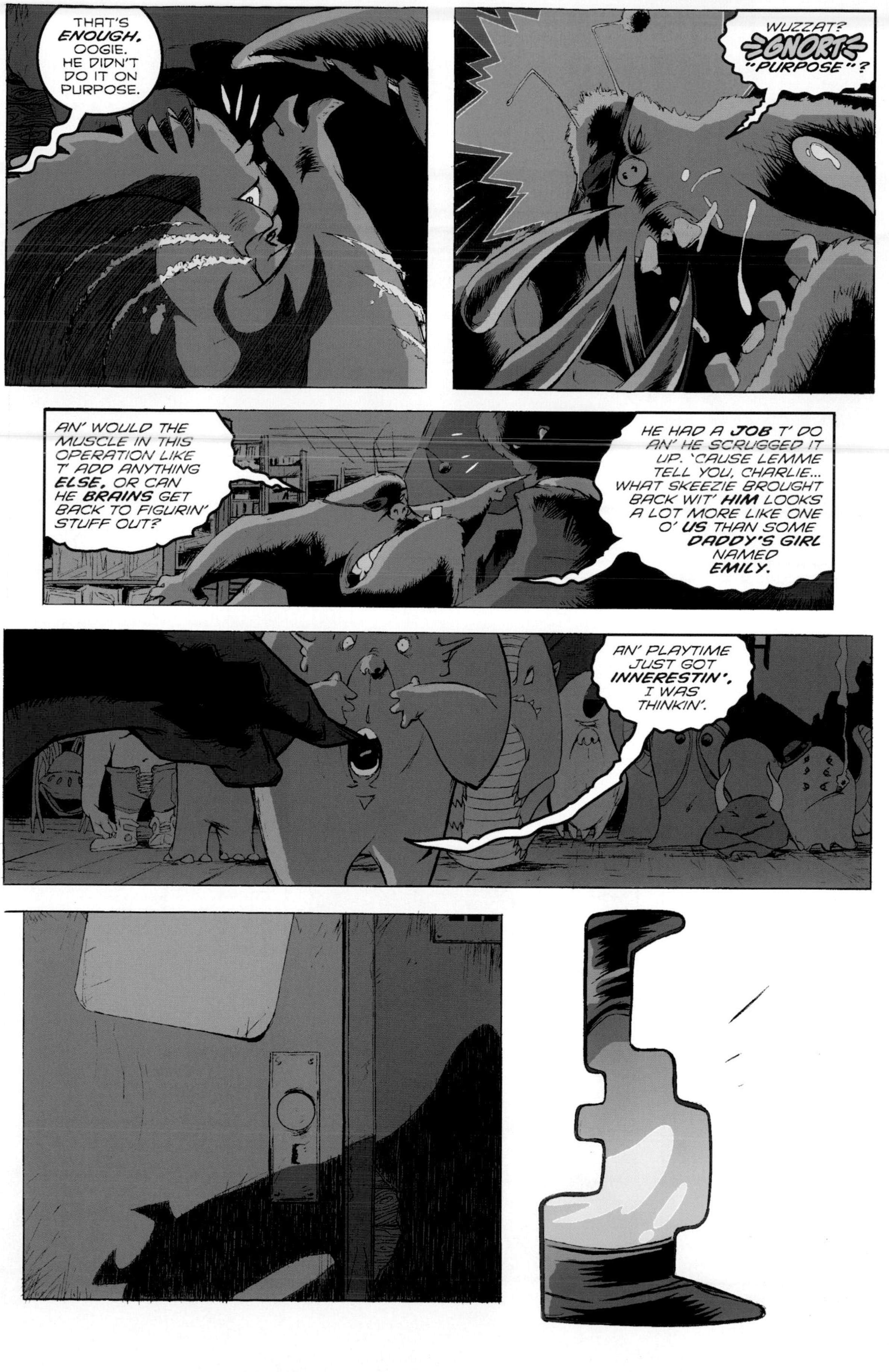
THAT'S ENOUGH, OOGIE. HE DIDN'T DO IT ON PURPOSE.
WUZZAT? GNORT "PURPOSE"?
AN' WOULD THE MUSCLE IN THIS OPERATION LIKE T' ADD ANYTHING ELSE, OR CAN HE BRAINS GET BACK TO FIGURIN' STUFF OUT?
HE HAD A JOB T' DO AN' HE SCRUGGED IT UP. 'CAUSE LEMME TELL YOU, CHARLIE... WHAT SKEEZIE BROUGHT BACK WIT' HIM LOOKS A LOT MORE LIKE ONE O' US THAN SOME DADDY'S GIRL NAMED EMILY.
AN' PLAYTIME JUST GOT INNERESTIN', I WAS THINKIN'.

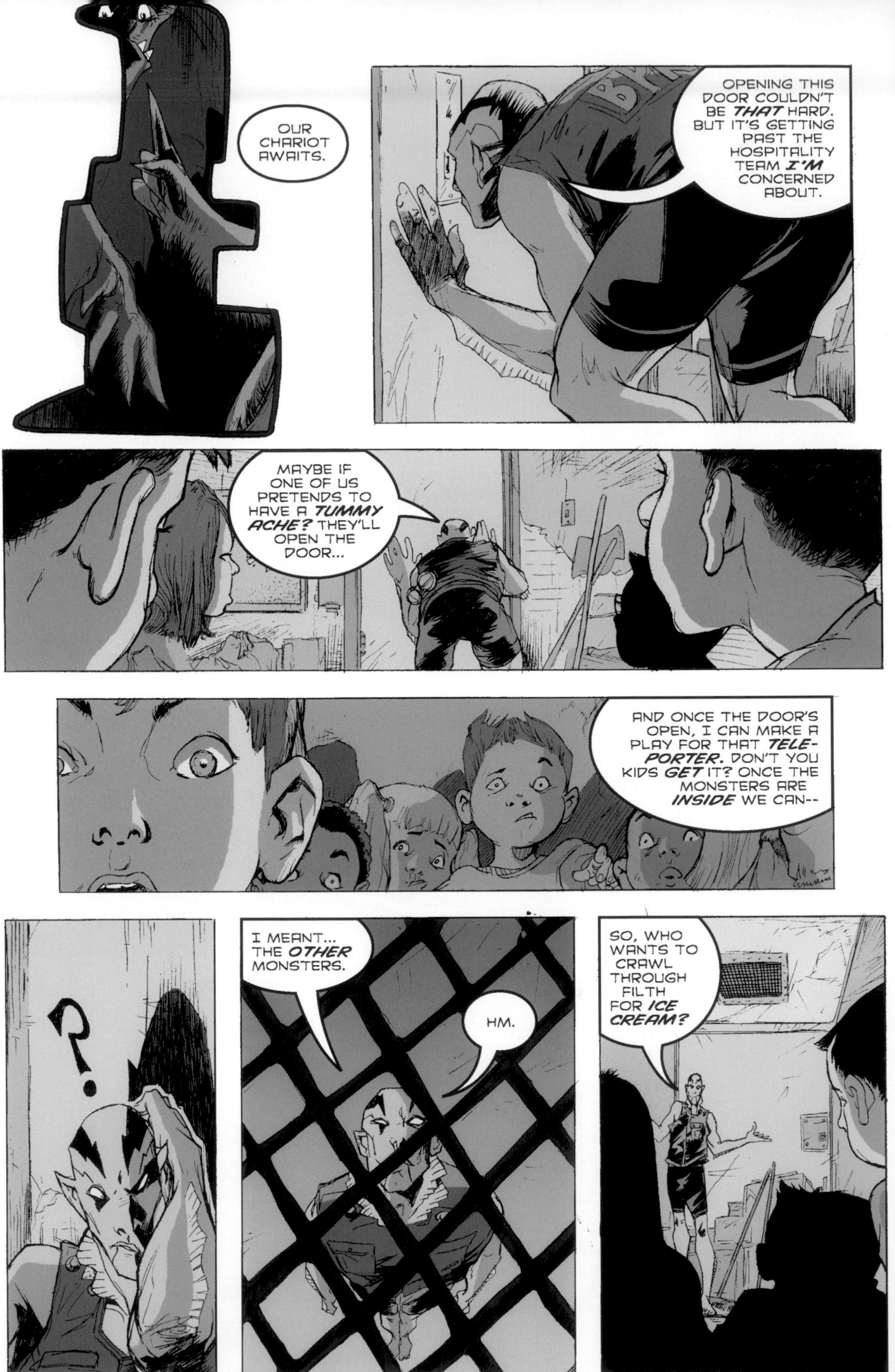
OUR CHARIOT AWAITS.
OPENING THIS DOOR COULDN'T BE THAT HARD. BUT IT'S GETTING PAST THE HOSPITALITY TEAM I'M CONCERNED ABOUT.
MAYBE IF ONE OF US PRETENDS TO HAVE A TUMMY ACHE? THEY'LL OPEN THE DOOR...
AND ONCE THE DOOR'S OPEN, I CAN MAKE A PLAY FOR THAT TELE-PORTER. DON'T YOU KIDS GET IT? ONCE THE MONSTERS ARE INSIDE WE CAN--
?
I MEANT... THE OTHER MONSTERS.
HM.
SO, WHO WANTS TO CRAWL THROUGH FILTH FOR ICE CREAM?

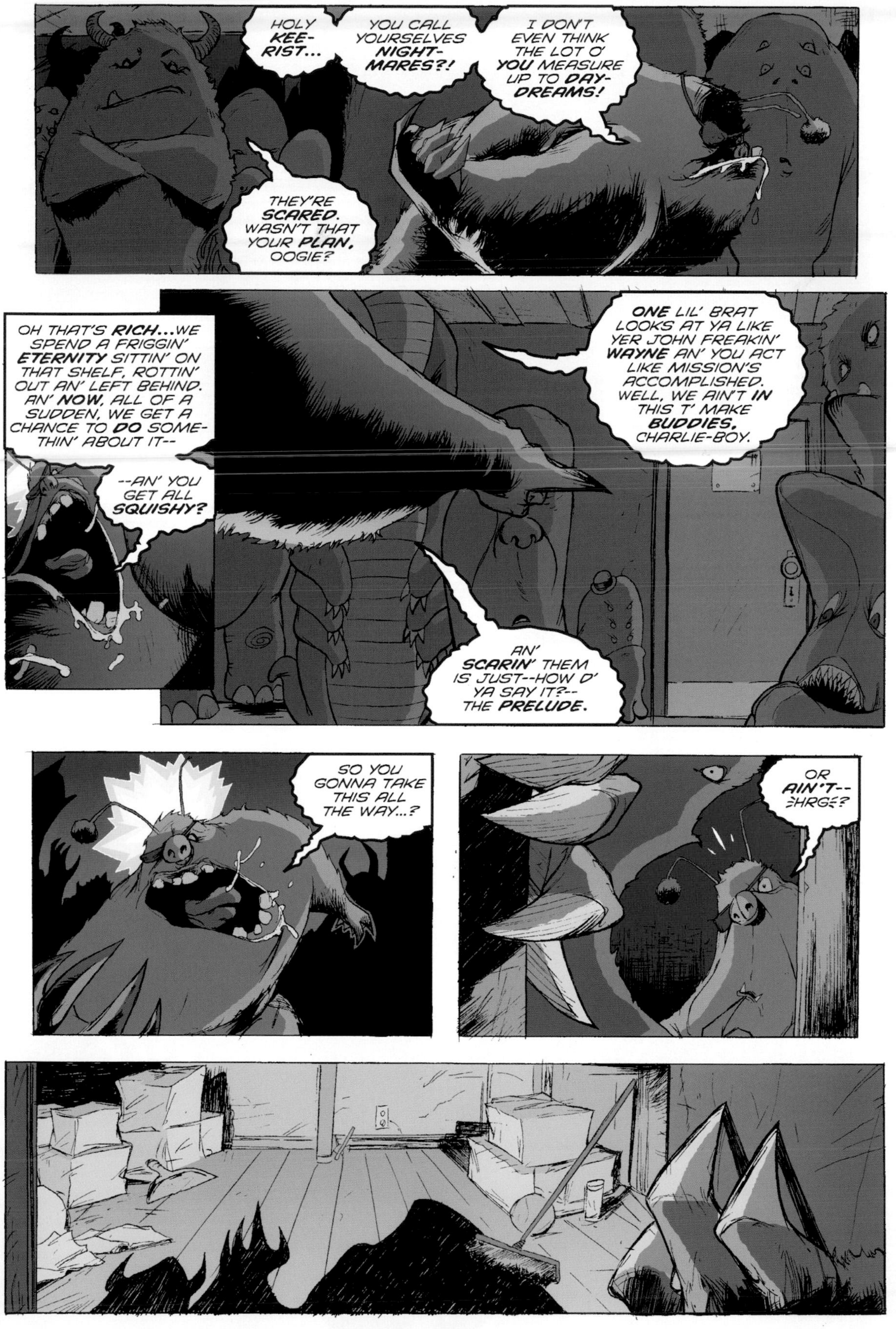
HOLY KEE-RIST...
YOU CALL YOURSELVES NIGHT-MARES?!
I DON'T EVEN THINK THE LOT O' YOU MEASURE UP TO DAY-DREAMS!
THEY'RE SCARED. WASN'T THAT YOUR PLAN, OOGIE?
OH THAT'S RICH...WE SPEND A FRIGGIN' ETERNITY SITTIN' ON THAT SHELF, ROTTIN' OUT AN' LEFT BEHIND. AN' NOW, ALL OF A SUDDEN, WE GET A CHANCE TO DO SOME-THIN' ABOUT IT--
--AN' YOU GET ALL SQUISHY?
ONE LIL' BRAT LOOKS AT YA LIKE YER JOHN FREAKIN' WAYNE AN' YOU ACT LIKE MISSION'S ACCOMPLISHED. WELL, WE AIN'T IN THIS T' MAKE BUDDIES, CHARLIE-BOY.
AN' SCARIN' THEM IS JUST--HOW D' YA SAY IT?-- THE PRELUDE.
SO YOU GONNA TAKE THIS ALL THE WAY...?
OR AIN'T--HRG?

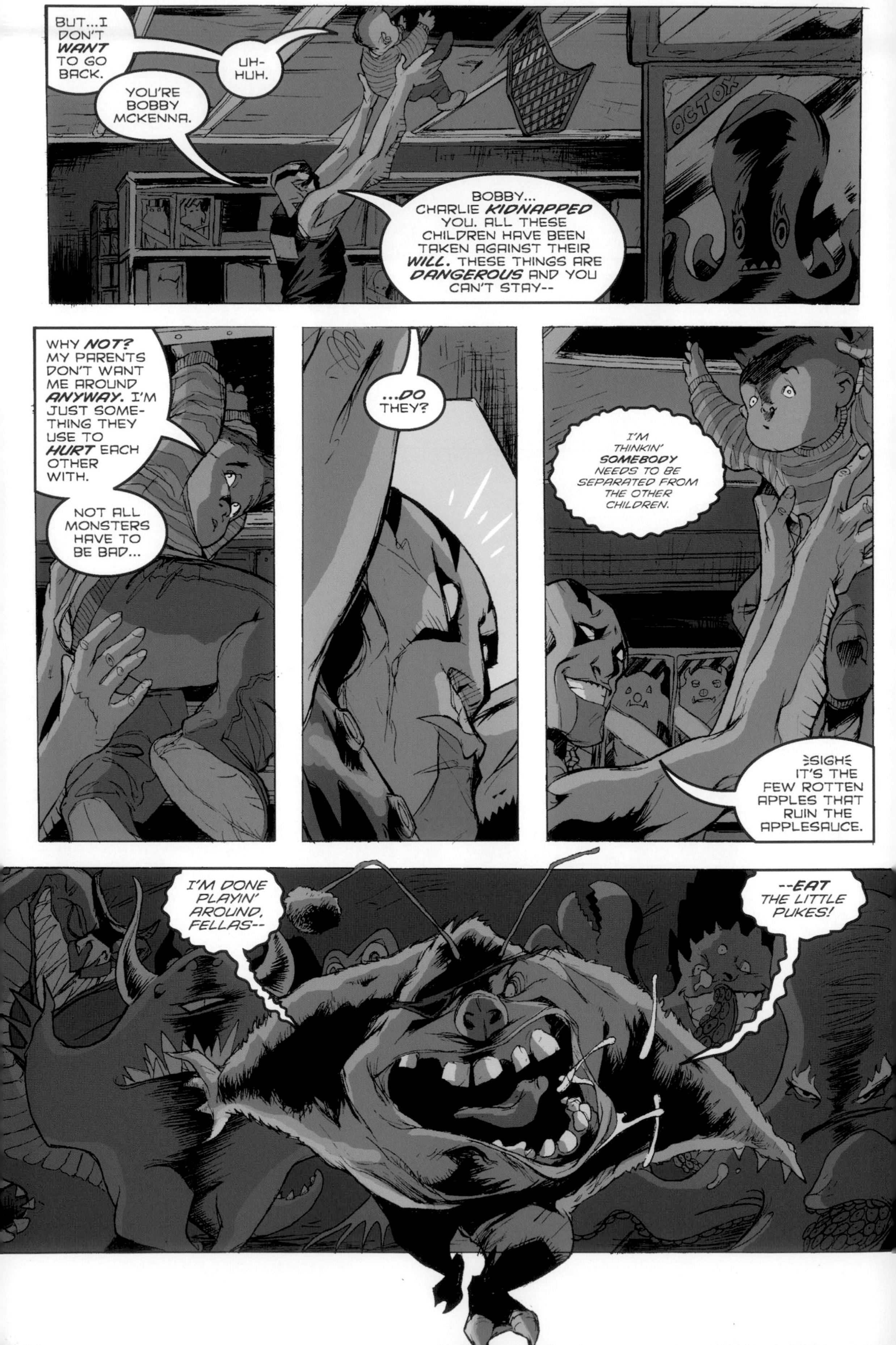
BUT...I DON'T WANT TO GO BACK.
UH-HUH.
YOU'RE BOBBY MCKENNA.
BOBBY... CHARLIE KIDNAPPED YOU. ALL THESE CHILDREN HAVE BEEN TAKEN AGAINST THEIR WILL. THESE THINGS ARE DANGEROUS AND YOU CAN'T STAY--
OCTOX
WHY NOT? MY PARENTS DON'T WANT ME AROUND ANYWAY. I'M JUST SOMETHING THEY USE TO HURT EACH OTHER WITH.
NOT ALL MONSTERS HAVE TO BE BAD...
...DO THEY?
I'M THINKIN' SOMEBODY NEEDS TO BE SEPARATED FROM THE OTHER CHILDREN.
SIGH IT'S THE FEW ROTTEN APPLES THAT RUIN THE APPLESAUCE.
I'M DONE PLAYIN' AROUND, FELLAS--
--EAT THE LITTLE PUKES!

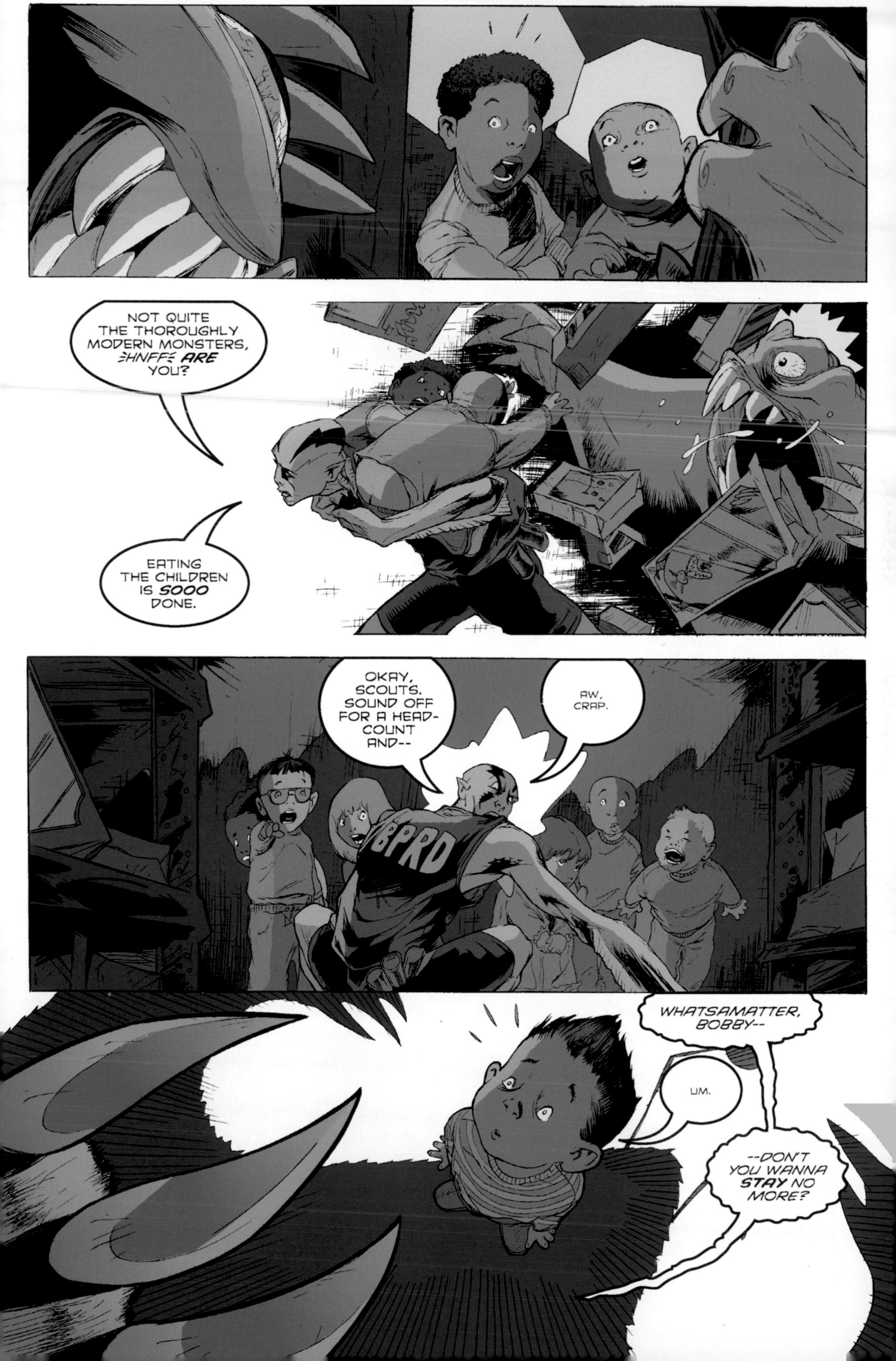
NOT QUITE THE THOROUGHLY MODERN MONSTERS, *HNFF* ARE YOU?
EATING THE CHILDREN IS SOOO DONE.
OKAY, SCOUTS. SOUND OFF FOR A HEAD-COUNT AND--
AW, CRAP.
WHATSAMATTER, BOBBY--
UM.
--DON'T YOU WANNA STAY NO MORE?

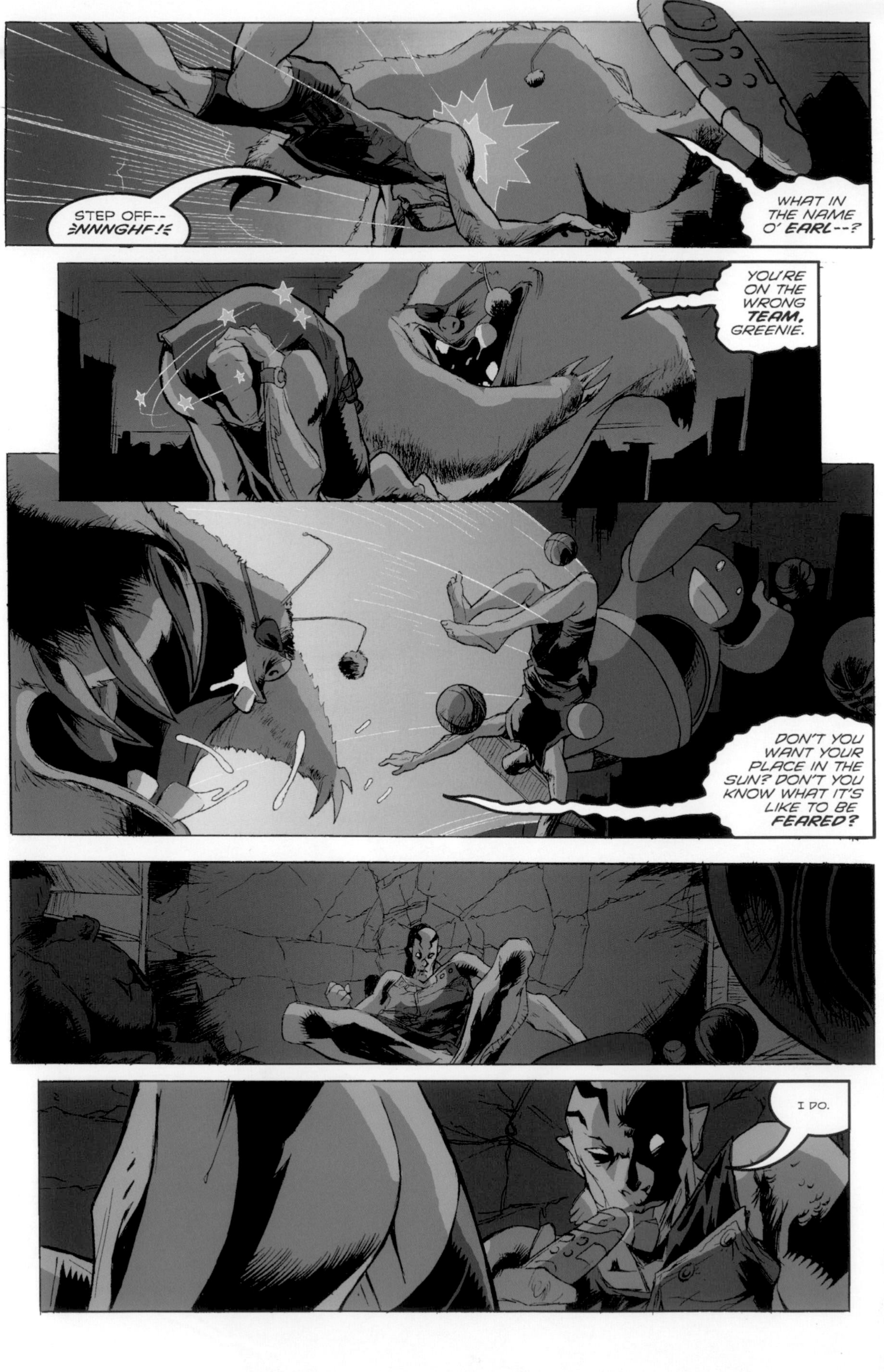
STEP OFF-- NNNGHF!
WHAT IN THE NAME O' EARL--?
YOU'RE ON THE WRONG TEAM, GREENIE.
DON'T YOU WANT YOUR PLACE IN THE SUN? DON'T YOU KNOW WHAT IT'S LIKE TO BE FEARED?
I DO.

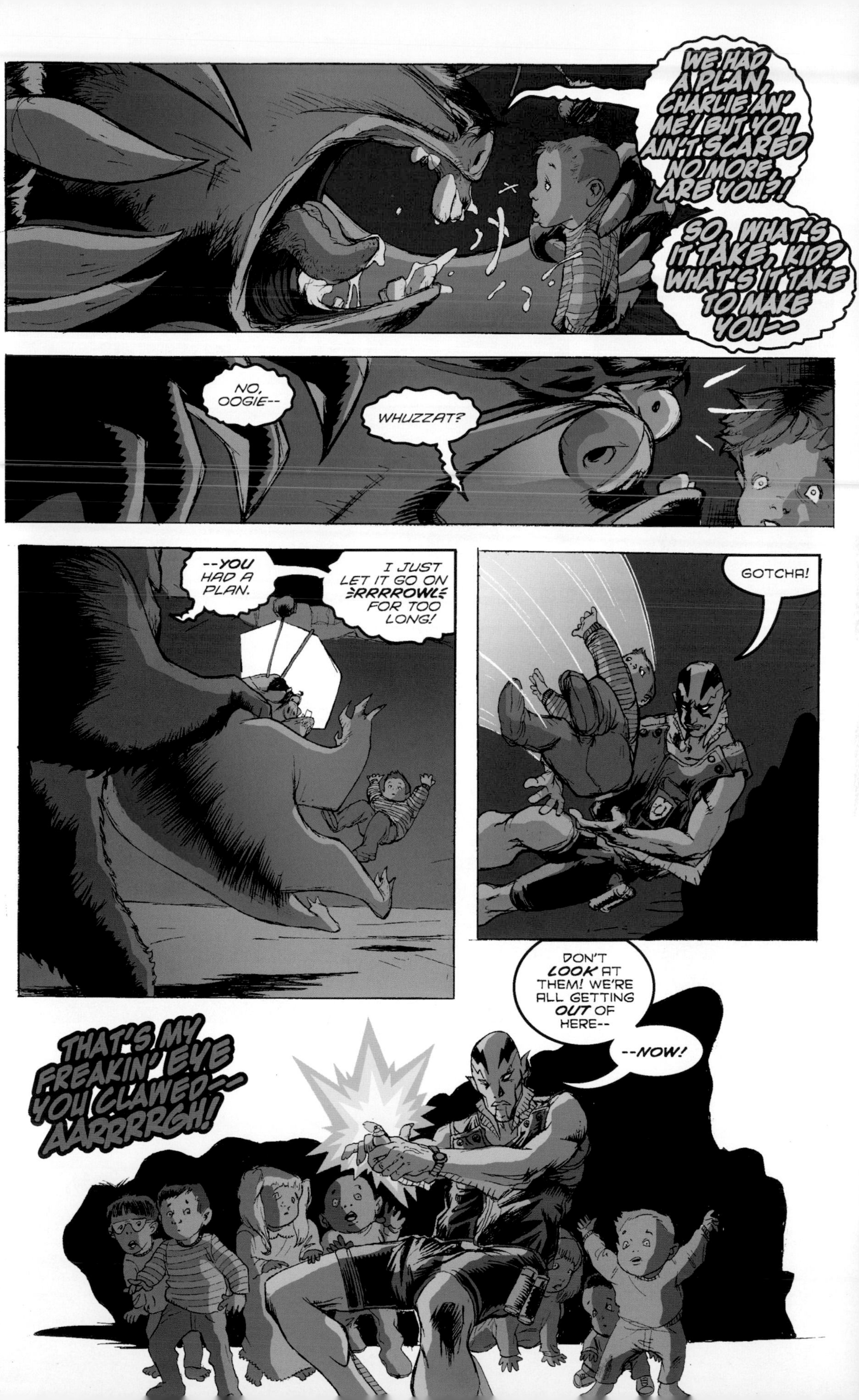
WE HAD A PLAN, CHARLIE AN' ME! BUT YOU AIN'T SCARED NO MORE, ARE YOU?!
SO, WHAT'S IT TAKE, KID? WHAT'S IT TAKE TO MAKE YOU--
NO, OOGIE--
WHUZZAT?
--YOU HAD A PLAN.
I JUST LET IT GO ON RRRROWL FOR TOO LONG!
GOTCHA!
THAT'S MY FREAKIN' EYE YOU CLAWED--AARRRRGH!
DON'T LOOK AT THEM! WE'RE ALL GETTING OUT OF HERE--
--NOW!

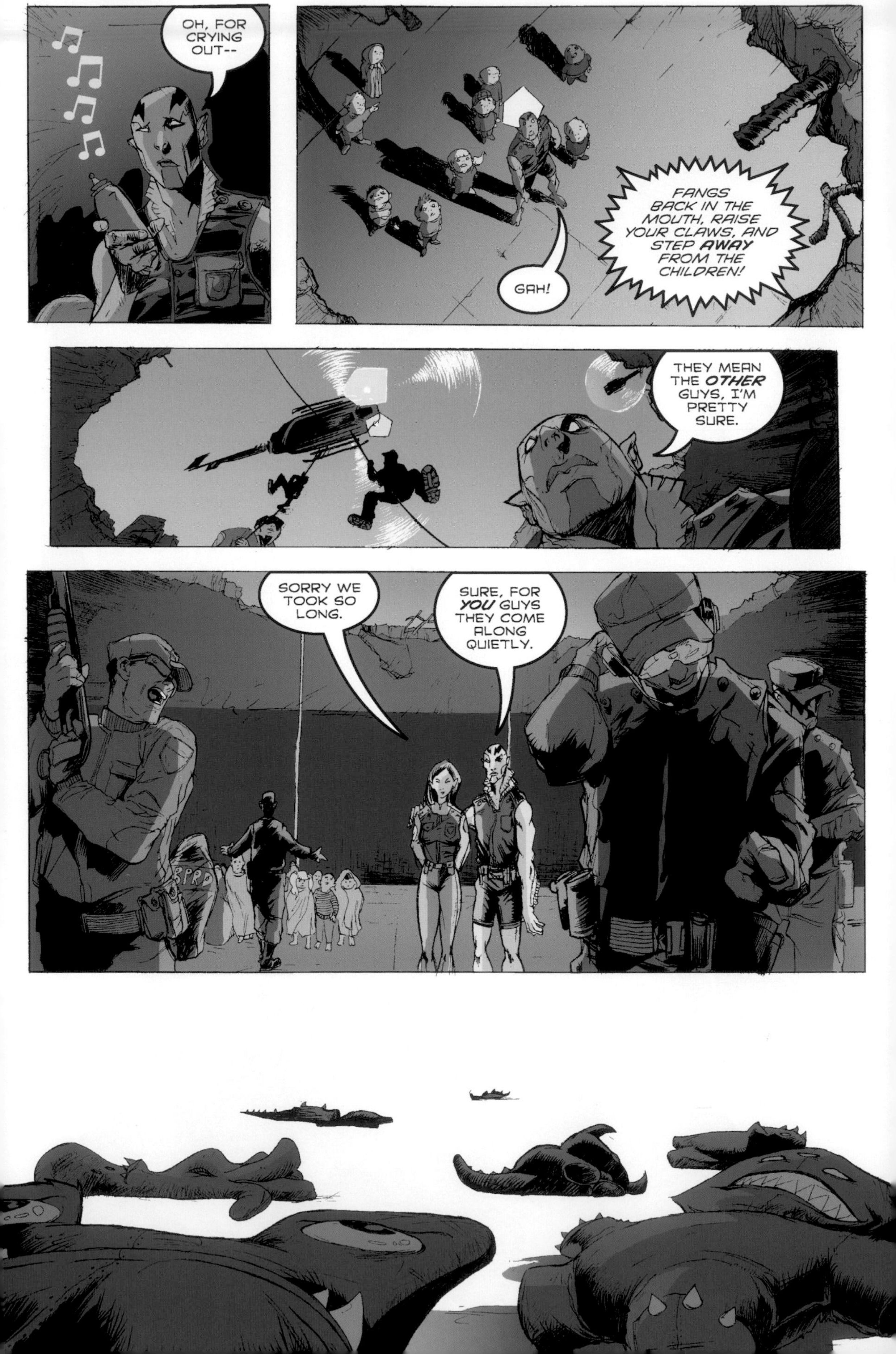

OH, FOR CRYING OUT--
FANGS BACK IN THE MOUTH, RAISE YOUR CLAWS, AND STEP AWAY FROM THE CHILDREN!
GAH!
THEY MEAN THE OTHER GUYS, I'M PRETTY SURE.
SORRY WE TOOK SO LONG.
SURE, FOR YOU GUYS THEY COME ALONG QUIETLY.
BPRD

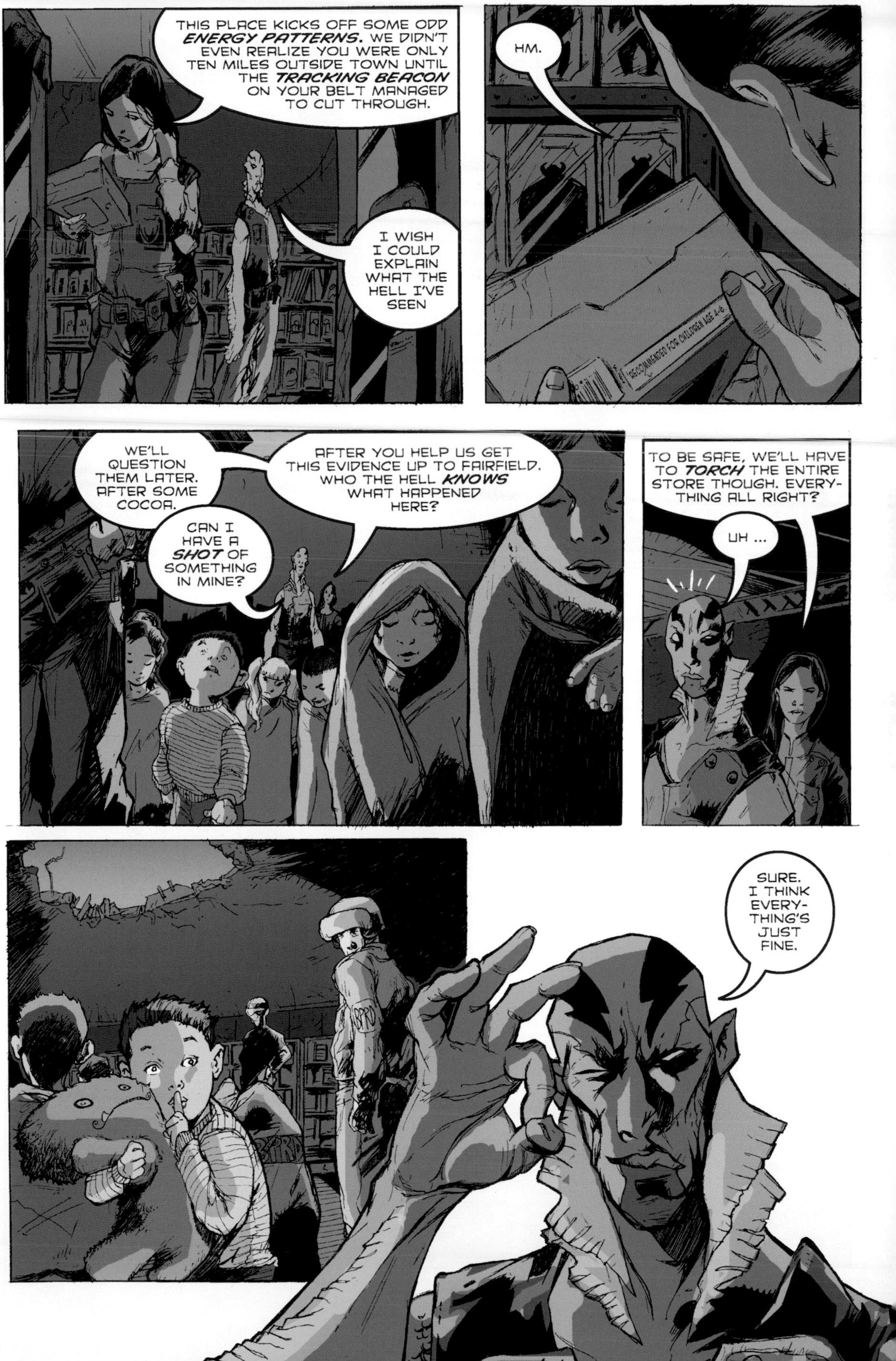
THIS PLACE KICKS OFF SOME ODD ENERGY PATTERNS. WE DIDN'T EVEN REALIZE YOU WERE ONLY TEN MILES OUTSIDE TOWN UNTIL THE TRACKING BEACON ON YOUR BELT MANAGED TO CUT THROUGH.
I WISH I COULD EXPLAIN WHAT THE HELL I'VE SEEN
HM.
RECOMMENDED FOR CHILDREN AGE 4-6
WE'LL QUESTION THEM LATER. AFTER SOME COCOA.
CAN I HAVE A SHOT OF SOMETHING IN MINE?
AFTER YOU HELP US GET THIS EVIDENCE UP TO FAIRFIELD. WHO THE HELL KNOWS WHAT HAPPENED HERE?
TO BE SAFE, WE'LL HAVE TO TORCH THE ENTIRE STORE THOUGH. EVERYTHING ALL RIGHT?
UH ...
SURE. I THINK EVERYTHING'S JUST FINE.

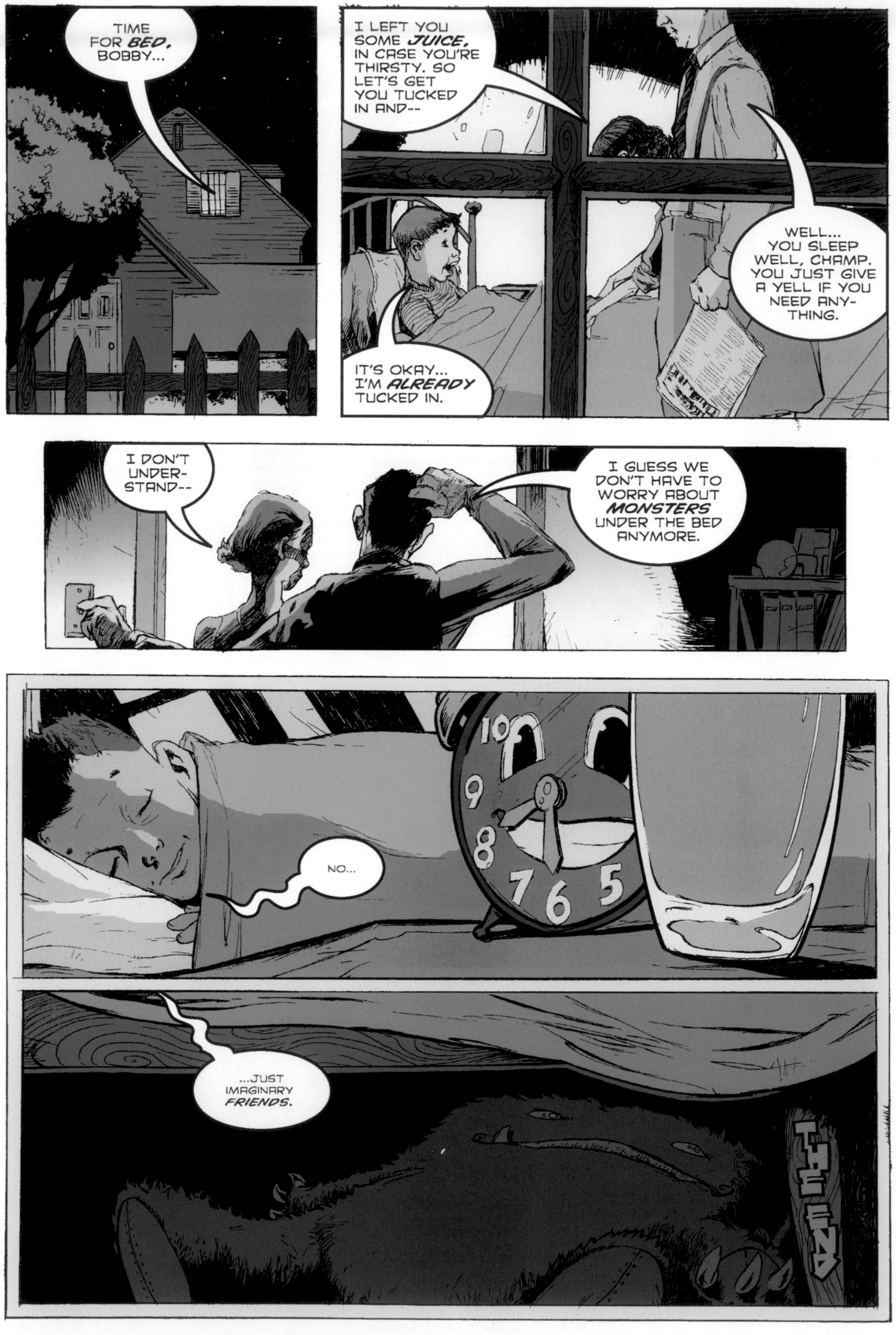

TIME FOR BED, BOBBY...
I LEFT YOU SOME JUICE, IN CASE YOU'RE THIRSTY. SO LET'S GET YOU TUCKED IN AND--
IT'S OKAY... I'M ALREADY TUCKED IN.
WELL... YOU SLEEP WELL, CHAMP. YOU JUST GIVE A YELL IF YOU NEED ANY-THING.
I DON'T UNDER-STAND--
I GUESS WE DON'T HAVE TO WORRY ABOUT MONSTERS UNDER THE BED ANYMORE.
NO...
...JUST IMAGINARY FRIENDS.
THE END

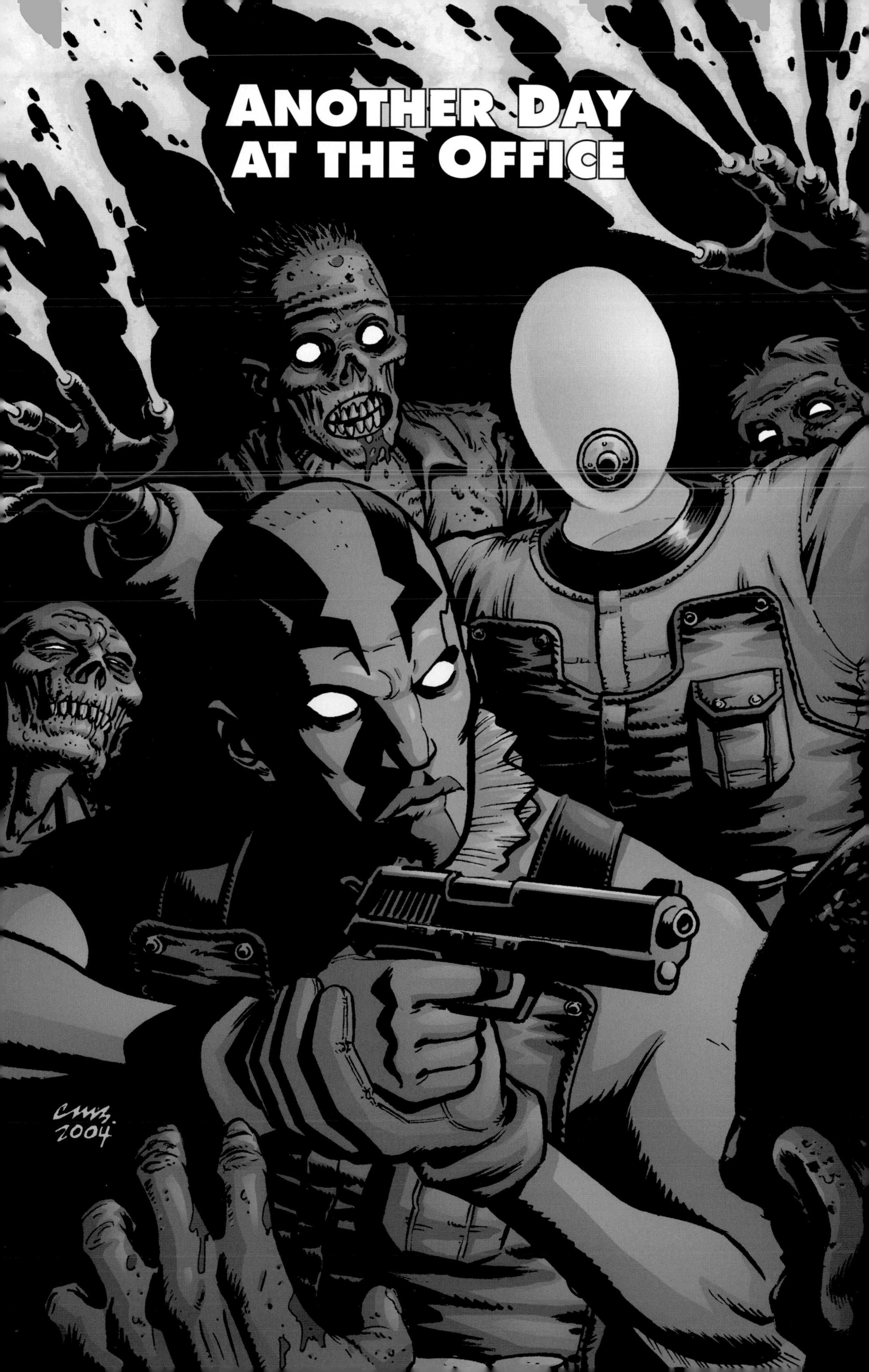
ANOTHER DAY
AT THE OFFICE

ANOTHER DAY
AT THE OFFICE

Story by
MIKE MIGNOLA

Art by
CAMERON STEWART

Colors by
MICHELLE MADSEN

Letters by
MICHAEL HEISLER

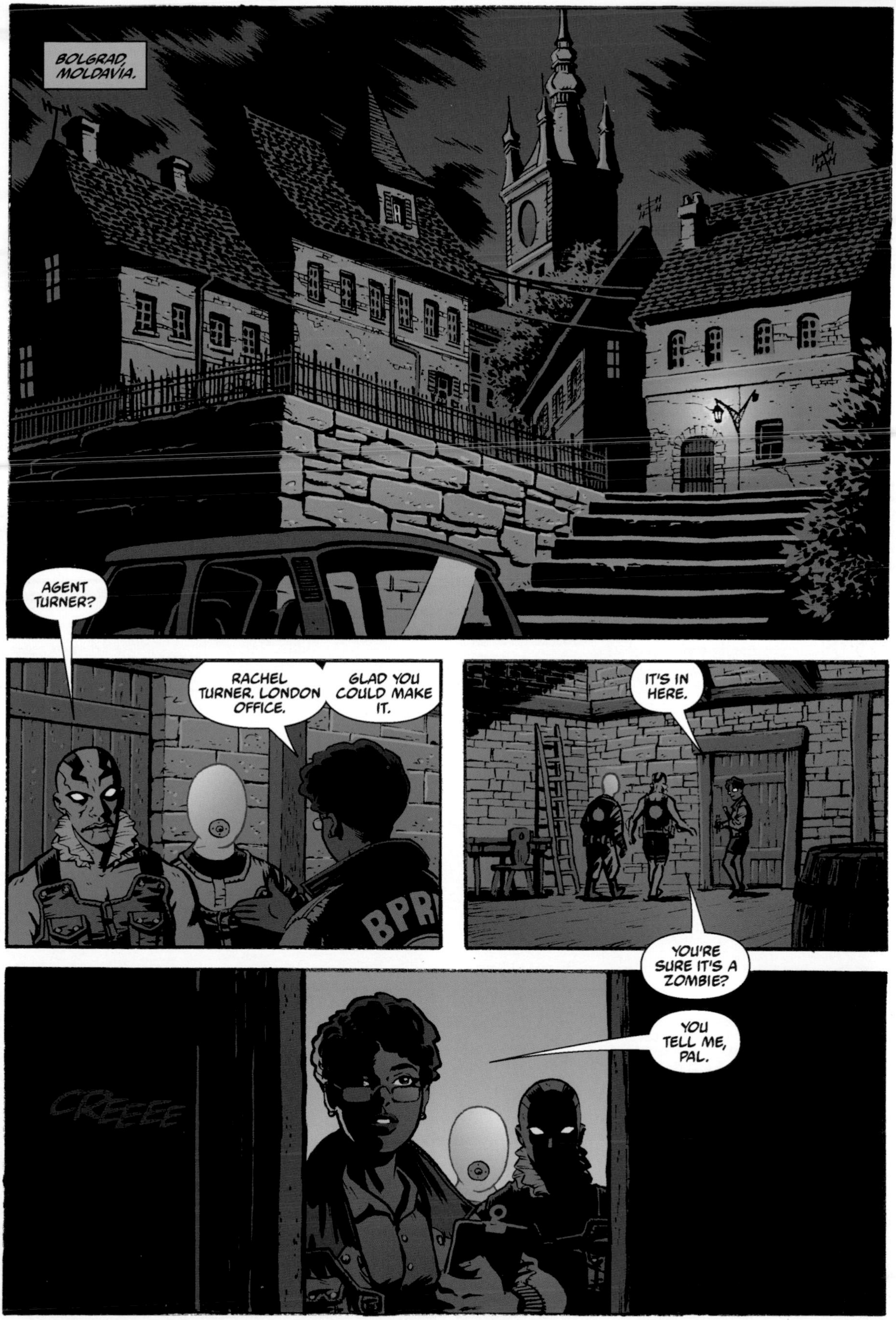
BOLGRAD, MOLDAVIA.
AGENT TURNER?
RACHEL TURNER. LONDON OFFICE.
GLAD YOU COULD MAKE IT.
IT'S IN HERE.
YOU'RE SURE IT'S A ZOMBIE?
YOU TELL ME, PAL.
CREEEEE

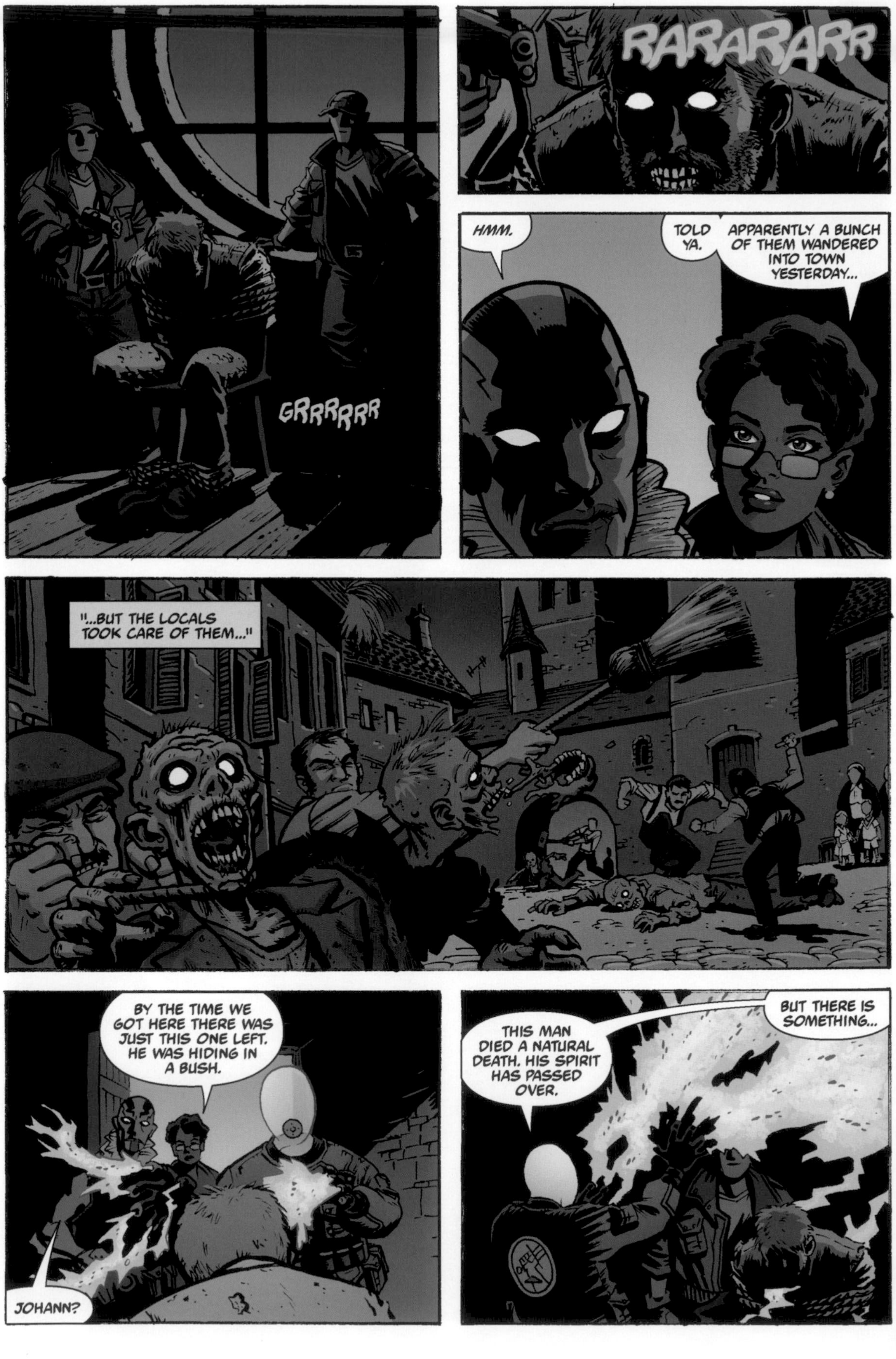
GRRRRRR
RARARARR
HMM.
TOLD YA.
APPARENTLY A BUNCH OF THEM WANDERED INTO TOWN YESTERDAY...
"...BUT THE LOCALS TOOK CARE OF THEM..."
BY THE TIME WE GOT HERE THERE WAS JUST THIS ONE LEFT. HE WAS HIDING IN A BUSH.
JOHANN?
THIS MAN DIED A NATURAL DEATH. HIS SPIRIT HAS PASSED OVER.
BUT THERE IS SOMETHING...

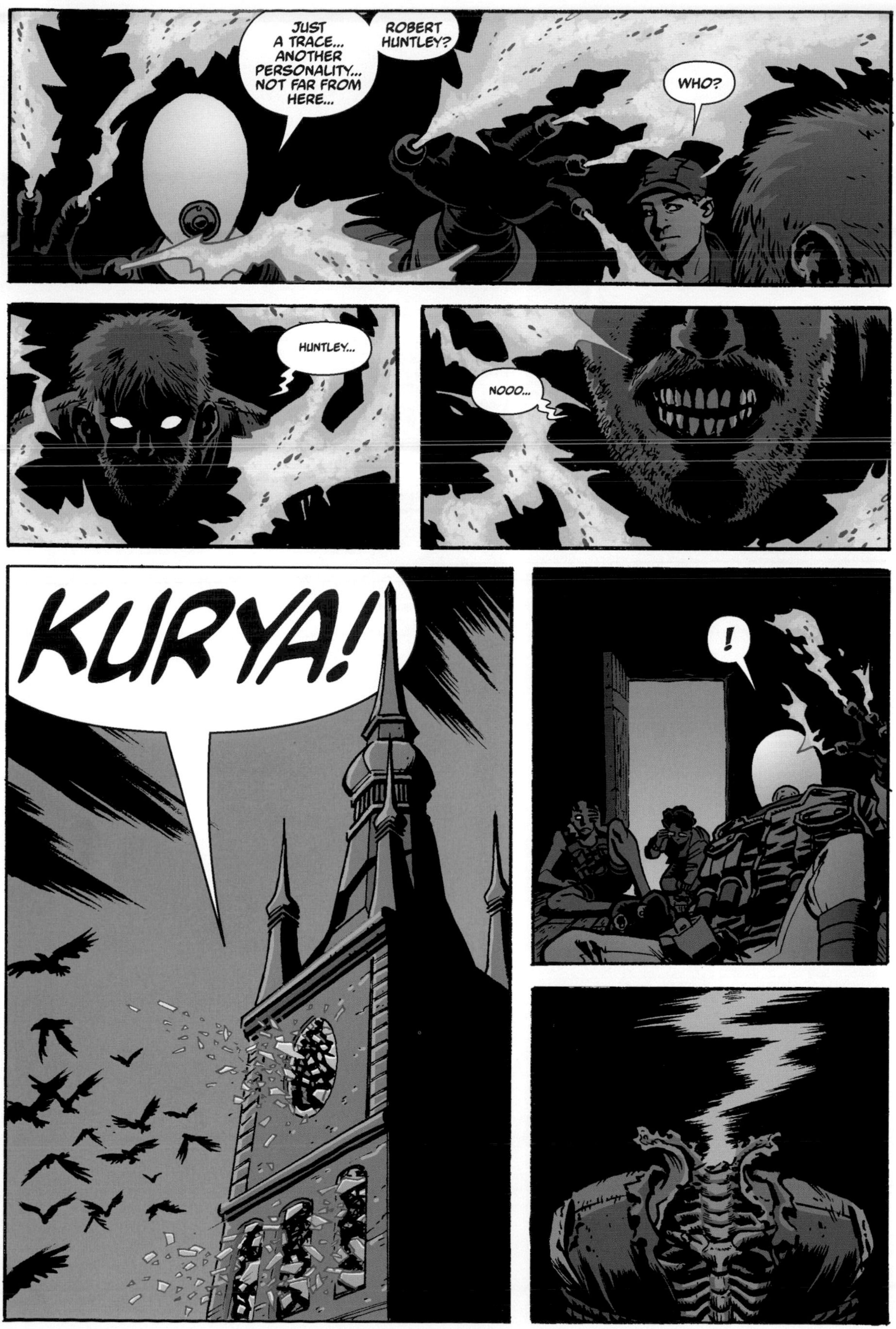
JUST A TRACE... ANOTHER PERSONALITY... NOT FAR FROM HERE...
ROBERT HUNTLEY?
WHO?
HUNTLEY...
NOOO...
KURYA!
!

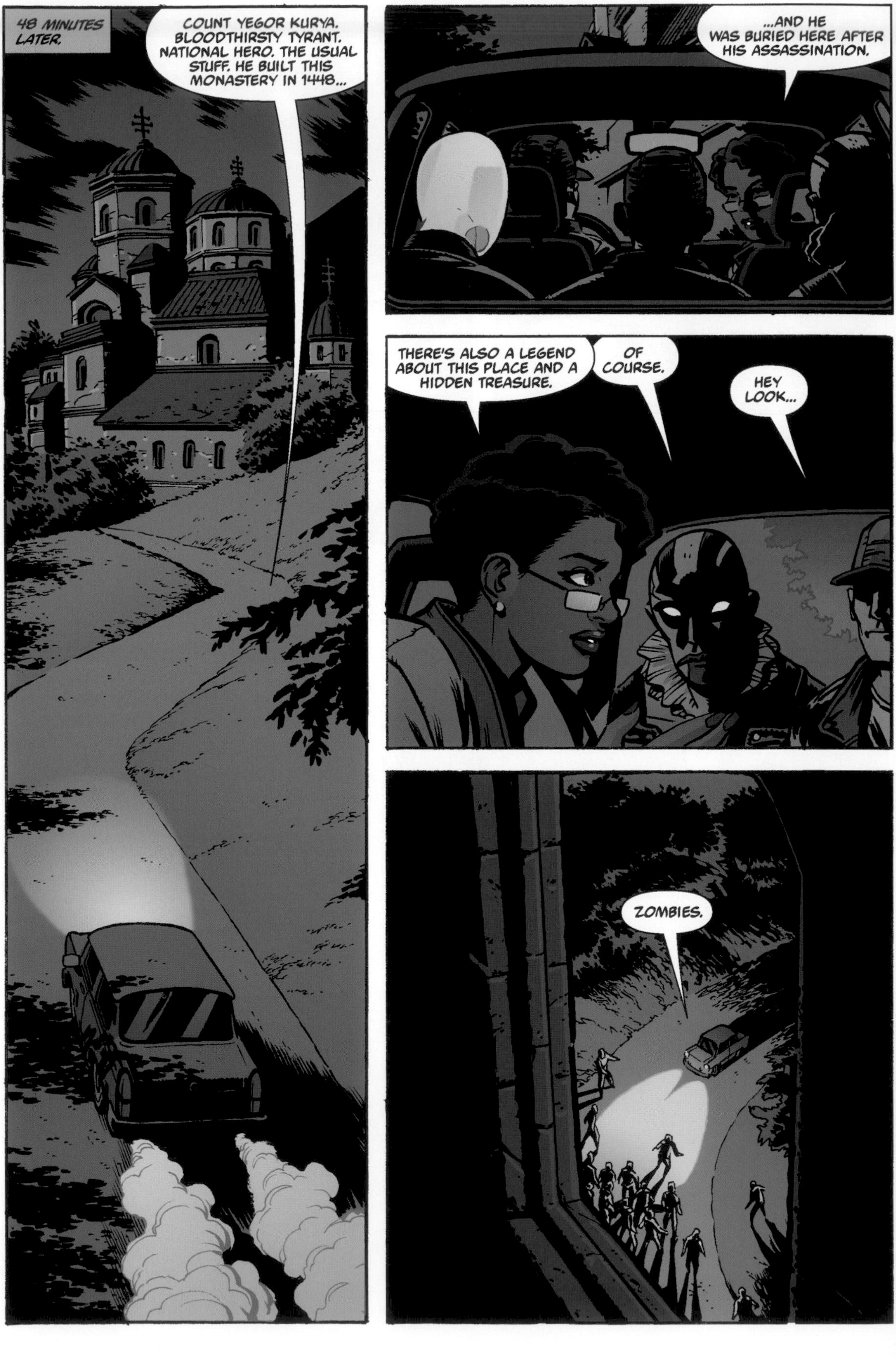
48 MINUTES LATER.
COUNT YEGOR KURYA. BLOODTHIRSTY TYRANT. NATIONAL HERO. THE USUAL STUFF. HE BUILT THIS MONASTERY IN 1448...
...AND HE WAS BURIED HERE AFTER HIS ASSASSINATION.
THERE'S ALSO A LEGEND ABOUT THIS PLACE AND A HIDDEN TREASURE.
OF COURSE.
HEY LOOK...
ZOMBIES.

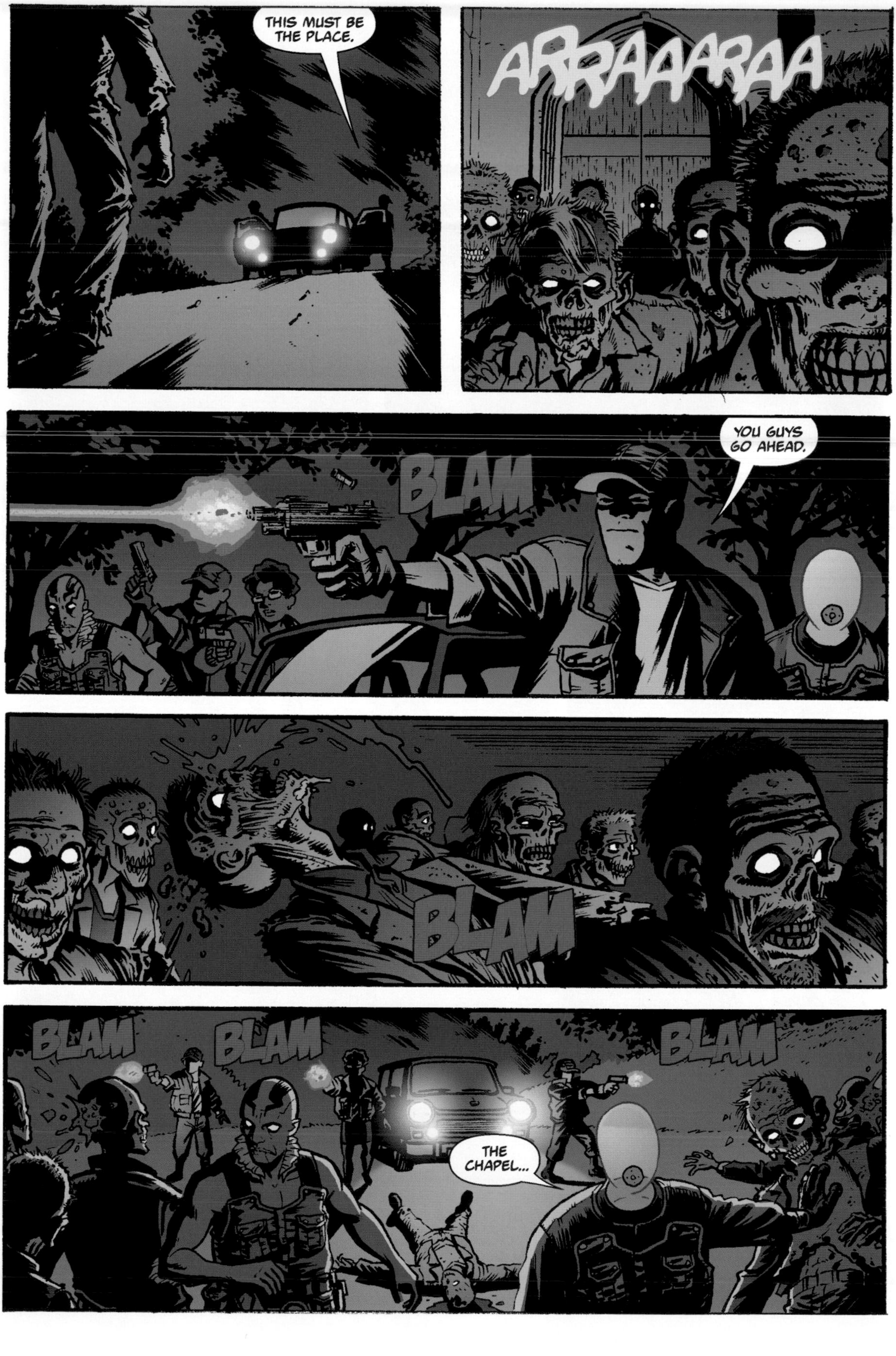

THIS MUST BE THE PLACE.
ARRAAARAA
BLAM
YOU GUYS GO AHEAD.
BLAM
BLAM
BLAM
BLAM
THE CHAPEL...

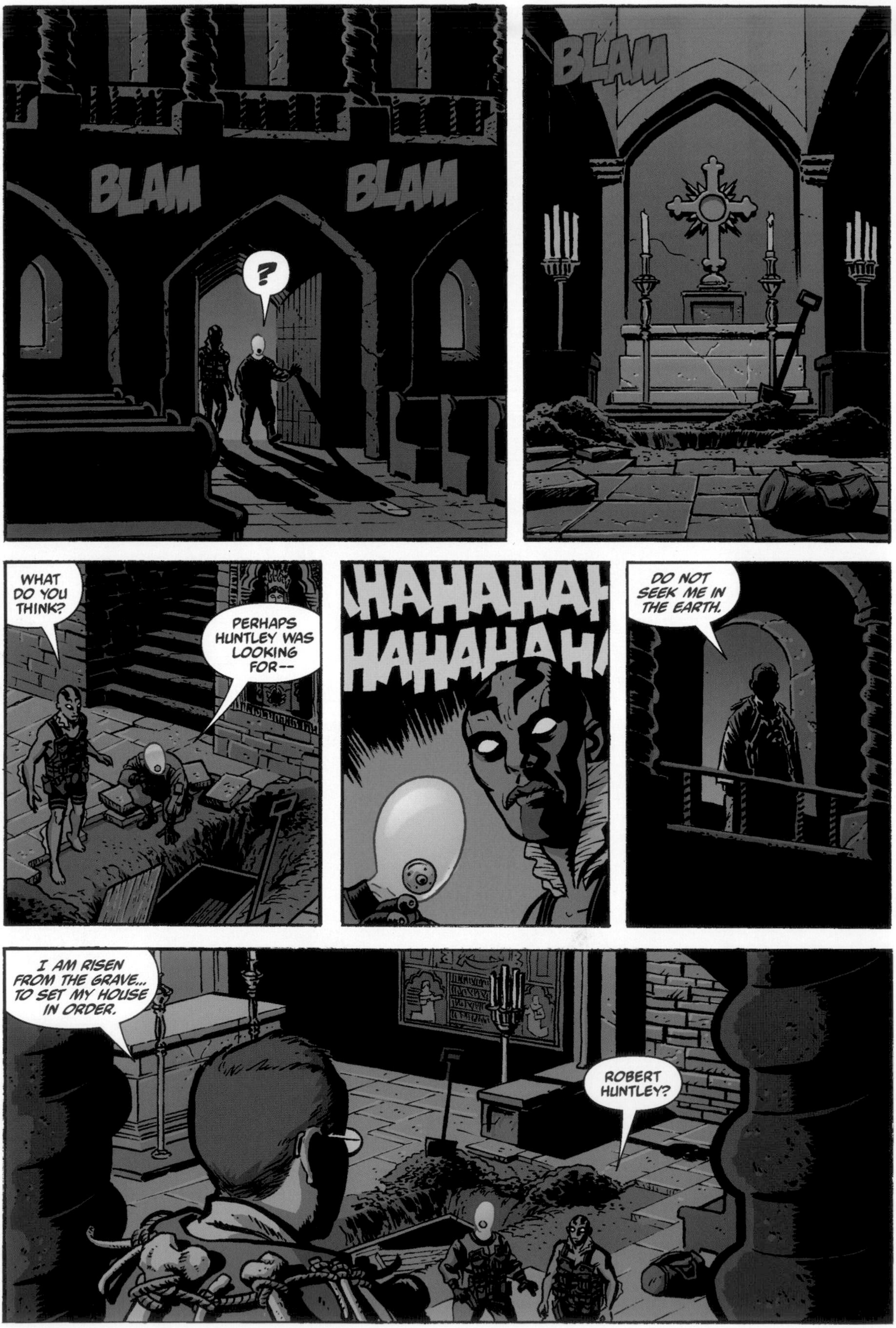
BLAM
BLAM
?
BLAM
WHAT DO YOU THINK?
PERHAPS HUNTLEY WAS LOOKING FOR--
HAHAHAHAH
HAHAHAHAH
DO NOT SEEK ME IN THE EARTH.
I AM RISEN FROM THE GRAVE... TO SET MY HOUSE IN ORDER.
ROBERT HUNTLEY?

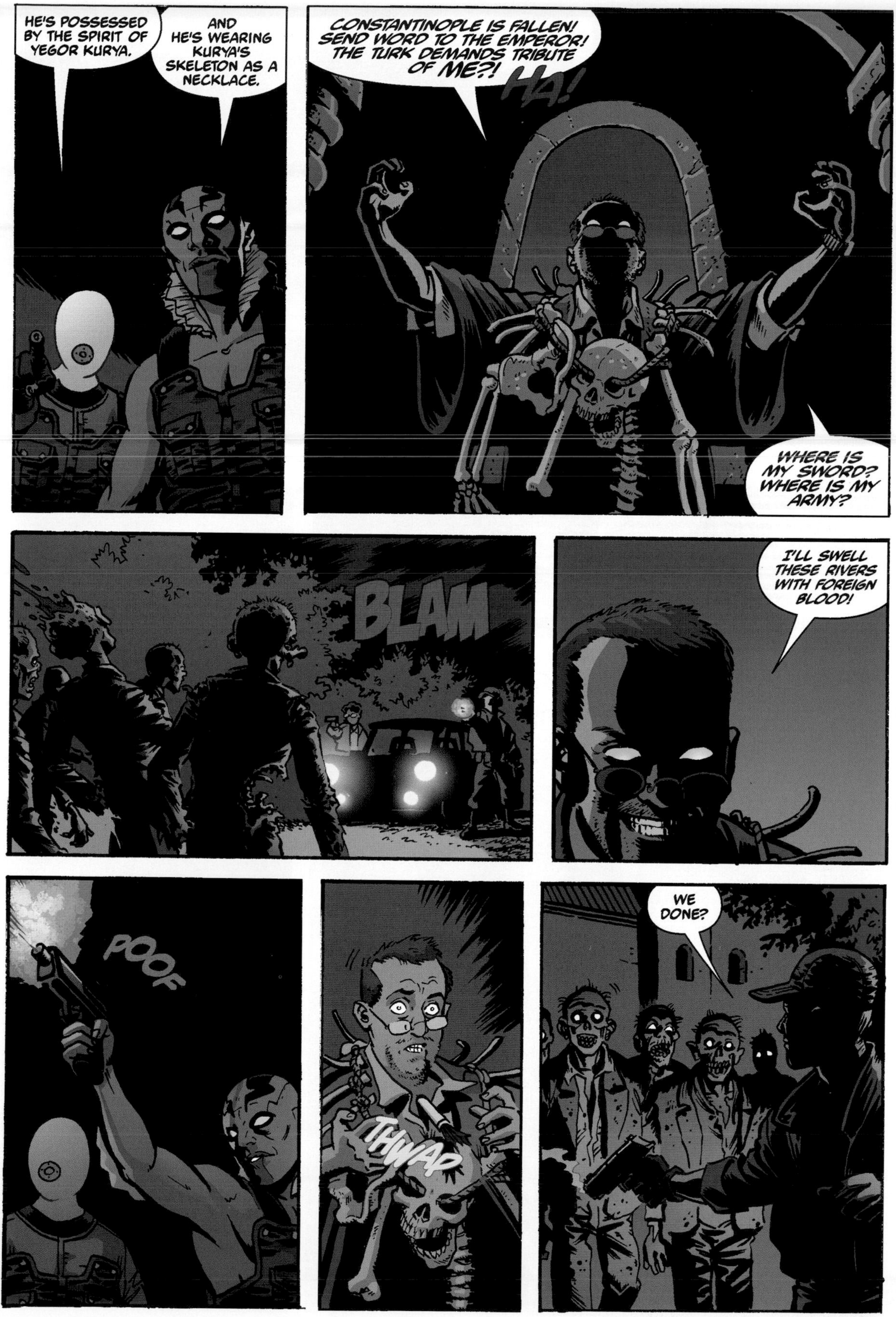
HE'S POSSESSED BY THE SPIRIT OF YEGOR KURYA.
AND HE'S WEARING KURYA'S SKELETON AS A NECKLACE.
CONSTANTINOPLE IS FALLEN! SEND WORD TO THE EMPEROR! THE TURK DEMANDS TRIBUTE OF ME?!
HA!
WHERE IS MY SWORD? WHERE IS MY ARMY?
BLAM
I'LL SWELL THESE RIVERS WITH FOREIGN BLOOD!
POOF
THWAP
WE DONE?

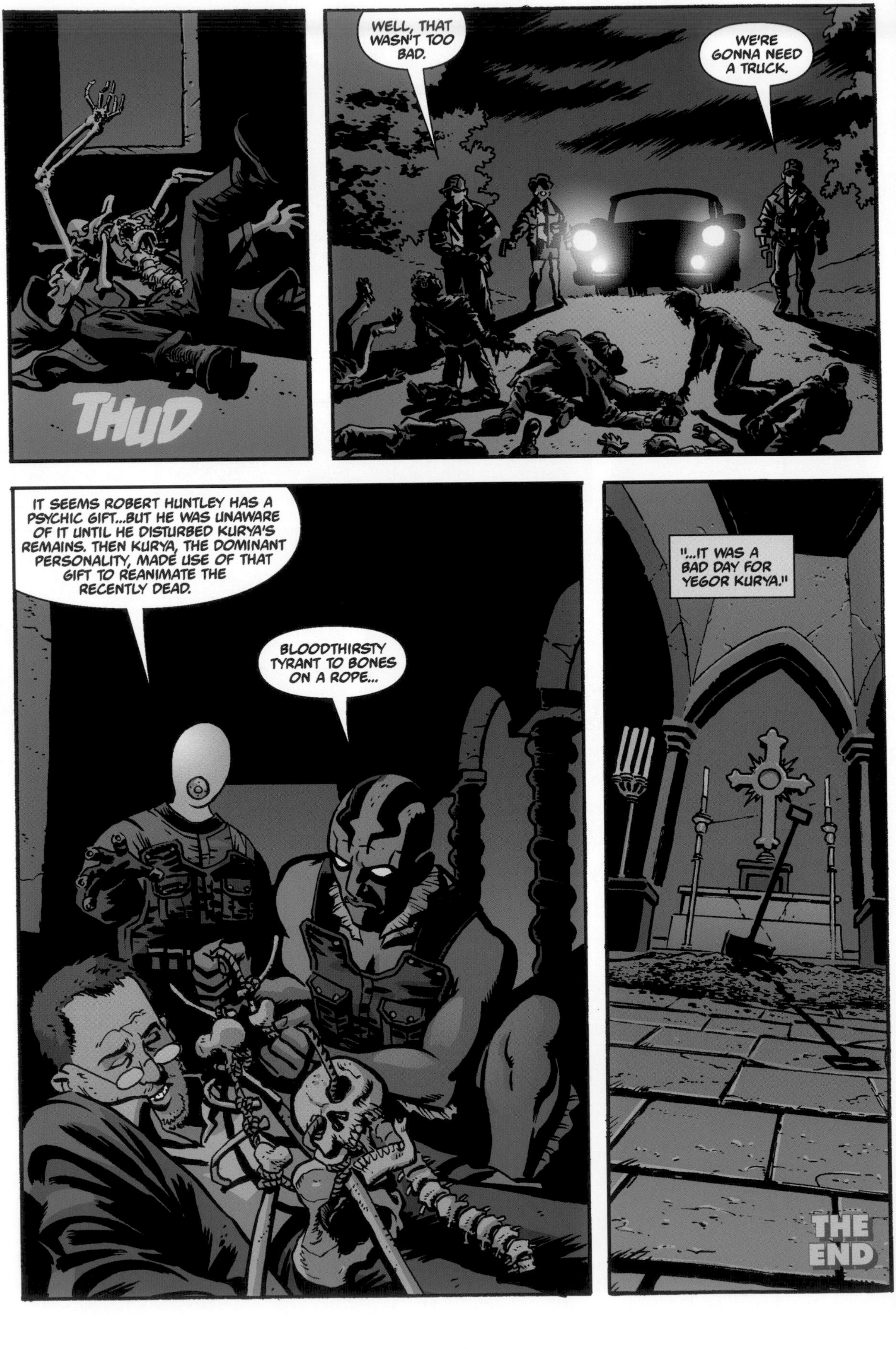
THUD
WELL, THAT WASN'T TOO BAD.
WE'RE GONNA NEED A TRUCK.
IT SEEMS ROBERT HUNTLEY HAS A PSYCHIC GIFT...BUT HE WAS UNAWARE OF IT UNTIL HE DISTURBED KURYA'S REMAINS. THEN KURYA, THE DOMINANT PERSONALITY, MADE USE OF THAT GIFT TO REANIMATE THE RECENTLY DEAD.
BLOODTHIRSTY TYRANT TO BONES ON A ROPE...
"...IT WAS A BAD DAY FOR YEGOR KURYA."
THE END

B.P.R.D.™

SKETCHBOOK

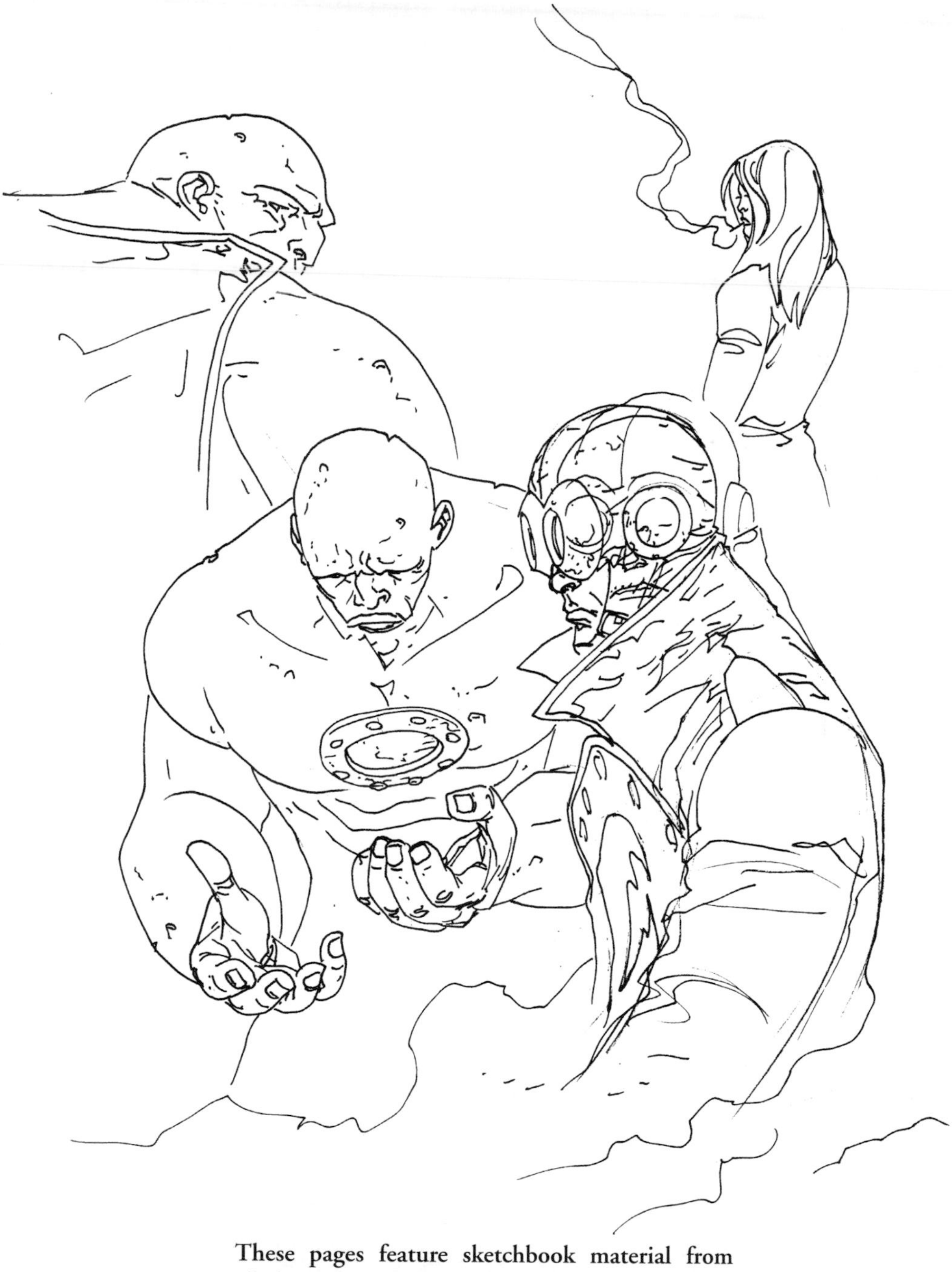

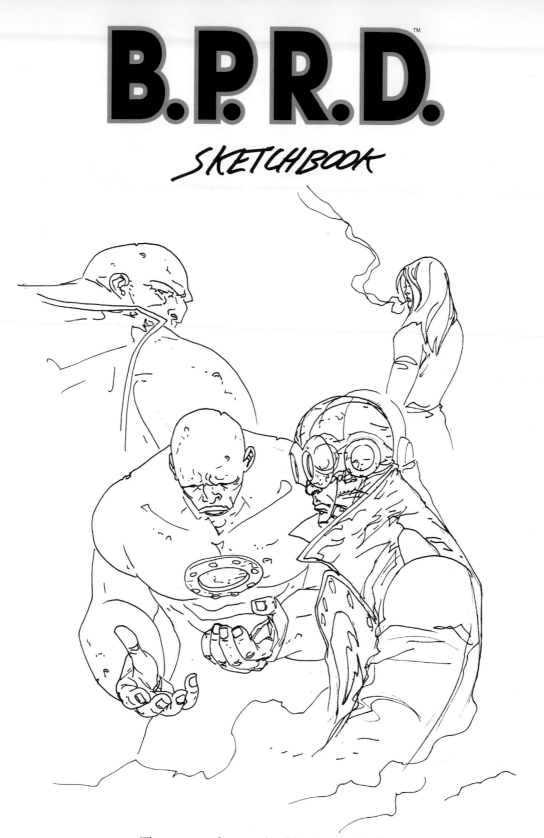

These pages feature sketchbook material from all the artists included in *The Soul of Venice and Other Stories.* While the book is *B.P.R.D.*, artists do tend to fill their sketchbooks with images of Hellboy.

—Scott Allie

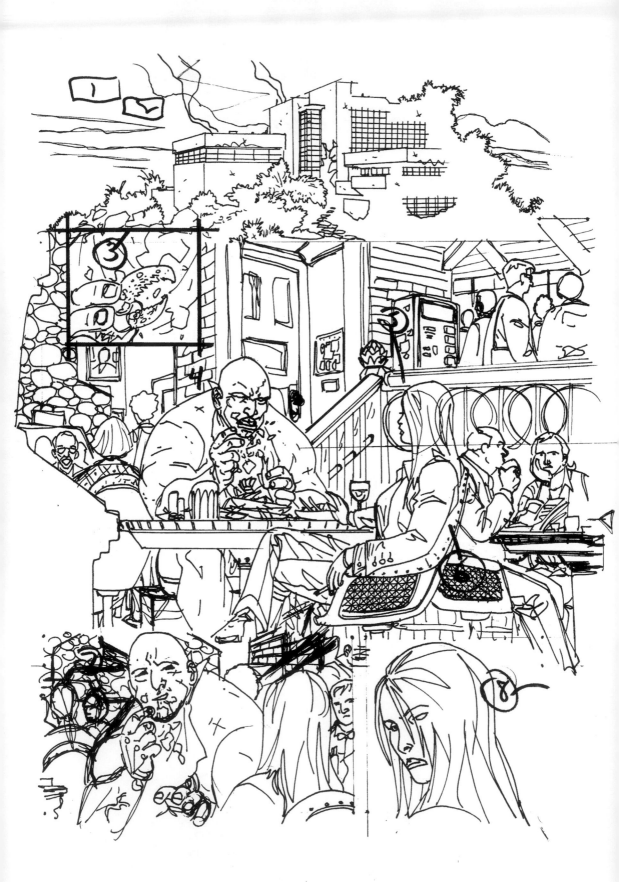

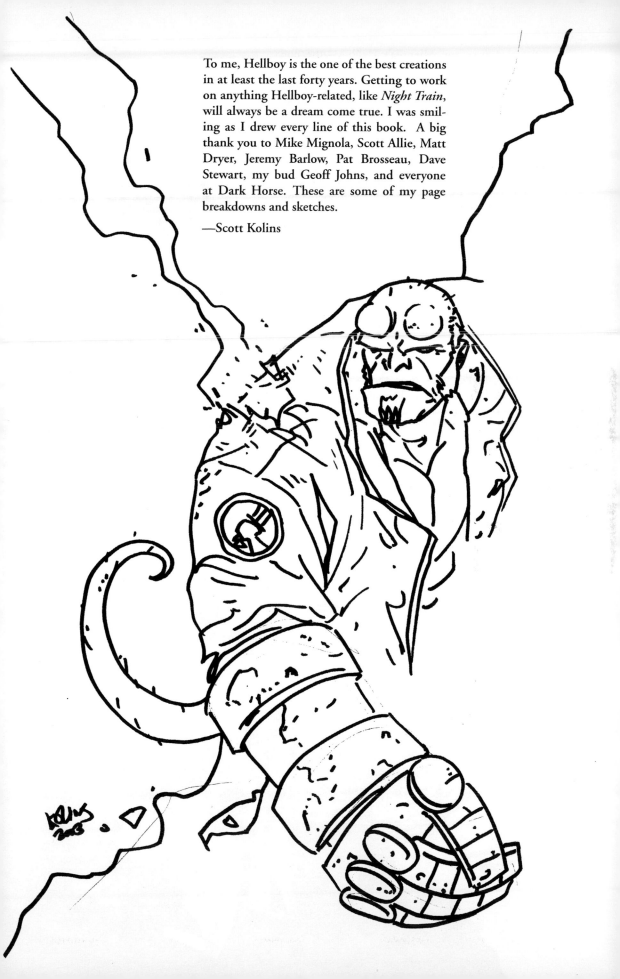

To me, Hellboy is the one of the best creations in at least the last forty years. Getting to work on anything Hellboy-related, like *Night Train*, will always be a dream come true. I was smiling as I drew every line of this book. A big thank you to Mike Mignola, Scott Allie, Matt Dryer, Jeremy Barlow, Pat Brosseau, Dave Stewart, my bud Geoff Johns, and everyone at Dark Horse. These are some of my page breakdowns and sketches.

—Scott Kolins

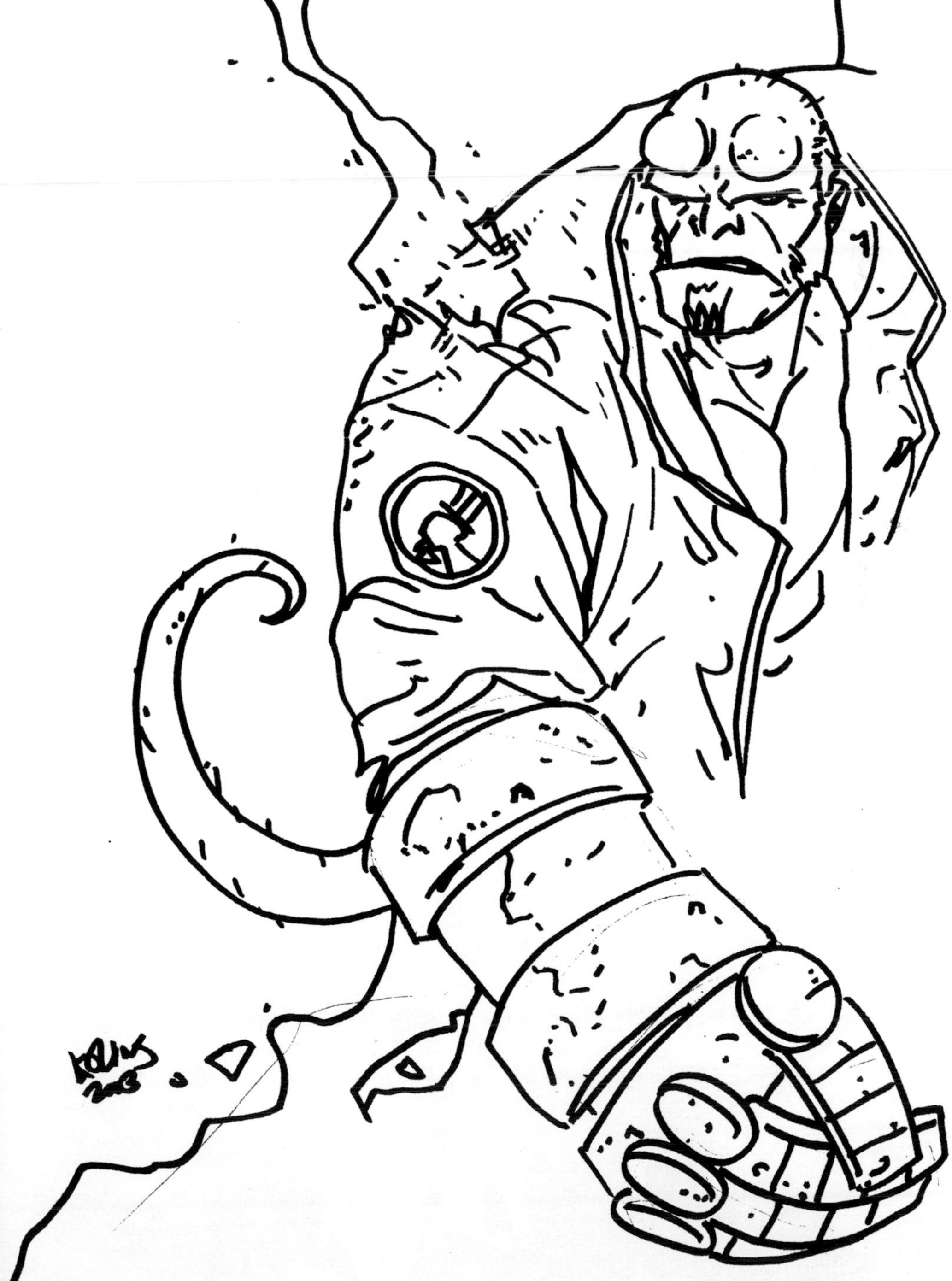

When I first saw Mignola's Hellboy—the one where he fights the giant dog at the gas station—I thought the same thing everyone else did: "Wow, that's cool, he wears goggles." It was a neat time, discovering Hellboy. I'd been a fan of Mike's since *Cosmic Odyssey* and watched him progress over the years. Now he was doing something uniquely him. Amazing stuff. Soon, this layered creation started to uncover itself, layers of mystery. First the visuals—Mike's use of black, the mood within his art. The environment, the backgrounds, that strange, semi-Victorian feel to his work. All that was new to me then, and the work shares a special place in my life with other great stories that reveal themselves in their freshness, and then sustain themselves over the years.

I was lucky enough to get to know Mike some, so when the chance came to work on *Soul of Venice*, not only did I want to impress the artist, but I wanted to make sure Mike the man was happy, too. He worked with us on the layout, and especially the cover, adding his own touch. Sitting in his studio, surrounded by books and unpublished Mignola art as he doodled on my layouts, is one of the best memories I've had in comics.

Mike—On behalf of myself, Kelsey, and Miles,
I thank you for such a great character and world,
and allowing us to play with them.

—Michael Avon Oeming

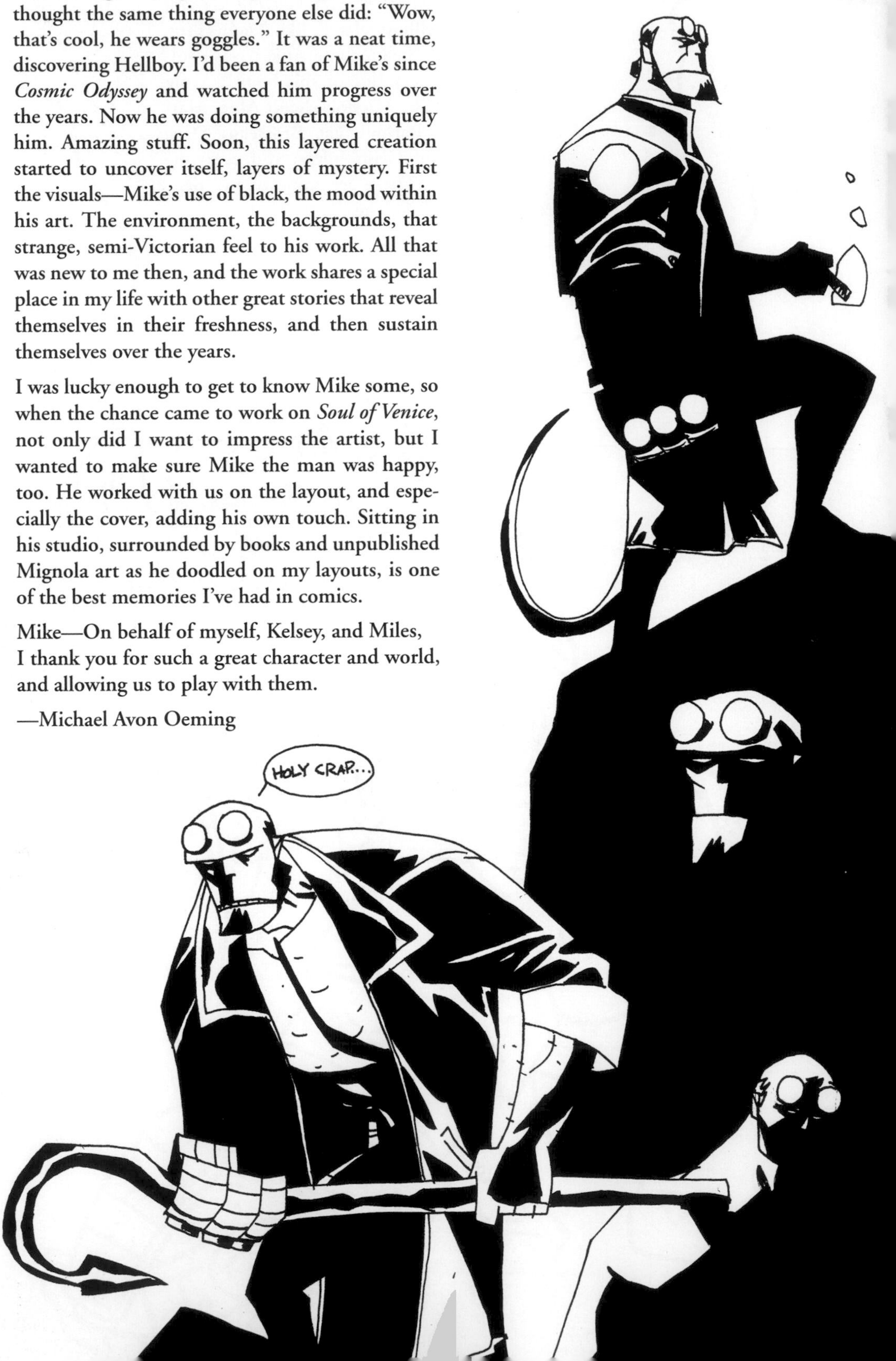
HOLY CRAP...

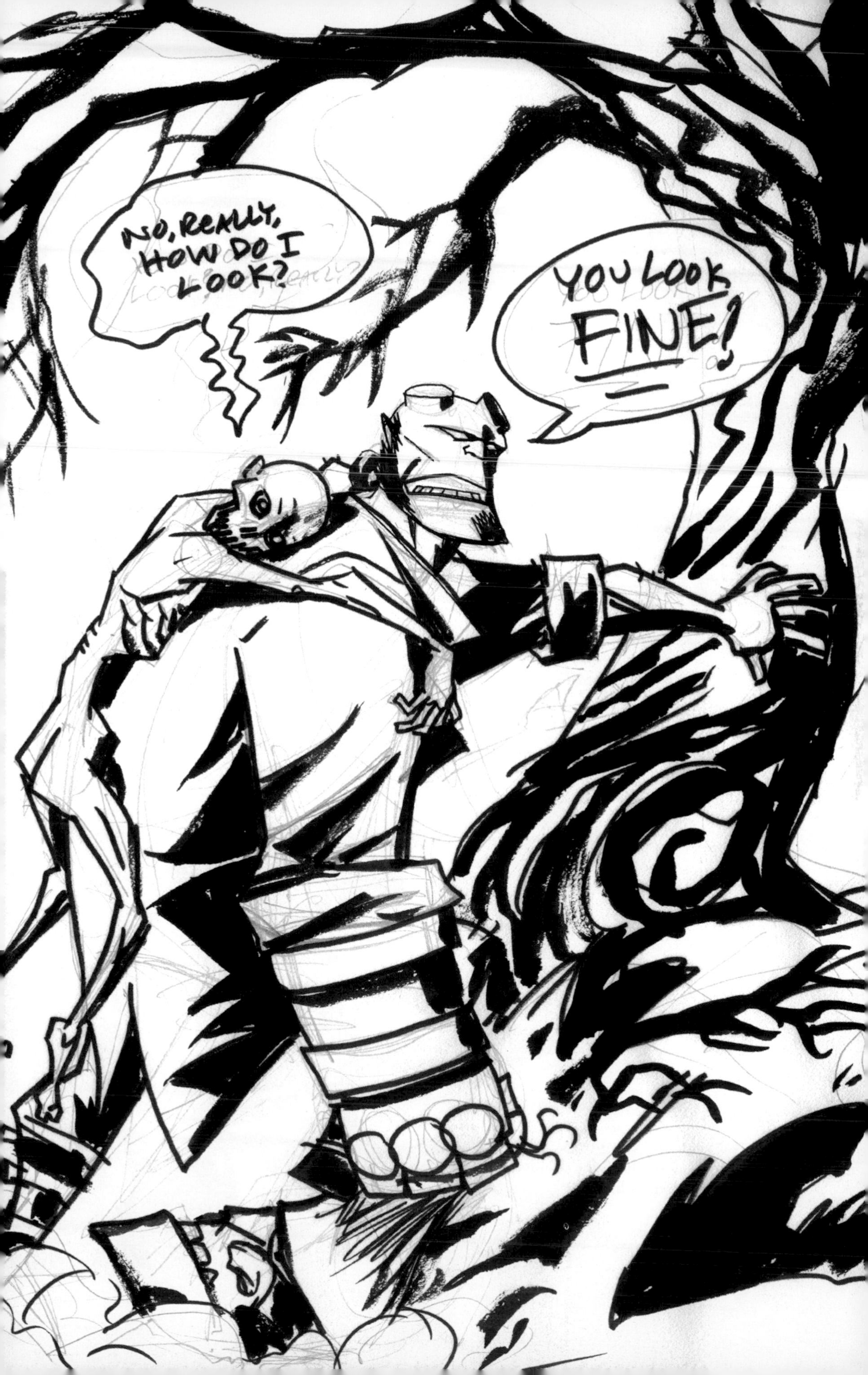
NO, REALLY, HOW DO I LOOK?
YOU LOOK FINE!

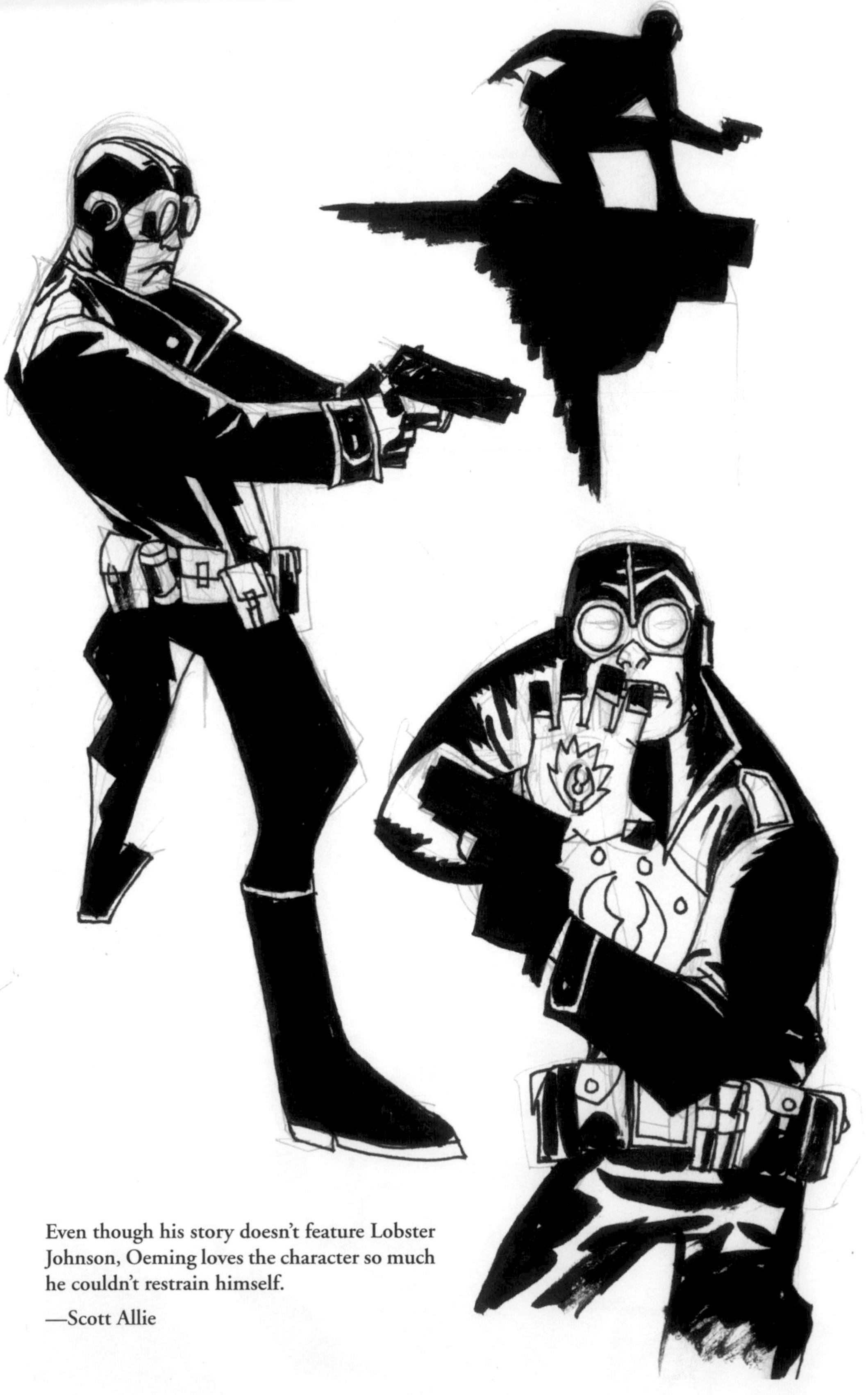

Even though his story doesn't feature Lobster Johnson, Oeming loves the character so much he couldn't restrain himself.

—Scott Allie

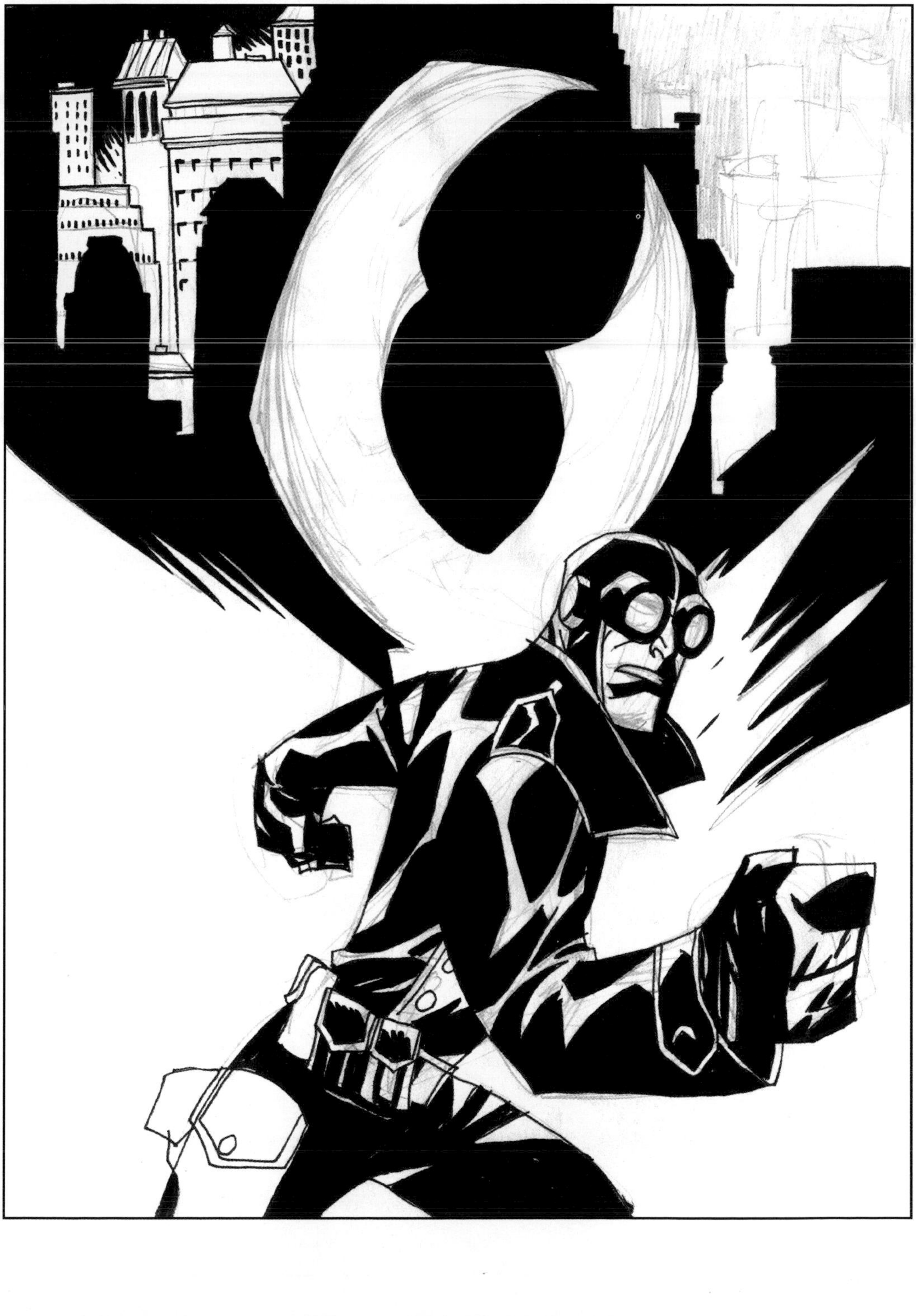

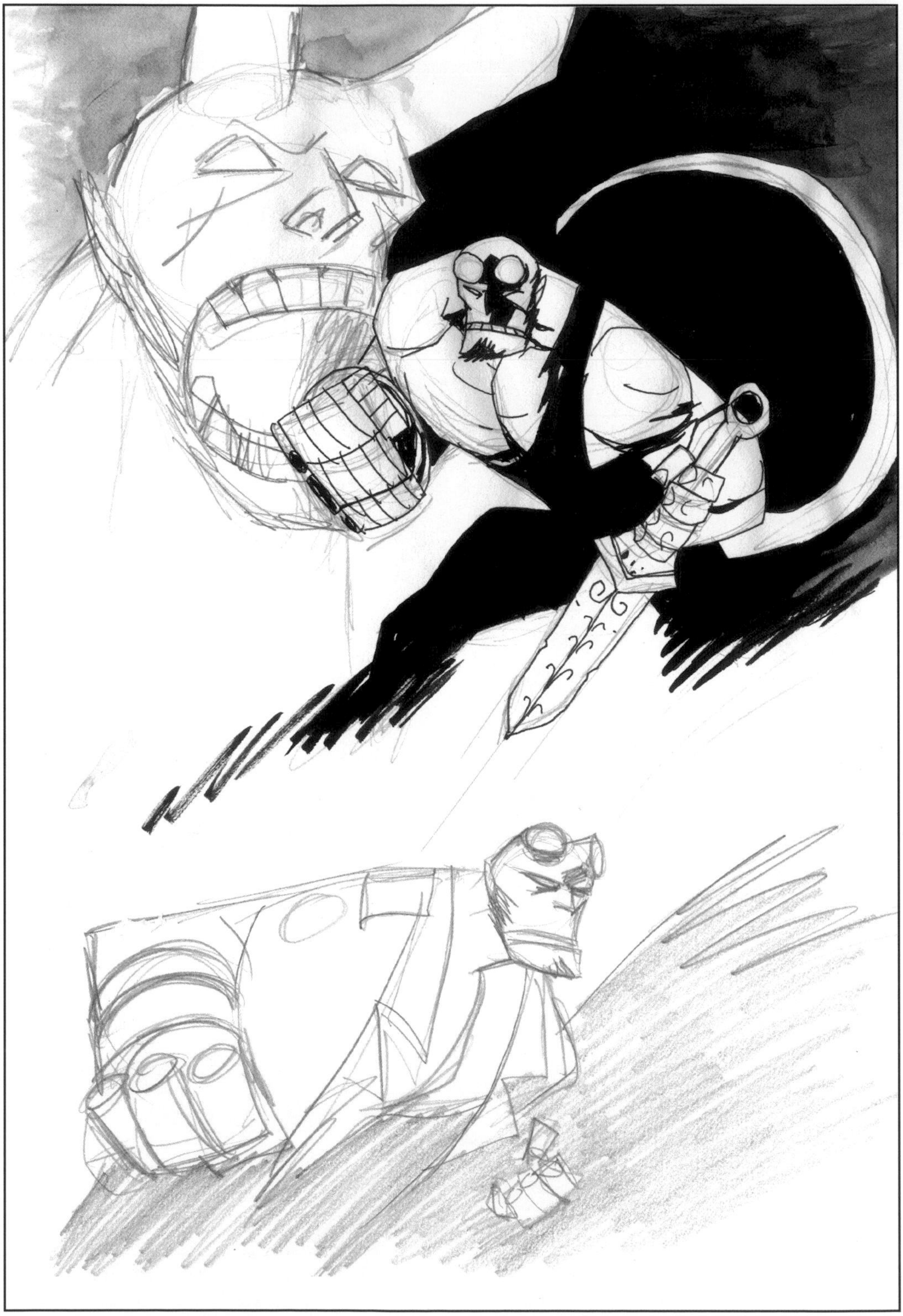

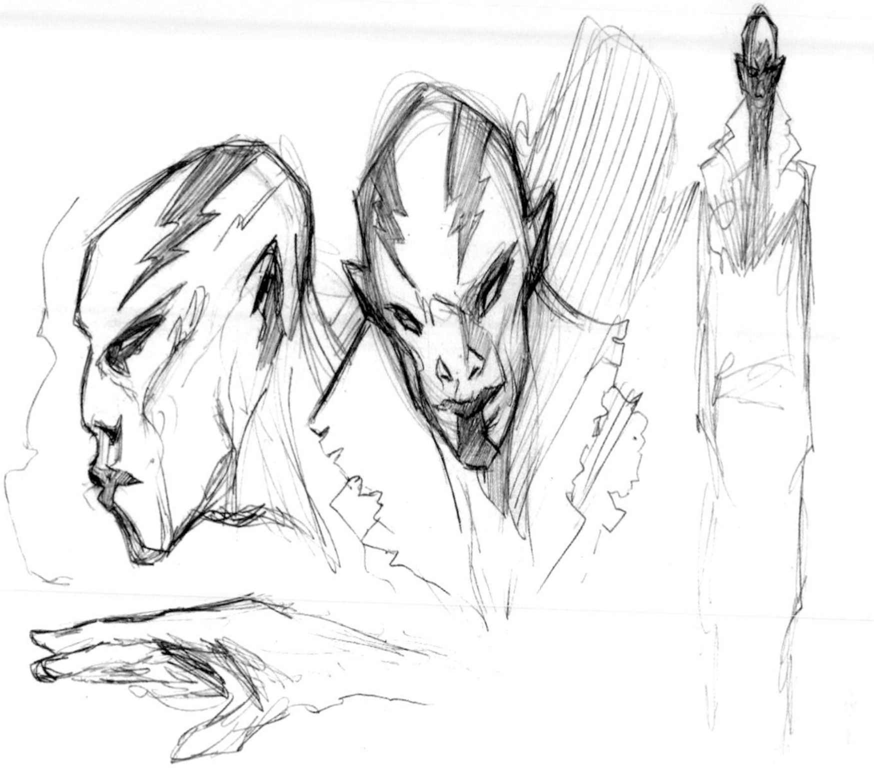

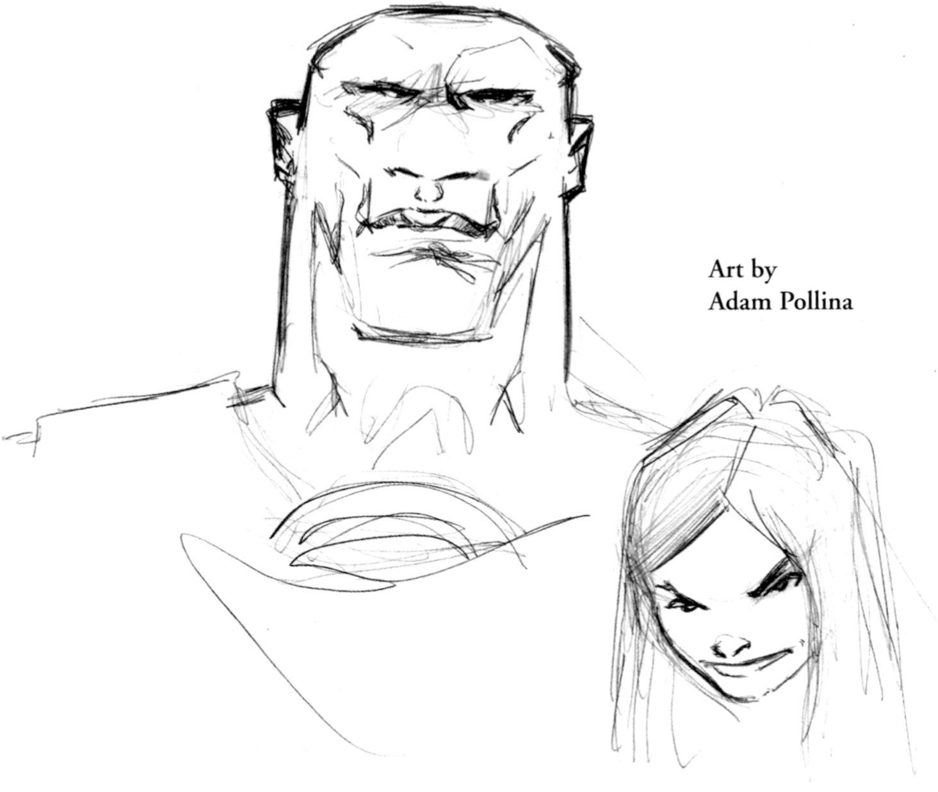

Art by
Adam Pollina

Unlike some of the other franchises we've had the privilege of working on in comics, something about Hellboy and the B.P.R.D. feels just as classic as the X-Men, etc., while feeling incredibly fresh and new at the same time. Both Adam and I were thrilled to bring our twisted mix of horror and playtime to the table.

—Joe Harris

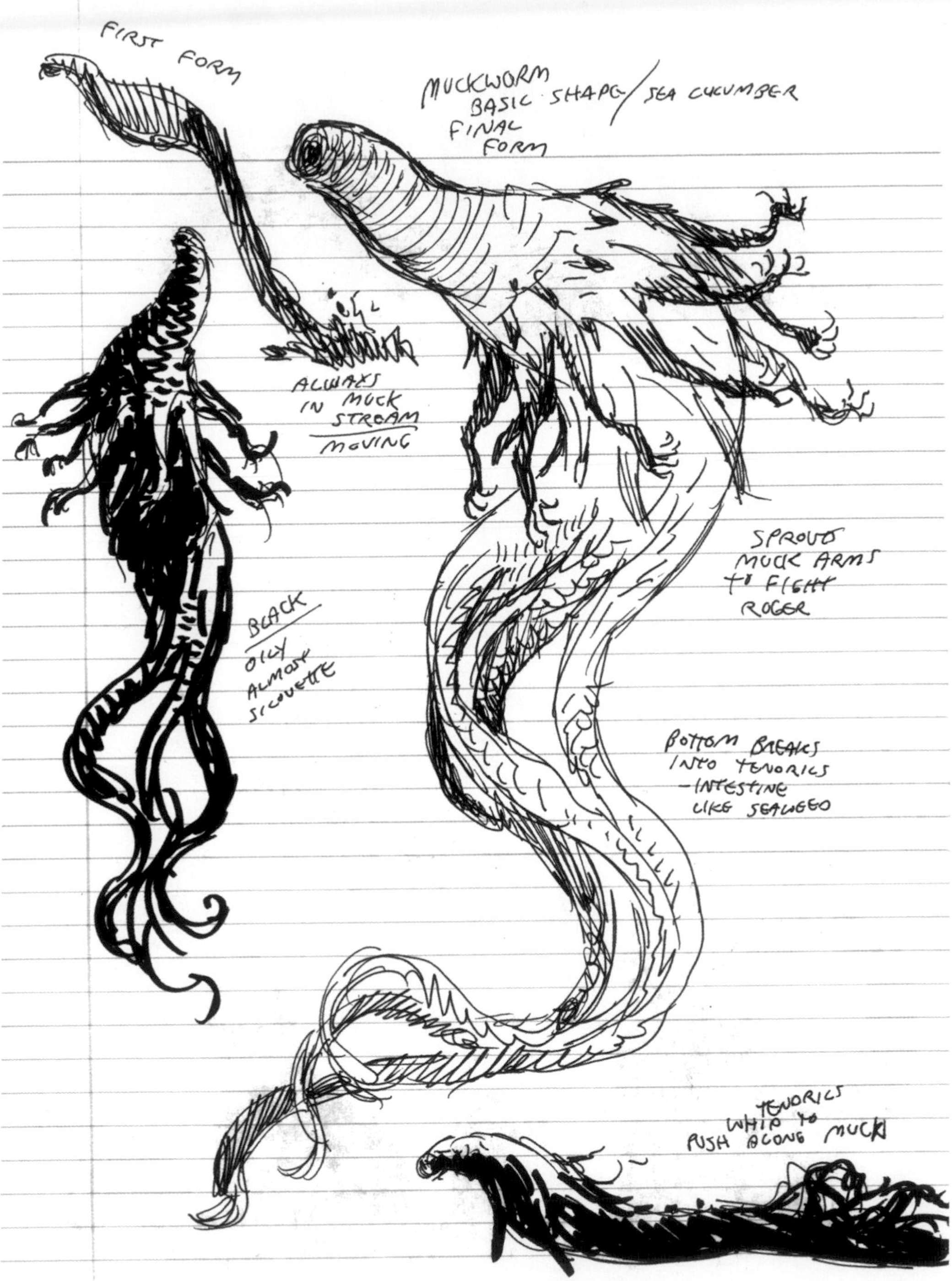
FIRST FORM
MUCKWORM
BASIC SHAPE / SEA CUCUMBER
FINAL
FORM
ALWAYS
IN MUCK
STREAM
MOVING
SPROUTS
MUCK ARMS
TO FIGHT
ROGER
BLACK
OILY
ALMOST
SILOUETTE
BOTTOM BREAKS
INTO TENDRILS
-INTESTINE
LIKE SEAWEED
TENDRILS
WHIP TO
PUSH ALONG MUCK

Mike's imagination and design has always been an inspiration, so I jumped at the chance to try my hand at drawing his characters—who wouldn't? Even a mundane backdrop like the small Massachusetts town in *Dark Waters* was entertaining to draw with the likes of Abe and Roger poking around in it. Aside from giving Abe a sleeveless rain coat, most of the new designs needed were centered on the mud men and giant muckworm. Both were pretty straightforward; the muckworm itself was toned down a bit in the finished art.

—Guy Davis

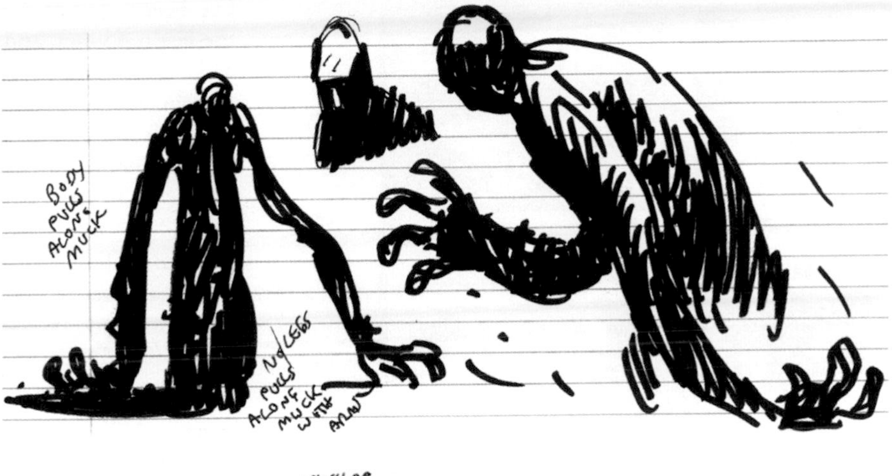
BODY PULLS ALONG MUCK
NO LEGS
PULLS ALONG MUCK WITH ARM

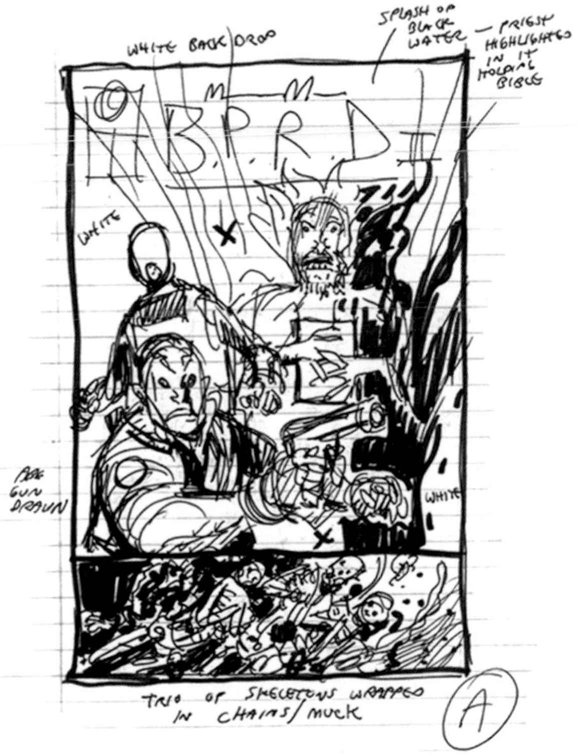
WHITE BACK DROP
SPLASH OF BLACK WATER
PRIEST HIGHLIGHTED IN IT HOLDING BIBLE
WHITE
ABE GUN DRAWN
WHITE
TRIO OF SKELETONS WRAPPED IN CHAINS/MUCK
A

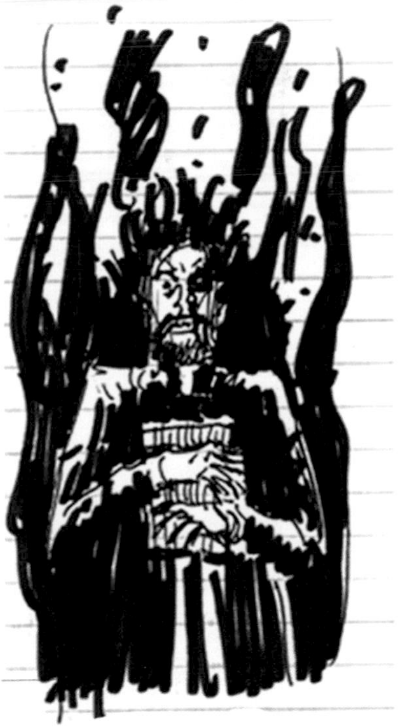

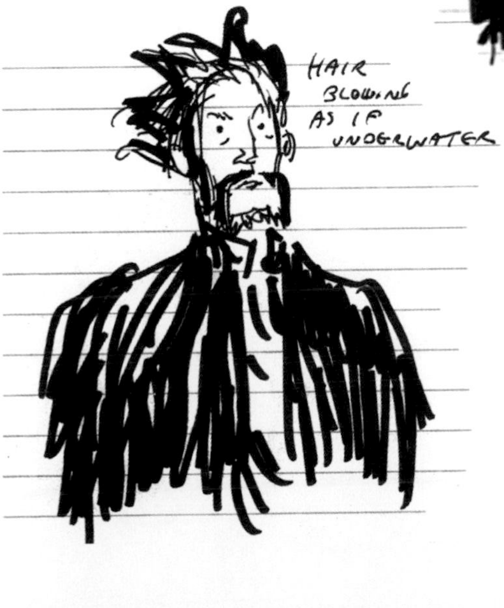
HAIR BLOWING AS IF UNDERWATER

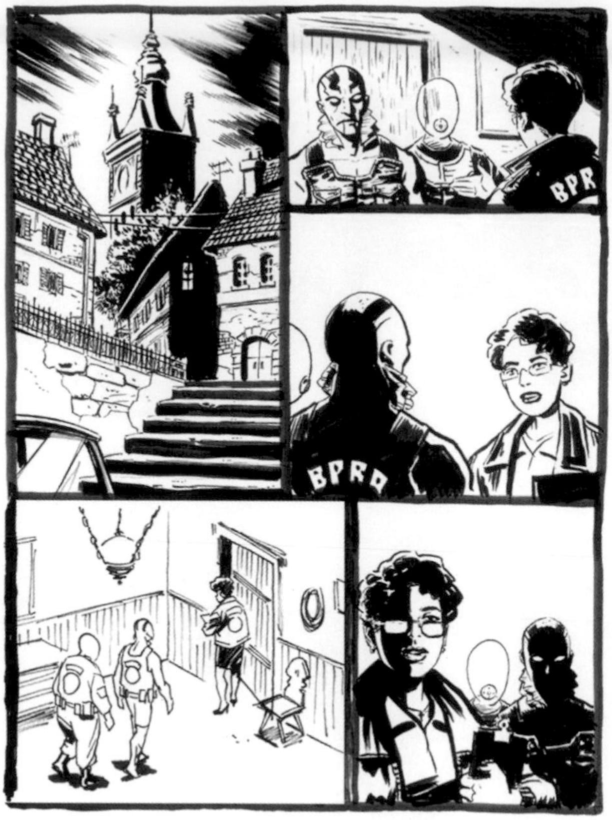
BPR

I've been a fan of *Hellboy* for the last ten years, and a fan of Mike Mignola for even longer, so being asked to contribute to this universe was both a thrill and an honor. I was kindly asked what sort of story I wanted to draw and decided that something to do with European zombies would be the most fun. Presented here are some of the preliminary sketches and rough layouts I produced for the story—if you compare the layouts with the final pages you can see a lot of changes based on Mike and Scott's suggestions.

—Cameron Stewart

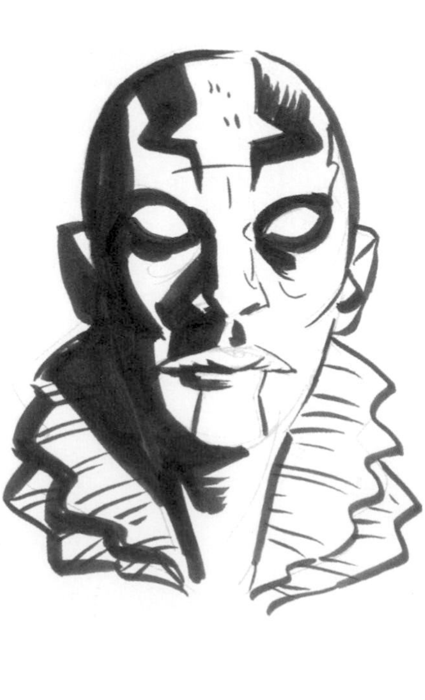

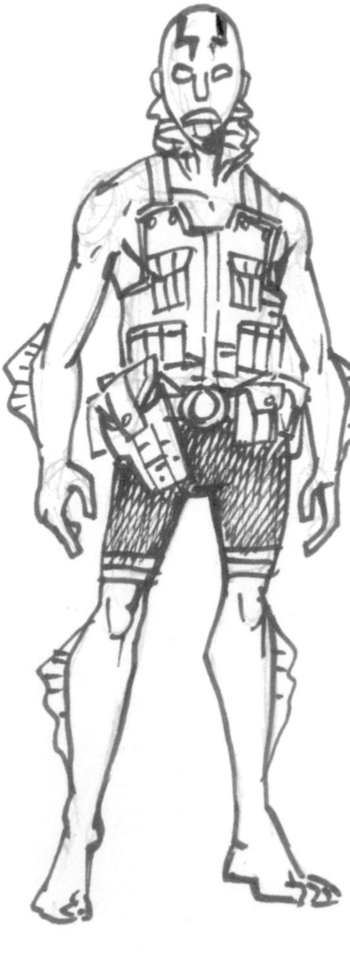

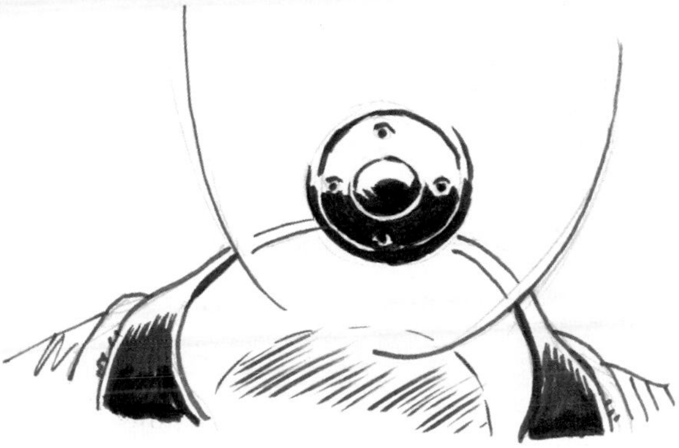
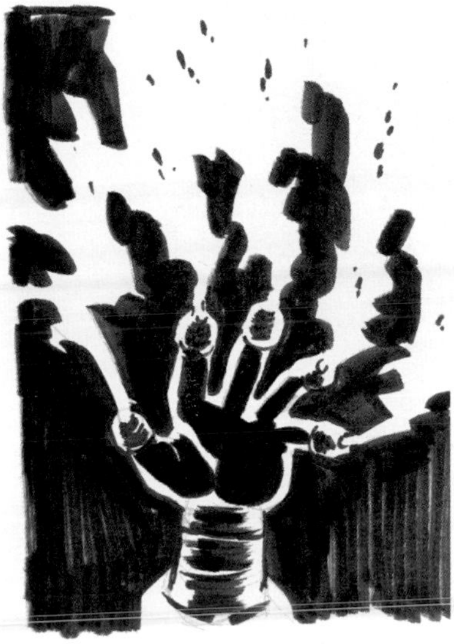
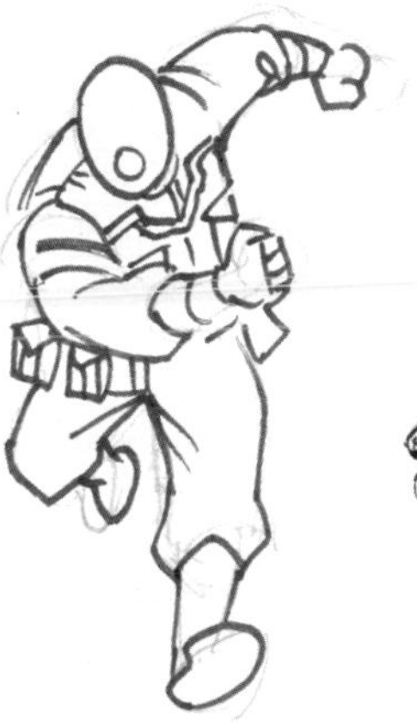
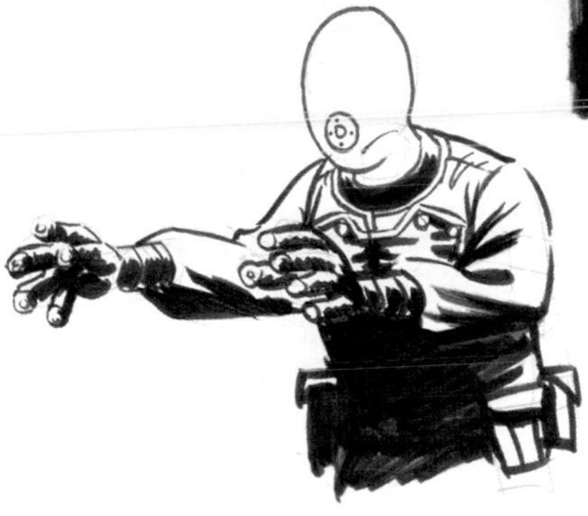
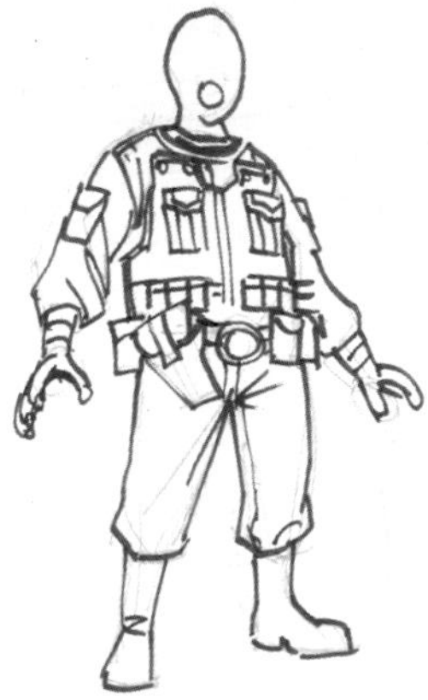
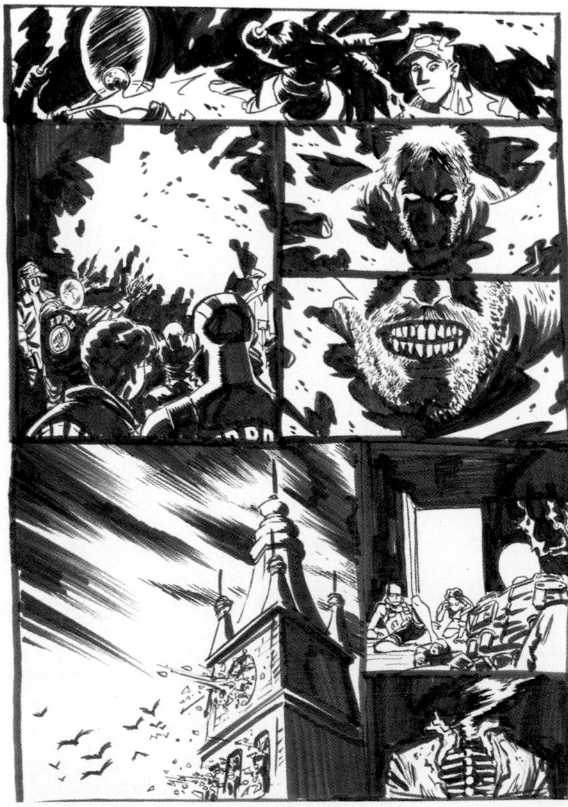
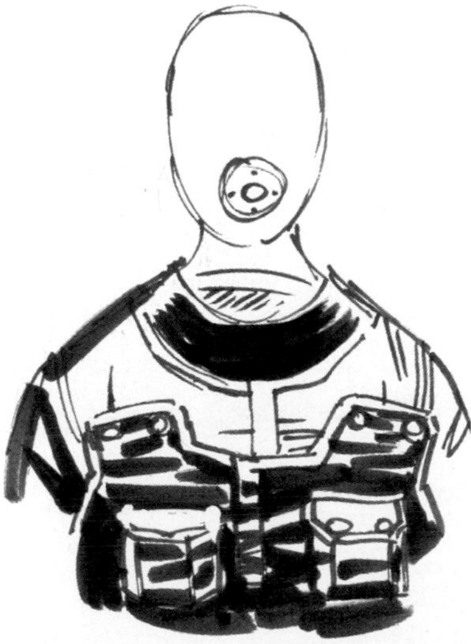

HELLBOY

by MIKE

SEED OF DESTRUCTION
with John Byrne
ISBN: 1-59307-094-2 $17.95

WAKE THE DEVIL
ISBN: 1-59307-095-0 $17.95

**THE CHAINED COFFIN
AND OTHERS**
ISBN: 1-59307-091-8 $17.95

THE RIGHT HAND OF DOOM
ISBN: 1-59307-093-4 $17.95

CONQUEROR WORM
ISBN: 1-59307-092-6 $17.95

THE ART OF HELLBOY
ISBN: 1-59307-089-6 $29.95

HELLBOY WEIRD TALES
Volume 1
By John Cassaday, Jason Pearson,
Eric Powell, Alex Maleev,
Bob Fingerman and others
ISBN: 1-56971-622-6 $17.95

HELLBOY WEIRD TALES
Volume 2
By John Cassaday, JH Williams III,
P. Craig Russell, Jim Starlin,
Frank Cho, Evan Dorkin and others
ISBN: 1-56971-935-5 $17.95

**B.P.R.D. HOLLOW EARTH
AND OTHERS**
By Mike Mignola, Chris Golden,
Ryan Sook and others
ISBN: 1-56971-862-8 $17.95

**B.P.R.D. THE SOUL OF VENICE
AND OTHERS**
By Mike Oeming, Guy Davis,
Scott Kolins, Geoff Johns and others
ISBN: 1-59307-132-9 $17.95

ODD JOBS
Short stories by Mike Mignola,
Poppy Z. Brite, Chris Golden and others
Illustrations by Mike Mignola
ISBN: 1-56971-440-1 $14.95

HELLBOY BASEBALL CAP
#17-106 $14.95

**HELLBOY LUNCHBOX
(& POSTCARD) 1**
Tin de-bossed full color
#19-012 $19.99

**HELLBOY LUNCHBOX
(& POSTCARD) 2**
Tin de-bossed full color
#11-836 $19.99

HELLBOY PVC SET
#10-666 $39.99

HELLBOY JOURNAL
#12-309 $9.99

HELLBOY SWEATSHIRT
Red-and-Yellow Hellboy Logo
#12-411 $39.99

HELLBOY ZIPPO LIGHTER
#17-101 $29.95

DARK HORSE COMICS™ *drawing on your nightmares*
darkhorse.com